Whispers of Hope:

The Story of My Life

A memoir

by
Bertie Simmons

To all those who have given me hope:

In memory of Mother, Ashley, Dorothy and Mrs. Ewing.

———————————

To my beloved family:

Paula, Brooke, Austin, and my great grandchild, Hank the Tank.

———————————————

—

To Craig Davis, Bena Kallick and all my former students, and especially to the most loyal and the best friend I have ever had, Sharon Koonce.

PREFACE

I Dream

I dream of a world full of hope
Where sunbeams sparkle with delight,
And raindrops wash away all hatred
While the moonbeams wrap us at night
In a blanket of peace.

I dream of a world of unconditional love
Where no one is judged by race, color, or creed,
And the fresh breeze delivers chances
While snowflakes provide the ambiance we need
To view the world with wonderment and awe.

I dream of a world of forgiveness
Where individuals can amicably disagree,
And all practice patience and civility
With no official order or decree
To follow the Golden Rule.

I dream of a world with no hunger
Where each has shelter and care,
And our doors are always open
In case someone is there
Who needs a helping hand.

I dream of a world where hope is not a whisper.
Where it is shouted around the earth,
And free to each individual
With no regard for one's place of birth
Or the number of one's zip code.

- Bertie Simmons
December 2017

PART I

"There are experiences in one's life that have a lasting impact and determine who the individual becomes. My improbable relationship with Dorothy McGuire at the age of ten changed my life forever and influenced my thinking and behavior in all my relationships. Let the story begin."

CHAPTER 1
That Strange Feeling

I had that strange feeling again. It was a mixture of excitement and suspense, like the one I'd had just before my baby brother, Johnny, was born. I sat on the front steps of my small frame country house with my chin nestled in the palms of my hands. My elbows rested on my bony, suntanned knees, and my gray-green eyes focused on a line of ants climbing up the steps. Mountains of brown curls were held captive in a ponytail. The brisk north Louisiana breeze played tag with the tall sea of grass beyond the hedge just outside the front fence. The sweltering sun caused small streams of sweat to run down my arms and legs. But I hardly noticed the heat. I felt restless and a little frightened.

I sprang up and began stomping the ants with my bare feet. I leaped from the steps, charged through the open gate, grabbed a yardstick from the back of my father's battered pickup truck, and began battling an imaginary enemy. Just as I lunged forward for the final blow, I heard a rustling coming from behind the hedge that lined my front yard. I froze in my tracks. Beyond the hedge, the tall grass hid a narrow trail leading to the vacant, weather-beaten, shotgun house that Mother had warned me never to enter. Now the grass looked like the ocean covered in white caps on a stormy day, just like in the picture books at school.

There was the loud rustling sound again! Something or someone was behind the hedge! I crept forward. I stopped to listen, running my eyes back and forth across the hedge. There it was again! Someone was there!

In my bravest voice, I demanded, "Come on out, whoever you are! Come on out! I got my sword here, and I'm not scared to use it. You hear me? I'm not scared the least bit!" I paused and waited for a response. Nothing. "Come on out and show yourself!" Silence.

I turned my body sideways and slipped, cautiously, through the hedge. At once I was swallowed by the towering, sun-bleached grass. I swept my yardstick dagger in front of me and struggled to part the swaying grass as I fought my way to the trail. "Where are you, and why don't you speak up?" I yelled again, my voice a little shaky. "What's the matter? You scared?"

The brisk breeze strummed the slender grass, and its rhythm started to give me that queasy feeling that I got when I let the front porch swing rock too hard back and forth or when I rode in the back seat of a car. I hoped I wouldn't vomit this time, but my head was beginning to spin. I turned to scramble back to my own yard, when I noticed a small, motionless mass huddled on the ground and almost covered by the grass.

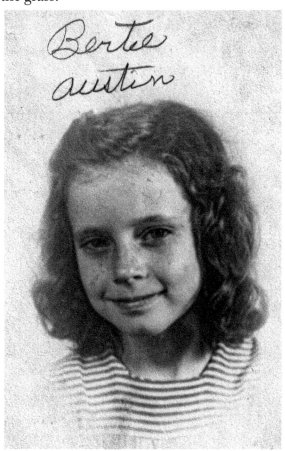

Bertie Austin as a child.

Hey, what's this? I said to myself. I was never one to turn away from an opportunity to explore and discover new things. Fighting off the nausea, I inched toward the mysterious mass until I could see more clearly. I leaned forward, trying as best I could to make out the shape in the rolling sea of grass. Suddenly, it took form: a little girl, with pigtails held fast with rubber bands, was crouched against the ground, her wide eyes staring out from her dark brown face. Her body was trembling, and tears were running down her cheeks.

I sighed, relieved. I knelt beside the girl, but she immediately jumped back, her big eyes fixed on me. I could clearly see that I had frightened her.

"Don't be scared," I whispered in a soft voice that forced itself over the nausea in my throat. "I won't hurt you. I was just pretending to be mean. Did you think I knew you were here? To tell you the truth, I'm about to vomit right now 'cause I get sick at my stomach looking at this grass swaying back and forth." I stood for a minute, swallowing hard. With my eyes closed, I held my head in my hands. I imagined myself standing in the middle of my father's vegetable garden right after he plowed it. I loved the way the freshly turned soil smelled, clean and sweet like laundered sheets when they were first brought in from the clothesline. I always used this trick when I was sick, and somehow, it always made me feel better. Finally, when my stomach stopped doing flip-flops, I reached for the little girl's hand and pulled her to her feet.

"Who are you? And what are you doing out here in this grass? I never saw you 'round here before."

"My, my name is Dorothy," she stuttered, her voice quivering. "I'm ten years old, and I live in that house." She was pointing in the direction of the forbidden building. "I have three brothers and four sisters. We just moved in last night. I heard you playing in front of your house and walked down the trail to try to see you, but when you heard me, I was scared and tried to hide." The words seemed to tumble from her mouth, and her eyes were still stretched wide.

"You moved in last night? Why'd you move in at night? How could you even see what you were doing?" I was amazed. "I didn't even know anybody lived in that house. I live in the house over there,"

I added, pointing in the direction of my small house. "I got two brothers. I'm the oldest," I bragged, placing my hands on my hips. "And I have to take care of them." But I was still confused and asked again, "Girl, you mean you moved in that house in the middle of the night? I don't get it."

"We always move at night," Dorothy replied softly, her head bowed. "I don't know why. I don't like to move but seems like we're doing it all the time."

Dorothy McGuire with friends.

"Oh well, so what does it matter? We can be friends!" I'd forgotten all about that queasy feeling in my stomach. "Now I know why I had that strange feelin' when I was sitting on the porch. I knew something special was about to happen," I grinned. Hanging onto my sword with one hand, I grabbed Dorothy with the other and pulled her through the grass to the hedge. We turned sideways and slipped, one at a time, through it. I rushed through the front gate and into the house to my mother, with Dorothy still in tow. "This is going to be the best summer of my life!" I exclaimed, as I introduced my new friend. And it was. It was the beginning of a special friendship and a glorious summer that changed my life forever.

CHAPTER 2
The Vines

Down the hill behind Dorothy's house was a swampy area that was cool even in the middle of summer. Dorothy and I spent endless hours swinging on vines and rolling and tumbling on the moss-upholstered ground. Tall trees blocked most of the sunlight, but a few rays slipped through. They cut into the shade like golden knives, glinting on our backs as we swung through the air, playing King of the Swamp. A small, slow creek wound through the swamp, and we would swing back and forth across it, occasionally letting go of the vine and splashing into its shallow depths. We named this spot "The Vines."

Many days that summer, Dorothy and I could be found at our secret place. Just at the edge of The Vines was a big oak tree we claimed as our own. A bough of the oak tree was shaped like a Y and hung near the ground. We sat, one of us on each side of the fork, and, kicking the ground, bounced up and down. Many secrets were shared as we sat in the Y of the old oak tree.

Every day, we played for hours until we were tired and then called it quits. We sat down under a tree and leaned back against its cool trunk. Birds were trilling, and the brook bubbled as it lazily tumbled over small stones half-submerged in the sandy bottom. Big cypress trunks jutted from the edge of the brook, like strangely formed soldiers standing guard.

"I love this place," I said, finally breaking the silence. "Let's make this our secret place. Don't tell nobody. Okay? If we do tell anybody, it can't be my brother Ronald 'cause he'll want me to bring him here all the time. He's too little to come here, and he might get hurt. We're big so we can come and have fun."

"I like this place 'cause nobody can see us here," responded Dorothy. "I don't have to worry 'bout nothing. That's why I like it here. I won't tell nobody nothing 'bout The Vines. Uh, uh," she insisted, shaking her head. "I won't tell."

Ashley and Brooke Fendley, Bertie's granddaughters, on a trip with Bertie back in time to the vines.

I didn't know you worried 'bout stuff. I worry too, but I don't tell my mother 'cause she has a lot to worry 'bout. I worry 'bout my mother all the time. Why do you worry?" I asked Dorothy, looking her straight in the eyes. "Why don't you want anybody to see you?"

"I'm just scared most of the time," Dorothy whispered, staring at the ground. "Just scared."

"Are you scared of things, or are you scared of people?"

"I'm scared of things and people," she replied. "I'm always afraid that I will do something wrong without meaning to make somebody mad. Sometimes we have to move in a hurry 'cause we're afraid something is going to happen. My mother and daddy are scared a lot of the time."

"If we come here a lot, maybe I can stop worrying and you can stop being scared," I replied hopefully. "I have to stop worrying 'bout when my father ties a rope around my waist and lets me down into the old dugout well—that's where we hang our jars of milk to keep them cool. When the jar of milk slips out of the rope and into the well, he drops me in to get the milk. I'm always scared that he's going to drop me in that cold and dirty water and that I'll drown. Maybe we can both stop being scared. I love having a friend like you. Let's make a pact so we will be friends forever." Then each of us licked our right thumb, slapped it into the palm of our left hand, made a fist of the right hand, slapped the butt of the fist into the palm of the left hand, and then we slapped each other's hands and shouted, "Friends forever!"

CHAPTER 3
The Drifters

It was early summer when the drifters came. Dorothy and I hid behind a huge oak and watched as they pitched their tents across the road from my house. They strung wire around the trunks of the tall, slender pine trees to make a corral for their horses. They were laughing and talking loudly as they took their belongings out of the horse-drawn wagons and put them into the tents. There were eight men, eight women, and six children. There were two girls who looked younger than Dorothy and me, and the others were boys who looked a little older. They wore brightly colored clothes, and Dorothy and I were fascinated as the men built a fire and set up a place to cook outside. The women then began preparing the meal. Everyone was working, even the young girl.

One elderly man named Old Tony was in charge, and he told all the others what to do. He had a crackle in his voice as he barked orders. He walked with a limp and had silver white hair and a long, gray beard. A young, dark handsome man yelled, "Old Tony, where should I put the Shetland pony? You want him in with the other horses?"

Old Tony with his cane.

17

"Just use a long rope and tie him to a tree for right now and feed him. He's walked behind the wagon for a long time and needs a big drink of water," Old Tony crackled. None of the men talked like us, and we thought they must not be from around here. We liked the way they talked.

"Where do you think these people came from?" I whispered. "They sure do sound different when they talk."

"I don't know where they come from, but I sure know it's not here. You think they're mean?" questioned Dorothy.

"Naw, they're not mean," I replied assuredly. "They really sound nice, the way they laugh and talk and all."

"Where can I get some water 'round here for the pony?" shouted the tall, handsome man. "Old Tony, I thought you said there was a creek around here."

Drifters on the pony.

I couldn't believe my ears. He was talking about our creek in The Vines. The Vines was our secret place, mine and Dorothy's! These people couldn't go there! It had to remain our secret. I had to do something and do it fast!

Without thinking, I jumped out from behind the tree. Dorothy followed. "I bet I know where you can get some water for your horses," I yelled. "I live right over there, and I know my parents won't mind if you get water from our well. That would be a lot easier than getting it from a creek. Anyway, it hasn't rained much lately, and even if you found a creek, it'd probably be dried up. I'll go ask my mother!" I headed off to the house, dragging Dorothy with me. Soon I returned to tell Old Tony it was fine to get water from our well.

"That's quite nice of you, young lady," remarked Old Tony. "Quite nice, indeed! I think we're going to like camping here." He grabbed a bucket and trudged to the well to draw the water.

"Girl, I sure thought our secret place was gone," whispered Dorothy, as we walked back to my house. "I sure did!"

"I'm not going to let anything happen to The Vines, Dorothy. That's our secret place, and nobody is goin' to mess it up if I can help it."

That night, the drifters danced around a big bonfire as Old Tony played an accordion and one of the women played a tambourine. As the women twirled, they held their full skirts, stretched out to each side, and swung them back and forth to the music. Their long, black hair glistened in the firelight and everybody was laughing and having fun. Dorothy and I watched them from the front porch of my house. My mother and two brothers joined us to watch the gaiety. I squealed, "This is better than seeing Hopalong Cassidy at the picture show!"

Bertie's mother in sailor cap with the Drifters.

"Yes, this is fun," replied my mother. "But you girls be careful because we don't really know these people. Don't go running off with them anywhere. I'm sure they're good people, but just be careful."

One day while Dorothy and I were playing in my front yard, Old Tony appeared outside the gate with the pony in tow. "Since you've been so nice as to share your water with us, I thought you girls might like to ride the pony. Why don't you ask your mothers if you can do that? He's a very gentle pony and won't buck. Would you like to do that?" Old Tony asked.

Bertie's mother, Ronald and John Austin with the Drifter's pony.

"Would I like to do that? Of course, I would. How 'bout you, Dorothy? Come on, let's ask our mothers," I shouted, running into the house. Both of us were back in a flash and ready to ride.

"Dorothy, you can ride first, and then I'll ride," I suggested.

"You can both ride at the same time," replied Old Tony. "Neither one of you girls weighs as much as an ant. Let me help you onto his back."

Dorothy and I rode the pony as Old Tony sat and watched. That was the beginning of a special relationship we had with him. He kept an eye on us all summer and warned us whenever he was afraid we were about to do something that would get us into trouble. Anytime we had a problem we couldn't solve, Old Tony was the person we ran to consult.

"I hope Old Tony lives here forever," I remarked one day after Dorothy and I had talked with him about our fear of tornadoes. My family had lived through a tornado that had destroyed our small town, and we often talked about how terrible it had been. "I don't think I'll be nearly as scared anymore when a storm comes. Old Tony has lived a long time, and he's never been killed. He's never even seen a tornado, so I'm going to stop worrying 'bout that. I got enough to worry 'bout without worrying 'bout that! It's over. The end!"

Tony was kind, gentle, and wise, and he would always help us find an answer. He was like a surrogate father to me.

Drifters.

CHAPTER 4
War

While Dorothy and I were having a wonderful summer, World War II was raging across the ocean. Each night after dinner when the dishes had been washed, dried, and put away, my whole family huddled around a big, brown, battery-operated radio. It had RCA VICTOR inscribed on a brass plate on the front, and it sat on the floor in the front room. When my father first turned it on, there was a lot of static, which disappeared once he found the right station. Then we listened to the news to keep up with what was going on with the war.

"This is Gabriel Heatter with the evening news," the voice on the radio declared in a matter-of-fact way. It was always serious and had a scary sound that made me feel uneasy. Every time I heard those words, I had a sinking feeling in the pit of my stomach.

After every newscast I asked, "Daddy, will you have to go off like Uncle Orvin and Uncle Allen did to fight in the war? Will you have to leave us?"

"No, I won't be going," he would always reply, but I was never sure. Later I learned it was because he had sight in only one eye. He lost the other in an accident when he was riding in the back of a pickup truck and going through the woods. A limb hit him in the face and struck his eye. He never regained the eyesight in that eye.

World War II gas ration book.

The war seemed far away to us, but we knew our parents worried about it. We overheard their discussions about the rationing of sugar, coffee, and gasoline and saw how hard they worked to make small amounts of those items last a long time.

After the newscast was over, when my mother was sewing and my father was reading one of his Zane Grey western books, I would turn on the radio and listen to music. I felt at peace when I heard the announcer say in a dreamy voice, "This music is being brought to you from the Blue Room of the beautiful Roosevelt Hotel in downtown New Orleans, Louisiana." I imagined myself there, swinging and swaying to the big band music. I glided across the floor, creating my own dances. Big bands were beginning to be scarce because so many of the men were going off to war, and there were times when solo artists performed instead. I liked them too, even though they sang sad songs about loved ones leaving. I could only listen a short while lest I use all the battery, but I loved to dance to the music and join in with the singers.

Soldiers who were training to go to war often camped just down the road from my house. They stayed there only a few nights before they moved on to another camp. Once the soldiers left, Dorothy and I would swoop down upon the campgrounds. We combed the area, finding small, round tins of coffee and sugar cubes that the soldiers had left behind. We raced to see who could find the most items. Once, Dorothy found a picture of a little girl. Scrawled on the back in a child's printing was "To Daddy, Love Amy." She handed the picture to me. I stared at it and tried to swallow the ball that had suddenly lodged in my throat.

Because of the war, people saved scrap iron, copper, brass, and other metals so they could be recycled. The old junk man came once a month in his rickety truck to buy the scrap metals. Dorothy and I decided to collect scrap iron to sell to the junk man.

"We can kill two birds with one stone," I remarked. "We can help our country win the war and make money, too. Besides, I think it would be fun! I already know where a lot of scrap iron is. Let's go! Good gracious, Dorothy, no telling how much money we can make!"

We spent days searching the countryside for scrap iron. I screamed with delight each time I found a huge piece of iron. "Look at this!" I shouted. "Can you believe how big it is? I'm going to need help with this!"

Dorothy rarely acted excited. She just went quietly about her job of finding all the scrap iron she could find. She had a keen eye and could spot pieces I missed, but she never said anything to hurt my feelings. Sometimes only a small bit of the iron could be seen, but when we dug the dirt away, we could free the entire hidden treasure and add it to our stack.

Both families joined in the effort, and the junk pile grew taller and taller. Even Old Tony joined in to help the cause. By the end of the month, the pile was almost as tall as our house and stood as an iron monster with many heads and tails. Dorothy and I could not believe our eyes! Everyone who passed the house commented on what a good job we had done. Old Tony always just shook his head and smiled as he watched us add more iron to the pile.

It was junk man day, and Dorothy and I got up early to wait for him. We sat on the ground under a tree near the road that ran beside my house. The sun was just coming up and turned the dew on the grass into shimmering liquid pearls. Birds flitted from tree to tree, singing loudly as if spreading the news of the good work we had done. A cool breeze played tag with the leaves of the sycamore tree where we sat, and the white underside of the leaves made the tree look like a giant snow cone.

"I'll bet he's going to be surprised when he sees how much scrap iron we've collected. He may not be able to carry all of it in his truck. I feel all jumpy inside! I even dreamed about an iron monster last night."

"Wonder how much money we'll get? I'm going to buy savings stamps with some of mine," replied Dorothy. "When I get enough, I'll trade them in for a savings bond. They sell the stamps at school, but I never bought none. They say it'll help us win the war. I can't for the life of me see why, but that's what they say."

"Wonder why we have to have war? I hate war! Every night Gabriel Heatter tells 'bout all the people who are killed in the war," I grumbled. "My mother said it's not right to hate other people. I don't hate nobody right now. I used to hate a girl, but I don't hate her now."

"The people in the war ain't the only ones who hate," Dorothy said soberly. "To tell the truth, they are not."

Urga, urga! Urga, urga! It was the junk man! We giggled as we jumped to our feet and waved our arms for him to stop.

"His old horn sounds like a rooster crowing," shrieked Dorothy, springing to her feet. She could get excited after all, and we jumped up and down as if we were doing jumping jacks.

"My, my!" remarked the junk man stepping from his old truck and looking at the pile of scrap iron. "Looks like you girls have been busy. My, my!"

"We have!" we answered in unison. We scrambled to keep up with him as he moved to the pile of junk and began setting up his scales to weigh the scrap iron.

Old Tony was standing in his camp, watching with a smile on his face. When the junk man tried to weigh some of the pieces, they were so large he couldn't lift them by himself.

"Look here," Old Tony shouted from across the road. "Let me help you with that. These girls have brought in some huge pieces of iron that will take more than one person to lift." He limped across the road and, still smiling, helped the junk man weigh the iron.

"These girls have really been working hard, as you can see," he remarked. "I'm amazed at how much scrap iron they've been able to find. Bet you don't find many places where two girls have gathered this much," he said proudly to the junk man.

"You're right." The junk man finished weighing all the iron and exclaimed, "My, my. You should really be proud of yourselves. Yes, indeed!" He handed us each four quarters and said, "If you girls get any more iron, just let me know. My, my!" With that he returned to his old truck and sputtered away. We looked at all our iron in the back of the rickety old truck as he drove away, and we laughed and laughed. Old Tony just smiled and shook his head as usual.

Dorothy held the quarters in her left hand and stared at them in disbelief. I licked the index finger of my right hand and rubbed the tops of the quarters to make them shine. Then off I dashed to show my mother how much money I had earned from all the hard work. A few steps from the door, I stopped and looked at Old Tony.

I looked at my quarters and then I looked at him again. I wondered if I should give him some of the money. As if he'd read my mind, Old Tony said in his softest crackly voice, "You girls deserve that money. You both worked hard. Buy yourself something fun with it." He reached out his arms and hugged me. It was the first time he had ever done that, and I thought I saw tears in his eyes. "Buy yourself something fun," he whisper-crackled and gave me a wink.

As Old Tony turned to limp back across the road to his camp, I thought he looked very old and tired. "Please don't let anything bad happen to you," I whispered, but he did not hear. "Please live here always." Then I ran to show my mother the quarters I had earned.

CHAPTER 5
The Taste of Injustice

As a reward for our hard work, Dorothy and I decided to walk into town to buy a cone of ice cream with some of the money we had earned. The town was about two miles away, down a winding dirt road protected by the shade from a phalanx of tall pine trees. We were so excited that we ran most of the way and finally reached the paved street bordered by white frame houses and sprawling oak trees on the south side of Chatham, Louisiana. We were almost there. Soon the sign Tom's General Store came into view. My heart was pounding! As we approached the front door of the store, Dorothy paused and stepped back.

"What's the matter?" I asked. "Let's go in and get the ice cream!"

"I can't go in there," she replied. "I have to go to the back to get mine."

"What?" I asked in dismay. "If I'm going in here, you're going in here. Now, come on in," I insisted, grabbing Dorothy by the hand.

"No! I'm not supposed to go in there," Dorothy insisted, pulling her hand away from my grasp. "I have to go in the back to get my ice cream. You go on in, and I'll meet you back here."

"Okay, if you're going in the back, I'll go with you, then." I clutched Dorothy's hand and headed for the back of the store.

Hand in hand, we skipped down the alley between Tom's General Store and the feed store next to it. We arrived at the back door, and Dorothy tapped on it timidly. Nothing happened. She tapped again. Nothing happened. I knew someone had heard the tap on the door, and I was determined that we were going to get our ice cream. I banged on the door with both fists shouting, "Open the door! We want ice cream! We want it now!"

Suddenly the door swung open, and there stood Mr. Tom, his face scarlet and his jaw quivering with anger. The whites of his big blue eyes were streaked with red, and they bulged as he shouted, "What do you mean pounding on my door and shouting at me? I'll get to you when I take a good notion to, but I don't want nobody pounding on my door! You understand?" He had been speaking to Dorothy, but then he spotted me. His eyes really bulged then, and swinging his arm toward the front of the store, he shouted, "Get back up front where you belong! You don't have no business back here!"

"We each want a cone of vanilla ice cream, and we earned our own money," I informed him, my hands on my hips and my jaw jutting forward. Mr. Tom stared at me in disbelief, his face still red and his big stomach shaking.

"I just don't believe this," he finally said, shaking his head. "I'm going to sell you the cream, but your parents will hear about this," he warned as he turned to get the ice cream. "You will pay for coming back here where you don't belong." He soon returned with two cones of vanilla ice cream and handed them to us. After we paid him a nickel each, we walked slowly back down the alley, licking the ice cream. Mr. Tom continued to glare at us as he wiped his hands on the white apron that stretched over his fat stomach. Then he slammed the door shut as we giggled and ran out of the alley.

As Dorothy and I walked back home, we talked about the signs she had seen over the drinking fountains and restrooms in some other Louisiana towns. She told me that one sign read Whites and the other, Colored.

"I drink from the Colored fountains and use the Colored restrooms. I don't mind really. That's just the way it is 'cause I'm colored."

"Does your fountain have Kool-Aid in it?" I asked, imagining her colored water fountain. Dorothy looked at me and told me it didn't. "I'll try it one day, just to be sure. I love red Kool-Aid!" I replied. We wondered why there were no water fountains or restrooms in Chatham that we knew anything about. We wondered…

As we walked down the road, we began to talk about school starting soon. "I wish we could go to the same school this year," Dorothy said after we had been walking for a while, just thinking. "It'd be fun to be in the same class. But I know that we won't be 'cause I have to go to Jasper Henderson."

"I don't even know why we can't go to the same school. Why can't we?" I asked.

"For one thing, I would be scared. You know how the white boys go down into the quarters and whop the colored boys in the back of the head with a two-by-four. They stick the two-by-four out the back window of the car and just go down the road, whopping all them colored boys in the head when they're walking down the road. Girl, I just remember! I don't want to go to a white school! And that's the truth!"

"Are you telling me the truth?" I stopped walking and placed my hand on my hips. I demanded, "Answer me! Are you really telling the truth? 'Cause if you are, I'm mad as hops!"

I stared at Dorothy and noticed her ice cream was melting and running down her dark arm. I compared the color of Dorothy's arm with mine and wondered why the color made so much difference. "There's nothin' right 'bout all this," I said after a while. "Why do you say that's just the way it is? Why don't you fight it?" I asked.

"I'm ten years old, and I'm scared," replied Dorothy looking at the ground. "I can't do nothin' 'bout it. Nobody can do nothin' 'bout it."

As we trudged down the dusty road that led back to our houses, I studied Dorothy's bare feet as little puffs of gray dust splattered from underneath them with each step and settled softly on their tops. I studied my own feet, and I wondered why color made so much difference. I wondered what Mr. Tom meant when he said I would pay for going to the back door of the store with Dorothy to get ice cream. I wondered...

Welcome to Chatham, Gateway to Caney Lake.

CHAPTER 6
A Friendship Pact

It was in November when I got that strange feeling again. I was sitting on my front porch, thinking about the stories Dorothy had told me and wanting to do something to change the bad things that were happening. But what could a ten-year-old do to make the world better? I wondered…

Suddenly, Dorothy charged through the hedge and ran through our front gate and onto the porch. "We're moving tonight," she sputtered breathlessly. "Girl, we're moving! I don't want to move!" she cried.

I sprang to my feet and began to shake Dorothy. I screamed, "No, you can't move! Tell me you're not moving!" But when I felt the tears touch my hands, I knew it was true.

"Mama said we're leaving right now!" Dorothy replied, swallowing hard. "Promise we'll be friends forever," she begged. "Promise!"

"I promise." I felt my eyes burning. "I really, really promise." I hugged Dorothy and could feel both our hearts pounding wildly. Then each of us licked our right thumb, slapped it into the palm of the left hand, made a fist of the right hand, slapped the butt of the fist into the palm of the left hand, and then we slapped each other's hands and shouted, "Friends forever!"

Dorothy, Bertie and their friends.

As Dorothy was running back toward the hedge, I turned my head to look at her one last time and she was looking back at me. "Friends forever," I whispered to myself. As I watched her run toward her house, I thought I would never forget the fun we had, and I was sure I had seen how scared she was as she looked back at me. I looked across the road and saw Old Tony watching us. For a moment I wondered if he could talk Dorothy's parents into staying. I decided he couldn't. I turned and ran into my house.

I didn't listen to the music from the Blue Room that night after the news. I didn't feel like dancing or singing. I lay in my bed instead and thought about Dorothy and the fun we'd had. I thought about how frightened Dorothy had looked when she turned back to look that last time. I wondered where Dorothy had been all afternoon. I wondered why she had not come out to play. We could have gone to The Vines one last time. I thought about the signs, Colored and White. I thought about the white boys with the two-by-fours. I thought about bad things happening to people. I thought until I fell asleep from exhaustion.

Later that night, I was awakened by a bright, flickering light through my window. I sprang from my bed and rushed to the window where I saw fiery tongues of flames leaping into the darkness. It was Dorothy's house! Figures in white hooded robes were running to get into a pickup truck, its engine revving. They were all laughing. As they sped away, my parents rushed to the front porch where they were joined by Old Tony in his long johns. I ran to the porch screaming, "This isn't funny! Stop laughing!" While they all talked about how awful it was that the house was burning, I was lost in my own thoughts. I wondered if this is what Mr. Fred was talking about when he said that I would pay for going to the back of the store with Dorothy. I wondered if it was my fault that they burned Dorothy's house down. I stood at the window and watched as the fire spread to the tall grass where I'd first met Dorothy. Dorothy's terrified face flashed before my eyes. I watched and wondered until there was nothing left but smoking embers. I now knew what my mother meant when she said she felt "empty" at times when she was lonely. I finished the night in a fitful sleep, dreaming of fire and the sadness I felt because Dorothy was gone.

The next morning, I arose just as the sun was peeking over the tops of the trees beyond the still smoldering embers. I slid out of bed, got dressed, and sprinted across the yard. I turned my body sideways and slipped through the hedge. The fire had burned the grass, so I had a clear view of where Dorothy's house had once stood. I ran past the embers to our secret place, my heart pounding, my mind exploding with thoughts that I could not understand. "Dorothy and I always felt safe in The Vines," I whispered to the wind as I ran. Once I had reached the big oak tree, I grabbed the familiar Y limb and was about to lift myself onto it when I noticed a folded paper tied with a piece of twine to Dorothy's side of the Y. I quickly untied the string that held the note, unfolded it, and read the message Dorothy had left for me. She told me she did not come out to play that last day because she had been too sad. She told me to stop getting angry about stuff and to stop worrying so much about things I couldn't change. We would be friends forever, she wrote.

I read the note over and over as memories flashed through my mind like the black and white picture shows I saw every Saturday night at the movie theater. But this picture show was different. This picture show was a private showing that could be viewed by me alone because it was a story about me and one of the best friends I had ever had. As the film ended and the reel spun wildly in my mind, I smiled, licked my right thumb, slapped it into the palm of my left hand, made a fist of my right hand, slapped it into the palm of my left hand, and then slapped into the wind as I whispered, "Friends forever!" And I meant it. I never saw Dorothy again, but throughout my life, that summer with her informed my beliefs, intentions, and actions as I, in my own way, worked tirelessly to give hope to the hopeless.

CHAPTER 7
Learning to Be Brave

Sometimes in our lives we are confronted with challenges, difficulties, and disappointment that cause us to lose confidence in ourselves and our abilities to overcome obstacles. It was during this time that I developed skills and knowledge that sustained me and brought hope and joy into my life. And now back to the beginning.

I was four years old, sitting alone on the bare wood floor in cotton panties and a white dress. Mother had made them from a flour sack, and she often laughed, "If you get out in the rain while I'm gone, you will be rolling in dough." I never knew what she meant, but she always laughed.

Bertie in homemade panties and homemade doll.

It had been some time since Mother had left for work. Before she left, we sang together the "bear" song, which she had taught me to sing throughout the day to keep from being afraid. The lyrics drifted softly through the room as we sang, "I'm just a bear, a brown baby bear. I roll and tumble everywhere without a care. And I am not afraid to be at home all day while Ma and Pa go stepping out and leave me here to play."

One of my favorite games was using sweet gum tree balls to build a magical structure. I took it apart and rebuilt it over and over again because I wanted my mother to say it was beautiful and creative when she came home. I also enjoyed looking out the window, watching and listening as the wind blew the limbs of the big oak tree. The sound was like a soft melody, and I often fell fast asleep.

I was usually startled from my sleep by a rap on the front door. A gust of wind swept through the room when the door opened, and as I sprang to my feet, my beautiful creation fell apart. I watched the balls rush across the floor as if to escape the intruder. It was my mother's sister Orell.

Aunt Orell Fuller, Bertie's mother's sister.

"Baby, are you okay?" she asked, as she bent over to pick me up. She always did the same thing and asked the same question.

My response was always the same. I tried to make my voice strong and replied, "Aunt Orell, I am not afraid."

"Baby, are you hungry?" I already knew what she was going to ask, and I always had the same answer ready.

"I'm not hungry," I replied, even though that was not exactly true. I knew I had a glass of milk in the ice box, but I wanted to save it for later, to make it last as long as possible. The day before, I'd gone to the back door of the house where my mother's other sister lived, and when she opened the door, I asked, "Sister, could I have a glass of milk?" I did that every day, and she always hugged me as she handed me a small bottle of milk.

I often heard my parents talk about not having any money. My mother cut and styled her neighbors' hair for twenty-five cents each, and Daddy worked at the time for the Works Progress Administration (WPA), the federal relief program for unemployed Americans started by President Roosevelt. He believed in fairness and justice, but he was highly opposed to giving welfare to able workers. While Daddy helped to build roads, bridges, schools, and hospitals, he often laughed that he worked for the We Poke Along program. His comment didn't bother me when I was young, but as I grew older and he continued to work for the WPA for several years, I thought he was making fun of the program. I didn't like it when I heard him make this joke because he was getting paid to do the work. I was happy that he was employed.

Every day, my mother rushed home to me after she finished her job and told me how beautiful my gum ball structure was. Though I was only four, she made me feel very brave and creative. She made me think I could do anything by bragging on me for not being afraid of being alone and for being able to create unique structures from gum balls. Even in the deep Depression of 1938, we refused to let it get us down, and our positive attitude and sense of hope were all because of Mother. She was very resourceful for her twenty years of age. When she came home after work, she was cheerful and always managed to put food on the table. She used any materials she could find to make clothes for herself and for me.

Even today, images of my mother flash through my mind. There she stands in front of the stove, a place where she spent much of her time and always felt comfortable. She wears an oversized man's shirt, which covers most of the length of her jeans, making her look even shorter than her five feet two inches. Her pixie haircut and playful green eyes give her the appearance of a teenager. The smell of frying bacon fills the room. "Hurry to breakfast, or I will throw it out!" We knew she would never throw away food, but this was her way of getting us out of bed and to the breakfast table. These words ring in my ears as thought birds flit through my mind, bearing images of mornings past. "She is dead," I always whisper to no one in particular. "She is gone!" I must accept it. No more mouthwatering scrambled eggs with cheese, fluffy homemade biscuits, and crisp salty bacon, all prepared by her.

Gently flitting thought birds will always calm me as they softly sing, "Sowing in the morning, sowing seeds of kindness." I can then laugh as a smile tickles my heart. I smile because I always remember this picture of her in the kitchen. Growing up, I thought she meant to be a seamstress because she was always singing the "sewing song." Hope, joy, and love surge through every sinew of my body and mind. This memory of my mother has sustained me and given me hope for a better tomorrow. The image of her was solidified in my mind as a four-year-old.

If a four-year-old were left alone today, Child Protective Services would step in and the child would be removed from the home. However, it was during that time in my life that I learned to be courageous, creative, self-reliant, caring, and a problem solver. This experience at four years of age played a major role in making me the person I am today. Mother's care, encouragement, and belief in me provided a strong foundation that would sustain me throughout the challenges of my life. She deserves all the credit.

First Grade

When I was four years old
My mother told me I was very creative.
When I was six years old and couldn't read
My teacher asked me
What I wanted to learn in first grade.
When I told her I wanted to learn to be more creative,
She told me they didn't teach that in first grade.
I asked the teacher if I could skip first grade.

-Bertie Simmons
December 2017

CHAPTER 8
School of Hard Knocks

I sat in my first-grade class and wondered why I had become so dumb. I had suddenly gone from deeply believing I could do anything, as Mother had assured me, to realizing I could not read. The teacher used round-robin reading as the method of instruction. The first student at the front of the class read a paragraph. That student was followed by the next, and next, and next. As it came closer and closer to my time to read, my palms grew sweaty, my face burned, and my heart pounded. I had already learned to hate Bob and Nancy, the children in the book, and their "clickety clap" horse.

And then it was time for me to read. I could not read a word. I just sat there feeling really stupid.

"Edna Jean, go help Bertie read," I heard the teacher say.

Then there came Edna Jean, with her ringlets and crinoline skirt bouncing as she walked. I always bowed my head and looked at her little "clickety clap" black patent shoes with white lace socks.

"Look at the book," she would always demand. I looked but could not read. She would then read the paragraph for me, turn, and bounce back to her seat, as I sat humiliated. I put my head down on the desk and longed for a stack of balls from the sweet gum tree so I could build another amazing structure and make my mother proud.

One day when I wanted to drop out of school in the first grade, I cried to my mother, "I hate Edna Jean Kennedy. I hate the clothes she wears, and I hate the way she always tells me to look at the book. I'm embarrassed and don't feel like looking at the book. I feel like going home and trying to build beautiful castles with sweet gum balls."

My mother put her arms around me and said, "You'll be able to read, and I'm going to teach you." Then she picked up a piece of paper and put a big black dot on it with a pencil. She turned to me and asked, "What do you see on this paper?"

I confidently declared, "A black dot."

She took my hands in hers and calmly explained, "This is what you are doing to Edna Jean. You are completely ignoring all the good she does, and you just zero in on the bad way she makes you feel. She is really trying to help you, but you are feeling badly about yourself and you just see the big black dot."

Mother then told me she wanted me to go to school the next day and find something good about Edna Jean. I became very upset because I didn't want to go back and find something good about the person who made me feel badly about myself. Later, I realized Edna Jean was very bright, and I liked smart people. She and I became close friends. When my mother passed away many years later, Edna Jean was there for me. I have spent my life looking beyond black dots and finding good in others.

By this time, Mother had received her GED, which allowed her to obtain a job as a nurse's aide. She was trying to learn the meaning of every word in the dictionary. She was also checking out books from a mobile library and devouring them. When I came home from school and she came home from work, she would read to me and then have me read the same passage to her. She read *Walden* and *Civil Disobedience*. I memorized passages and particularly liked the one on time: "Time is but the stream I go a-fishing in. I drink at it; but while I drink, I see the sandy bottom and detect how shallow it is. Its thin current slides away, but eternity remains."

I also loved when he said, "If a man does not keep pace with his companions, perhaps it is because he hears a different drummer. Let him step to the music which he hears, however measured or far away." I have always stepped to the music of my own drummer.

While Mother read and discussed other authors such as Walt Whitman, Edgar Allan Poe, and Ralph Waldo Emerson, it was Thoreau who captured my interest and heart. I loved the way he talked about independent thought, because I did not think the way most of my friends did. Somehow in my mind, this gave me the right to think my own thoughts. It somehow never occurred to me at the time that the books were far beyond a first-grade level. But I liked them so much more than the stories about Bob and Nancy and how much they enjoyed riding their horse.

It was during that time that Mother remembered that when I was a baby, I never crossed the mid-line of my body as I moved my arms when I wanted to be picked up. She told me she thought that might have something to do with my inability to read with fluency and ease. She had also noticed that I pitched a ball with my right hand and batted the ball with my left. She thought this also contributed to my difficulty learning to read. She had my father make a balance beam and I walked it every day. After I was grown and teaching, I read about the studies of Newell Kephart and reflected on my mother's insights and how she had helped me. Kephart reported studies that confirmed the relationship between a child's perceptual-motor development and its impact on the ability to learn to read. He also suggested the use of a balance beam and other movement activities in order to improve perceptual-motor skills. Mother may have read something like this while she worked as a nurse's aide. I did begin to be able to read better, but I think it was because Mother read to me and had me read to her.

Why?

Shattered dreams stitched
Together with broken promises
Whether or not they are real.
Unsung love songs
Rotting in a liquor cesspool
Fermenting to produce
Sweet words of deceit
And the charm of a cobra.
Why?

-Bertie Austin
September 1947

CHAPTER 9
A Tattered Life Quilt

"Your father is a dishwasher in a paper plate factory? Bertie Frances, what are you talking about?" shouted my teacher.

She had asked each of us in our third-grade class to tell how our father was employed. I thought the question was inappropriate because my father was unemployed. I was too embarrassed to say in front of everyone that he did not have a job.

"You are not telling the truth, and you are just a smart-aleck!" she screamed. "You will be punished for this. You will write lines which will say, 'I will never tell a lie again.' You are to write it one hundred times."

Daddy was frequently unemployed. He often said he was not afraid of work. He said, "I could lay down beside it all day and go to sleep." So Mother continued to work as a nurse's aide. While many people were struggling financially, we would have been dirt poor except for Mother's minimal pay. We were often hungry. I never forgot how I felt when my teacher made me reveal such an embarrassing, painful situation. These experiences stayed in the back of my mind for many years as I became a teacher, principal, and superintendent and was dealing with poor, under-served students.

Although he couldn't hold down a job, my father was very intelligent and a great vocalist and musician. He also designed, constructed, and carved all kinds of wooden toys with complex and intricate parts. He only had a fifth-grade education, but he loved to read and subscribed to the *National Geographic* magazine even though we were poor. He loved to debate politics, and his views were usually controversial. Finding ways to avoid a consistent job was where he dedicated his curiosity and intellect.

**Ronald's first day of school – age 6.
Bertie – age 10.**

When my younger brother, Ronald, entered first grade, my mother made me responsible for taking care of him. I was in fourth grade, and Mother still thought I was capable of anything. She told me to make sure he was always safe. That became quite a task because Ronald suffered from school phobia and would often escape from school. As soon as I would find out that he was gone, I would run home in search of him. I often found him squatting under the tall front porch of our rented house.

When I was in fifth grade, I was still responsible for Ronald's safety. One day I smelled smoke and was sure the school was on fire. I charged down the hallways, shouting at the top of my lungs. "Fire drill, fire drill! The school is on fire!" I jerked open the door of Ronald's room and yelled for him to run.

The entire school evacuated, and the teachers were angry and shouted insults at me when it was discovered there was no fire. When I returned to my classroom, my teacher held me in her arms and told me she understood why I had taken such drastic action. Yet what she told me next broke my heart. She told me it would be best if I didn't help any more after school because the other teachers thought I should be punished. Until that day, I had been her after-school helper, which made me feel important because she had chosen me. The pain from that day stayed with me as I grew older. I never found punishment to be an effective way to handle discipline. As a teacher, I built strong relationships with students and worked to discover and address the root of the problem when a student exhibited inappropriate behavior.

I loved living in Chatham, Louisiana in spite of my problems in school. A rippling creek ran just north of the town, and I often went there to sit on the banks and listen to the melody of the lazy water trickling off the rocks in the stream. I also went there every spring during my elementary and middle school years to pick the blackberries that grew in profusion, and I sold a gallon of the berries for one dollar to ladies who used them to make blackberry pies. Huckleberries and persimmons also grew in the area, and I picked and sold them in gallon syrup buckets. I always gave the money I earned to my mother.

We moved to Eros, six and a half miles north, during the summer after my fifth-grade year and lived in a house that belonged to Uncle Keith, Mother's brother. Mother joined the Church of Latter-day Saints. My father was not a member of any church, but he occasionally attended services at the Pentecostal Church. I begged Mother to let me attend a different church because I found both of their churches to be scary. Mother gave me permission, and I chose to attend the Methodist Church where I was made to feel safe and welcome. One day I rushed home from church and climbed high up in a tree in our backyard.

"What are you doing in that tree?" Daddy yelled. "You get down right now!"

"I'm looking for the Lord," I yelled back. "I just learned about Zacchaeus. When the Lord saw him there in the tree, he told him to come down because he was going to his house. I even learned a song about him. Maybe the Lord will come to our house if he sees me here. He might be able to help us with our problems, like not having enough food. And Daddy, he might be able to help you stop drinking beer."

"You get down immediately," Daddy hollered. "Get down now, and nobody is going to tell me when to drink beer."

I immediately began climbing down, mumbling, "I may be missing my last chance to get the Lord to help us." I rushed into the house and sang the Zacchaeus song to my mother, who already knew all the lyrics. We then sang together and laughed and laughed about me in the tree.

Every year, we moved into a house owned by my mother's Aunt Mag. Nobody lived in the house during the school year because her two daughters were school teachers, who lived and worked in another town until the summer. We lived there for free during the school year in exchange for taking care of the property. Mother was described by many at that time as being able to turn a sow's ear into a silk purse. She was always able to make Christmas a memorable time. We would go into the forest and find a beautifully shaped cedar tree, cut it down, and load it into our homemade sled, which our horse would pull back to the house. We decorated the tree with sweet gum balls covered with foil that we had stripped from the backs of chewing gum wrappers. Mother helped us collect the foil all year so we would have enough to decorate the tree. She helped us make colorful paper chains to hang on the tree and a cardboard star for the top. Santa usually brought us an apple or an orange, but it was when I was in elementary school that he brought me a pair of store-bought panties. All my panties had always been made by my mother from flour sacks. I was thrilled by Santa's unexpected and magnificent gift and often sat alone quietly rubbing the two sides of the tag on the elastic waistband together. I thought we were living as rich people lived.

Much of my time was spent watching over Ronald. I always wanted to know exactly where he was and that he was safe. There were times when I put him in harm's way even though my intentions were good. Once on a snowy day, I hooked the sled to the horse and took Ronald for a ride. The horse was going a bit fast, and the sled hit a bank of snow and turned upside down. I managed to jump out, but Ronald was trapped under the sled. I started screaming and ran home to get Mother to help me rescue Ronald. I was panic-stricken as we rushed back to the horse, which I had tied to a tree. When we turned the sled right side up, Ronald was lying there peacefully as if nothing had happened.

Living at Aunt Mag's meant that Ronald and I had to ride a school bus. At the end of each school year, the bus driver would stop at the store and buy ice cream for each student who had passed. I always passed, but Ronald failed. This meant I had to stay on the bus with him and neither of us got ice cream.

"Please, Ronald! Please pass!" I begged.

His response was always the same: "I don't care about school."

Even though Ronald always struggled in school, he grew up to be highly successful and one of the best men I ever knew. He became the man my father never could become.

CHAPTER 10
More and More Broken Promises

As the lyrics of the famous country western song drifted through the room and ended, the announcer interrupted, "There you have it, ladies and gentlemen. The singing cowboy Claude Austin and his band from Swartz." It was Daddy singing over the radio. He was extraordinarily talented and played almost any musical instrument. He had a wonderful band, and when I was a teenager, they often had me sing with them. I never knew what to do with my hands and always felt uncomfortable and fake. I was sure the audience would know I didn't care for country western music.

Bertie and John.

Daddy began to drink more and more liquor and often came home drunk after performing in a club, and I seldom saw him when he was not stumbling and cursing. He was an embarrassment to me, and I stopped inviting anyone to my house. He drank every day, and it became apparent that he was an alcoholic. He lost his job on the radio and began to use Mother's money to purchase his drink. We all begged him to stop drinking, and even though he promised that he would, sadly he never did. He became more and more aggressive toward Mother, Johnny, and me. When he hit Mother, I sprang into action, jumped on his back, and hit him with my fists, as I screamed at him to leave Mother alone. He turned on me and pulled his belt from his pants. I rushed to a corner of the room where he wouldn't be able to hit me as easily. He always whipped me with the buckle end of the belt. The belt hit each side of the wall because he was so drunk. My legs were a mass of cuts and bruises. This became a way of life for us, and the abuse continued until I left home.

I should have known Daddy would grow more and more abusive the more he drank. Even when I was friends with Dorothy, I would awake in the morning and defend Mother because he would have a gun, threatening that if she left the house to work as a nurse's aide, he would kill her.

"You're not really going to work," he shouted in accusation. "You're just going there to meet some men!"

Eventually, Daddy rode to work with her and watched her all day. All he ever saw her doing was working to get money so we could have food.

Daddy also had a clear disdain for me and for Johnny, the younger of my two brothers. He whipped us often but never touched Ronald, who was the middle child. Daddy loved him and called him "son," but Johnny was always called "boy." Ronald and I began to tease Johnny, telling him that he had been adopted. There were also times when I felt that I had been adopted, but I looked too much like my father for that to be true. Johnny and I did not feel jealous of Ronald because we also loved him.

Daddy was creative in his cruelty toward Johnny. Once, Johnny was able to obtain a small pony, which he loved with all his heart. He loved him so much that he was impatient to get home at the end of each school day to ride his horse. One day he rushed home, and his pony was missing.

"Where is my pony?" he screamed. "I've been waiting all day to ride my pony."

"Hell," Daddy replied. "I sold that damn horse for twelve dollars and fifty cents. Hell, that'll buy three jars of snuff. That horse was just one more mouth I had to feed. You didn't need him anyway."

Johnny, whose nickname was Chum, was heartbroken. He cried and cried and asked Daddy to get the horse back. He never saw that pony again.

On one occasion Mother had prepared a dinner for the family. She'd set the table, with meatloaf and vegetables ready for us to eat. Daddy came into the kitchen drunk, grabbed the edge of the table and flipped it upside down, breaking all the dishes and destroying the food. My two brothers and I screamed. We were all hungry and scared. I ran down the dirt road until I reached the clay pits. I worried about what was happening to my mother and my brothers, but I hid there and cried for hours. I did not try to protect anybody. I felt that I needed to flee and protect myself.

Bertie – age 16.

This terrifying turmoil was commonplace in our home and grew more violent as the years passed. In the spring of my junior year of high school, I had the female lead in the junior play. I had worked for hours on my lines and was sure I would make my mother proud. I hoped that my father would be sober and that my family would attend the play with me. I wanted so badly to feel like a family.

"Daddy, it's just one hour before the school play starts. Don't you think we should leave so we won't be late?"

"What do you mean leave? I don't plan to go anywhere, and you're not either."

"Claude, she has a major role in the play, and it's very important that we're there to see her perform," Mother explained.

"Important, hell! We're not going!"

"I am going!" I shouted, running from the house. I sprinted three miles to the school and arrived breathless on stage just in time for the rising curtain.

I could not believe my father would not take my mother and brothers to see me perform in the play. And, I could not understand why Mother stayed with him. Things got worse and worse, and I often begged her to leave him. I promised her that I would make sure we could survive. She would always respond that my father had many good points and that it was against her religion to get a divorce. She would then remind me that she married him when she was only sixteen and that she had taken a vow to stay with him forever. I couldn't understand what religion would require her to stay with someone who was so abusive to the entire family. I thought God was love.

In the middle of that summer after my junior year in high school, I was awakened by the sound of my father's voice. "We're moving again." It was Daddy telling us to get up and help pack things into the truck.

"Where are we going?" I asked.

"We're moving to the empty house across the road from Mama and Papa Austin. The house is in bad shape, but we'll fix it up. Hell, we can sweep trash from the floors right through the cracks between the boards."

"What?" I screamed. "That means I'll have to change schools, and it's my senior year. That school isn't as good as my school. I just can't go to another school."

Daddy stared at me with his one good eye. "What in the hell difference does it make to you? You are never going to amount to anything anyway. All you're going to do is get pregnant and have babies. You can't keep the boys out from between your legs." I felt nauseated. His words brought back memories from years before when I'd told him that I was getting sick and that the bones in my legs were always hurting. I was terrified that I was getting rickets because our diet was so poor. I couldn't understand why he always refused to take me to the doctor, but I could hear him saying the same thing that he was saying to me now.

Somehow, I found the courage to say, "That's not fair, Daddy. I have never had sex, and I am going to college." I had never mentioned college before, because I really thought he would laugh at me. My mother's family had pursued post-secondary education and talked with me about the possibility and encouraged me to think about it. Mrs. Ewing, my high school mentor, also told me that I should go to college, and I always wanted to please her.

"How the hell are you going to college? You got no damn money. I sure as hell won't help you."

"I'll find a way to go to college, and I am not just going to have babies." I calmly replied.

"Claude." It was Mother in her soft voice. "I wish you would not talk to her like that. She is going to make you proud someday."

"Proud, hell," Daddy replied as he loaded the last mattress and tied it down with ropes.

We were on our way to our new home, a shack filled with spiderwebs and trash. I had been in that house when I had visited my grandparents, and it was scary. I had seen cracks in the floor wide enough for snakes and other creatures to crawl into the house. I knew I could not live in that place and feel safe.

It was in late July that I decided to run away from home to get back to my school in Chatham, where I could receive support from caring people like Mrs. Ewing. She was my choir and history teacher and my basketball coach, and she was my favorite high school teacher. I attended the Methodist Church in Chatham so I could sing in her choir. "Bertie can do anything she makes up her mind to do," she often said. She was beautiful and always dignified and smiled often. She always encouraged me and believed in me, and this changed my life.

Bertie's inspiration and favorite teacher, Mrs. Ewing.

On the day that I left, I placed on my mother's pillow a poem I had written.

Mother

Bertie's mother.

Did I ever thank you, Mother,
dear,
For all the things you've done for
me?
For saving me from all the frights
That crept into my dreams at
night.
For being there in constant care
To help in times of deep despair?
With never-dying love for me
To help to determine my destiny?
Did I ever say the good things I do
Go back to the training I received
from you
And I hope that I will never do
Anything to cause you shame?
This I tell you so when I go
Deep in your heart you will always
know,
Mother, I love you so!

-Bertie Austin
1951

I told her I was leaving and hugged and kissed her goodbye. She was crying, and I assured her I would be alright. When Daddy heard me, he grabbed his single-barrel shotgun. "You try to leave this place, and I'm going to shoot you right in the ass. I'm going to kill you!" he shouted. I calmly replied that he had already killed my spirit as I walked out the door.

Daddy rushed outside with the gun, and my brother Ronald followed. I turned and saw the two of them standing behind me. Daddy lifted the gun to his shoulder. I heard him cock the gun, and I began to run, zigzagging back and forth down the path, believing it would be more difficult for him to hit me. He never pulled the trigger. I think he thought he could scare me into staying at home. I had no money, but I had a deep desire to learn and go to college.

Alone

Wrapped in the warm
blankets of my courage,
I contemplate the future.
Where will I be and with whom?
I mark time by the whelps on my legs and arms.
The burning, searing
Pain as the belt strikes.
The tears that refuse
To spill from determined eyes.
No flinch, no indication of
Suffering. Just anger.
But I hate anger! I
Will not have it steel my heart.
I think love and forgiveness.
I think understanding and patience.
I think of dancing. I think of singing.

-Bertie Austin
December 1949

CHAPTER 11
Help Wanted!

There are times in one's life when events are so devastating that one could easily give up on one's dreams. It was during this period in my life that determination, perseverance, and hope sustained me. These qualities were fueled by my reading of all the works of Langston Hughes. They enabled me to hold fast to my dreams. Nobody was going to stop me from reaching my dreams!

I was deathly afraid that, even if I escaped his shotgun, Daddy might follow me in his truck to keep me from leaving home. The terrain was hilly, and the pathway from my house to the highway was a dirt road, which was muddy due to a recent rain. After running for what seemed to be hours, I finally reached Chatham and walked down the street breathlessly. I saw a Help Wanted sign in the window of a café. I thought, I need help! I went inside and applied and was given the job of cashier. When I explained that I had run away from home, someone called my mother's sister who lived there in town. Sister and Uncle Henry, her husband, came and rescued me. They told me I could live with them.

My job was short-lived. One of my tasks was to lift cases of soft drinks from the floor and place the entire twenty-four-bottle case in the serving window each night at closing. I weighed less than ninety pounds and could hardly lift the cases. I was always afraid that I would drop the case and break the bottles and then be required to pay for them. I asked if I could just be the cashier and let the boys who worked as dishwashers help me lift the cases. I was told it was part of the cashier's job, and I knew that I would not be able to continue.

Sister and Uncle Henry had a grown son, J. L., and two daughters, Bobbie and an adopted daughter, Charlotte. They also had a parrot, who always squawked at me when I passed, "Brighten the corner where you are! Be a little sunbeam!" I hated that parrot, but I loved living with Sister. She canned the best sweet pickles, and I lived on pickle sandwiches so I wouldn't cost Sister much money. They shared gifts at Christmas and included me, even though I had nothing for them. I received five yards of forest green gabardine, which I sent to my mother, who had become an accomplished seamstress. I was filled with joy to be able to send her this fabric as a gift because I knew she could use it to make a skirt for herself.

We lived in the Bible Belt, and Sister was very religious. We attended the Methodist Church every Sunday, and I loved singing in the choir and attending Sunday School. I tried to memorize the entire Bible, one chapter at a time, but I was confused by the scriptures. I was especially confused when I saw people profess Christianity but behave in unchristian ways. They didn't walk the walk, and I struggled to make sense of it.

One day I was walking in the woods near Sister's house. A black man was hanging from the limb of a tree. His eyes were bulging, and his face was distorted and a strange color. My first impulse was to try to cut the rope, but instead I started running and screaming. Overcome with fear, I ran back to the house and breathlessly told Sister and Uncle Henry what I had seen. I ran into my room and cried and cried. I never knew why this man had been lynched, but I had heard rumors about the Ku Klux Klan being active in the area. I had nightmares about the man for many nights. Did the people who did that to him profess to be Christian? I wondered…

Our high school basketball team made it to state finals during my senior year. Each player was required to have a physical examination to qualify. Everyone passed except me. I was told that I must be examined by a cardiologist. I had no money to pay for the examination, so Mrs. Ewing took me for the exam and paid the doctor. The physician diagnosed me with what he called "soldier's heart," and he said that I should be able to participate. I made All State that year in basketball even though I was only five feet tall. I think my accomplishment was because I wanted to make Mrs. Ewing proud and to prove I was strong.

Years later I learned that "soldier's heart" was a term from the Civil War era, describing abnormal blood pressure and heart rate in veterans. In the 1970s, the condition was labeled post-traumatic stress disorder (PTSD), as large numbers of Vietnam War veterans with these symptoms were diagnosed. I could only assume that some of my experiences had altered my blood pressure and heart rate.

It was widely known around town that I was determined to go to college. We knew nothing about scholarships, but I kept hanging on to my dream. I asked Mrs. Ewing and my mother's family what I could do to be able to go to college. I told them I would work to help support myself while I was in college if I only knew how to do it. Uncle Henry suggested I join the armed forces because I would be able to attend college on the GI Bill that President Franklin Roosevelt had signed in 1944. This was a reoccurring conversation he had with me. I was determined to find a way to enter college immediately after graduating from high school and work my way through. But I had no desire nor intention to join the armed services.

One day some ladies from the church told me they wanted to help me realize my college dream. They also told me I had received a scholarship from The Broadmoor United Methodist Church in Shreveport, Louisiana. I would receive twenty-five dollars a month for as long as I was in college. They had also collected enough money to pay my tuition until I could get a job. I was overwhelmed with joy and gratitude. One of the ladies was the mother of my high school friend, Algene Anders.

Bertie as a high school graduate.

I graduated from high school in 1952, and that summer, church members drove me the ninety miles to Natchitoches and dropped me off to enroll in Northwestern State College, which later became Northwestern State University. I was a first-generation college student and had never been to Natchitoches. I chose that college even though there were other colleges closer to home. I had done research and found that Northwestern was a renowned teacher's college, and I thought it would better prepare me for whatever area I decided to enter in education.

I began immediately looking for a job. I found one the first day, working in the college cafeteria. I would serve breakfast, lunch, and dinner, and what I earned would enable me to pay my tuition, room, and board. I gladly accepted the job and was on my way.

I had no money for books, so I made friends with other students and borrowed theirs. I took their books to the basement of the dormitory after lights out and studied there every night. I continued working in the cafeteria, studying in the basement at night, and attending summer school for the three years it took me to graduate from college, except for one extension course, which I completed during my first year as teacher. I attended school every summer since I had no home and no place to go, and I was eager to graduate from college and obtain a job so that I could begin to support myself.

I entered Northwestern with a burning desire to be a high school dance teacher. I had loved to dance, since I had envisioned myself in the Blue Room of the beautiful Roosevelt Hotel in New Orleans, dancing to the big band music as it streamed from our radio. This desire was fueled as I watched Mother's father, Gene Yeager, move so gracefully. He was a dance teacher and choir director, and the Yeager family had a quartet. They were all multi-talented and were highly successful as adults. They all became successful members of the community and civic leaders in Monroe, Louisiana.

Yeager choir: Calton, Sam, Keith, Sister, and Orell.

My goal of being a dance teacher was never to be, however. During my first dance class, I watched the lithe dancers who could lift their legs high over their heads and point their toes. Their gracefulness was reflected all around the room, in the mirrors on the walls. My short, stiff legs would barely come up to my waist, and I knew I would never make it in dance. I had the Yeager talent for movement and was great at social dancing and interpretative dance, but ballet was well beyond my ability.

"Perhaps as a teacher I can help other students who struggle in school as I did," I told my friends. "Maybe I can make a difference in a kid's life the way Mrs. Ewing did in mine." I decided to give up ballet and become an English teacher. I decided to dedicate my life to making a difference in the lives of others, especially those who were poor and minority.

W. R. Roberts, college friend, and Bertie.

I loved college and found time to date and build relationships despite my heavy work schedule. I had no spending money except the twenty-five dollars a month I received from the church, and I visited the church once a year to thank them for their generosity. I always felt that, in a way, I was betraying my mother and negating her influence on my life. She had always done so much for me, and I valued her support and love more than the church scholarship. I had this feeling for years. This experience gave me a better understanding of how events in life can undermine the pride of struggling students.

The Yeager family was always supportive of me and a real source of encouragement and inspiration. Once while I was in college, I used the twenty-five dollars I had saved from the church's monthly allowance for a bus ticket to go home. It had been so long since I had seen Mother. I had spent all my money and had no way to return to school, so Mother asked my Uncle Calton to drive me back to college. That was in 1954, and Uncle Calton's car was a faded blue 1941 Ford that he had bought for $350. The car's headliner had come loose and hung on the heads of the passengers. My grandmother had covered the car's ceiling with cloth from flour sacks and stuffed it around the edges of the windows to secure it. It looked good, but the engine was well worn. We were both afraid the entire trip that the car wouldn't make the ninety miles. Calton's willingness to help despite the condition of the car was an indication of the spirit of the entire Yeager family.

In August 1955 I left college and obtained a teaching job in Kinder, 120 miles further south from Natchitoches. I completed the extension course I needed in order to receive my college diploma in January. I taught English and mathematics in the high school, and because the administration knew I had made All State in basketball, they also made me the girls' head coach. In my spare time, I volunteered to teach social dance at the local recreation center and loved every minute of it. My favorite dance was the tango, and I soon had most of the young adults in town tangoing and jitterbugging. I also taught a dance class in the school and worked with students to compose and perform "Sneetches on the Beaches" and other Dr. Seuss stories. I loved improvisation and being creative. This provided me with the opportunity I had always wanted to teach dance to students in school.

Designating me the basketball coach turned out to be a mistake. I did not like it. I had no idea how to coach, nor what instructions I should give the players. I would see other coaches writing on a small chalk board as they coached the team, and I longed to know what to write on my board. Finally, I wrote, "Put the ball in the basket!" That did not work, and we only won three games and lost thirty-three. I was fired as a coach.

After losing the last game of the season, I awakened the next morning with a strange feeling in my body. I had difficulty moving my left leg and arm, and my speech was slurred. When I tried to drink water, it ran out one side of my mouth. Frightened, I rushed myself to the doctor, who said I had had a slight stroke. Perhaps it was from the pressure of wanting to win games and my inability to coach. The stroke affected the left side of my body, and it was many years before I stopped experiencing an extreme weakness in my left leg, arm, and eye.

Bertie and college friends.

CHAPTER 12
A Whole New World

It was in 1955, during my first year of teaching in Kinder, that I met Kerry Simmons. He had grown up in the town where I was teaching, and we began to date when he was on furlough from the navy. We eventually married and moved to Houston, Texas in 1957. The thought of moving from a small town in Louisiana to a large city in another state filled me with terror. The only state I had ever visited other than Louisiana was Arkansas, which was very much like my home state. I had never been to a large city before, and the place he had rented was a basement apartment downtown. There were no windows, and the rooms had a musty smell. I was panic-stricken and wondered why he had selected such an unwelcoming place. I knew, though, that I would not stay there long. At night Kerry had nightmares, and often, in his sleep, he kicked me out of bed. I began to realize that he thought he was still in the service. That old feeling of being alone crept into my being.

We went to the grocery store once we had unpacked our belongings. I had never been grocery shopping and had great difficulty deciding what to buy. I did not know what Kerry liked to eat and had no recipes. I was embarrassed and reluctant to choose anything.

"What is wrong with you?" Kerry barked. "Don't you know what food we need? I'm expecting you to cook the food and have supper ready when I come home from work. Now, what do you want to cook?"

I had never learned to cook, and I didn't have a clue what to cook nor how to cook it. While in college, I had eaten all my meals in the school cafeteria where I worked. While I was teaching, I was renting a single room and did not have access to the kitchen, so I did without food or ate in a cafe. I wondered if I was ready to be a housewife. Fortunately, Kerry chose what he wanted to eat, and we made it through our first grocery shopping experience. I called my mother, who sent me recipes. I slowly began to get better and better at preparing meals.

Kerry and I both had cars, but I had never driven in a city. I struggled with the one-way streets and the fast-moving traffic. I practiced when Kerry was at work because I did not want him to criticize me. Finally, over time, I grasped the hang of it.

Fortunately, the central administration building for the Houston Independent School District (HISD) was downtown and close to where we lived. I made my way there and applied for a job. Kinder was a small town, and I had been hired directly by Kinder High School. I didn't know if Kinder even had a school district office. It was quite different in Houston. I felt as if I were being swallowed by the enormous district office and the numerous departments. I struggled to find the personnel office and understand the process of applying for a job. Eventually, I filled out an application and was called in immediately to be interviewed. I was hired on the spot as a fourth-grade teacher at Hartsfield Elementary School. I could hardly wait to get started.

The school was in southeast Houston, just down the street from MacGregor Park and the Palm Center shopping center, which had been created to meet the needs of middle-class white suburbanites. Kerry and I moved closer to the school, and thank goodness, I could easily walk to school. I especially enjoyed walking in the park and eventually took a summer job there, teaching archery and swimming, thanks to my experience in the water ballet program at Northwestern.

The student body at Hartsfield Elementary was all white when I began teaching there, and the community surrounding the school was majority Jewish. Later while I was still teaching at Hartsfield, I had three black students in my class. It was my observation that they were well received by the white students and parents, even though there was much racial unrest in the city. We had heard stories about how other black parents had been cursed and threatened in other schools. Black students in those schools were still required to drink from separate water fountains and use separate bathrooms. That did not happen at Hartsfield, where they were treated with respect.

I was always eager to discover the passion of each of my students and found time during the day to let them pursue their interests. One black student, Isaiah, loved to write songs and sing them to the

72

class while playing an imaginary guitar. The lyrics of one of his songs had been locked in my memory bank since then. It was a call and response with the entire class responding to the omm pah pahs in the chorus. He said he learned this approach at church, and you can decide where he learned to write the lyrics.

Oh, my baby, omm pah, omm pah,
Yes, my baby, omm pah, omm pah,
Went to the bar, omm pah, omm pah,
Got me a beer, omm pah, omm pah,
Saw this girl, omm pah, omm pah,
Come over here, omm pah, omm pah,

(Call)
Omm pah, omm pah,

(Response)
Omm pah, omm pah,

(Call)
Omm pah, omm pah

(Response)
Omm pah, omm pah.

Bertie's Hartsfield class of 1966.

All the students and I always joined in the response, and then we all applauded Isaiah and cheered him. In retrospect, I never had a white parent complain about our out-of-the ordinary class offerings nor did the black students suffer any jeering or rude remarks. Several of my students kept in touch with me through the years and visited with me often. David Poffenberger and Sandy McArthur were two of my stars. I thought David would grow up to be a businessman because he was an entrepreneur by the age of ten.

Paula Simmons and Brown Bear praying.

I was still teaching at Hartsfield on November 23, 1963, when we received the message that President John F. Kennedy had been shot to death in Dallas. Paula, the one child that Kerry and I would have, was two years old at the time. I had been deeply concerned about the atmospheric nuclear testing that had been going on since 1945 and the effects the atomic fallout would have on the milk my daughter drank.

President Kennedy appeared to be trying to do what he could to control the testing. When I told my students President Kennedy had been killed, many of them wept. That was a very sad period in our history. What would Vice President Lyndon Johnson do about the nuclear testing that was at its highest rate in 1961? I wondered…

While Paul Simon has clearly stated the lyrics of his song "The Sound of Silence" were not a response to the assassination of President Kennedy, they reflect the silence that occurred in my life during that time. I called Mother when I heard about the assassination. She stated, "I am sorry, I cannot talk now. I am too overcome with sorrow." That sentiment was shared by all my friends. Again, I was alone.

CHAPTER 13
Blankets of Courage

I enjoyed teaching the students at Hartsfield, but I was concerned about the continued turmoil in the city of Houston. The 1954 Supreme Court decision on Brown vs. Board of Education had declared that separate but equal schools were unconstitutional. The daily newspapers and radio programs all described efforts being made by black students to enroll in white schools. But these students were always rebuffed, and the HISD was slow to end the separation of white from black students in public schools. It was clear to me as I observed the snail's pace of desegregation that I had moved into a city that was attempting to avoid adhering to the requirements of the law. I remembered Dorothy and her struggles. I remembered how we both wished that we could attend the same school and that Dorothy decided that she would not want to go to a white school because of the way some whites treated blacks. I wanted to learn more about the integration issues in Houston, so I delved into studying Houston's past and current integration initiatives and have kept up with them continuously. It has become clear to me that we cannot legislate the heart.

In 1956, the HISD school board held a meeting concerning the integration of the public school system. That meeting was filmed by KUHT TV and is archived in the current YouTube library on that period of history. The president of the board, Mrs. Olan Rogers, is seen making this statement to begin the meeting:

> I am in favor of segregation because I firmly believe that God in his supreme wisdom created the different races of man and intended them to remain as he created them. I believe that races should witness to God as races, and that each one has something to contribute to his eternal plan. But if whites and Negro children attend the same schools, interracial marriage will occur and that will be the destruction of both races.

Although Houston slowly began to implement the law in 1956, it appears, even today, that the attempt has never been successful. HISD continued to find ways to avoid integration. A federal judge in 1960 ordered the district to integrate one grade level at a time.

I was surprised when in 1958 Hattie Mae White was elected to the HISD Board of Education. She was the first black person elected to a public office in Texas. She had significant support from blacks but only a few whites. When a cross was burned in her front yard and the windshield of her car was shot, I was shocked, but many were not. Still, she served on the board until 1967, when she was defeated. During her tenure, she had fought tenaciously for equity. Gertrude Barnstone, former HISD board member, made remarks at Hattie Mae White's funeral about her having more courage and intelligence than anyone she knew. Eventually, the district named the HISD Administration Building on Richmond Avenue in honor of Hattie Mae White. The new administration building on 18th Street continues to bear her name.

In 1960, I watched as a group of students from Texas Southern University carried out a very strategic plan to participate in a sit-in at the lunch counter of a local Weingarten's supermarket. They were neatly dressed and had obviously planned to remain nonviolent. Their plan was unsuccessful since the counter was closed immediately by the cafeteria manager, and they were not served.

One unintentional consequence of the sit-in was personally devastating to me. Two white young men captured a young black man who was not involved in the protest. They beat him with chains, even across the face and head, and then left him hanging from a limb of a tree, assuming he was dead. Even though he survived, I was horrified and kept seeing in my mind the black man I had found hanging from a tree when I was sixteen. I felt deeply depressed and alone. There was no one I could discuss it with in Houston because most white people saw nothing wrong with beating a man so violently simply because he was black.

That same year, a group of students marched to the City Hall cafeteria. I was so proud of Houston Councilman Louie Welch because he ordered the manager to serve the students. The story was on the front page of the local newspaper the next morning.

In 2000, I published a book titled *Wind for New Wings*, A Message from the Leaders of Today to the Leaders of the New Millennium. I personally interviewed 214 Houston leaders, four of whom had a personal perspective on the days of "Jim Crow" and the efforts to integrate HISD. Conrad Johnson, John Biggers, Melanie Lawson, and Reverend Bill Lawson all had a story to tell that informed our understanding of the events of the 1960s.

Melanie Lawson

John Biggers was an accomplished artist who taught at Texas Southern University. In Bigger's paintings, the figures' hands are exaggerated in size to symbolize the fact that most of the jobs blacks were permitted to have in the Jim Crow South involved the use of their hands—plumbing, teaching, preaching, or embalming. Biggers said, "Racial discrimination was so horrible that one does not want to remember it because it is so painful. We had to get off the sidewalk if we met white people. We were threatened with death, and there was no protection. The police did not protect poor people, white or African American."

The Gleaners, 1943 by Biggers.

John Biggers

Dr. Biggers continued to explain that he grew up in a small mill town, Gastonia, North Carolina. It was a typical small, segregated Southern town, and he lived on the "other side" of the railroad tracks. "That is why I have railroad tracks in most of my drawings and paintings. The track became a visual symbol to me because it was the quickest way to leave town and go to another town. There were no highways at this time, and the little 'Bob train' ran north and south carrying produce from the hill country of North Carolina. We kept time by the train."

Conrad Johnson was the band director of the world-renowned Kashmere High School band in Houston. He recalled, "I suffered racial discrimination, and my band did, too. I remember once we were in competition in Huntsville, Texas. We won, but because we were African American, the judges said it was a tie with another school. In 1972, we went to Mobile, Alabama, to compete for the best stage band in the nation. They tried to say it was a tie again. I would have no part of it. I told them I came there to win, and if we did not win, give us second place. After one hour of deliberation, we were awarded first place."

Melanie Lawson reflected on her experience as a young African American girl in Houston, Texas. She attended Turner Elementary, an all-African American school, until sixth grade when she transferred to Edgar Allen Poe Elementary, an all-white school, as a part of the school district's effort to integrate the schools. "I can remember some very tense moments in that classroom with only one other African American in the class. The teacher was a lovely, very Southern gentleman who, on the first day said, 'Now we got a couple of colored kids in here, and I don't want y'all picking on them. They're here because the law says they have to be here so y'all just treat these like everybody else.' Because of his statement, we became novelties."

One of the most influential leaders in the city of Houston during the time of desegregation and for years after was the Reverend Bill Lawson. His story is an important one from which we can learn. In 1965, the NAACP protested the HISD because the city had not desegregated the schools, nine years after Brown vs. Board of Education. The Houston branch of the NAACP sent a letter to HISD demanding they desegregate the schools by September 1965. Dr. Lawson remembers, "The letter was referred to committee, which meant it was going into the trash can. It was decided we would have a march on HISD. My job was to go to the schools and try to get the kids to be a part of this march. Our strategy was to ask them not to go to school on May 17, 1965. They were to gather at the South-Central YMCA. We were all given assignments to get various groups involved in the march. When we got to the YMCA, there were about 2,000 high school students there. We were horrified to find that there were few adults who were going to join us. We finally decided to march anyway. That day, civil rights came to Houston, Texas. We marched to the HISD headquarters, which was on Capitol Street. As we marched down Dowling Street, the African American adults saw all the kids going down the street with a thin layer of adults. They joined us. The crowd swelled from 2,000 to 5,000, and this was the first protest march held in Houston."

Reverend Bill Lawson

Dr. Lawson continued, "Dr. King had taught us to remain nonviolent, and we were not to resist arrest, and if we were retaliated against, we were not to retaliate in kind. There really was not that much resistance. The school board began a serious desegregation, one grade at a time, and by September, every school in Houston was desegregated. Civil rights came to Houston in the most peaceful, nonviolent fashion possible, rather than the way it went to Watts, Harlem, and Washington, DC. There had been, between 1959 and 1963, several sit-ins led by Stearns, Allen, and Curtis Graves. They had run into some serious difficulties, had been arrested and that early movement, which was led primarily by college students, had been rebuffed. But as professionals became involved in civil rights protest, doors opened almost magically."

I remember the role George Oser, an HISD board member, played to accelerate the desegregation of schools. Though he was white, he co-founded a citizen group called Citizens for Good Schools, which worked to keep integration moving forward. Oser was joined by Eleanor Tinsley, Reverend Leon Everett, and Leonard Robbins. All four won seats on the HISD Board of Education in 1969. They had put together a group of blacks, Hispanics, and progressive whites to accomplish this task. The decisions made by this board significantly increased integration while white flight numbers soared.

As I wrote *Wind for New Wings* in 2000, I had to think back to the many brave leaders in our community who were wrapped in blankets of courage as they created what seemed like magic in a time of change in our world. I felt fortunate that I had experienced these brave leaders, black, white, and Hispanic, who worked to bring about equity. Sadly, white flight has continued to soar, and presently the HISD has fewer than nine percent white students.

CHAPTER 14
Taking Chances

I moved from Hartsfield School in 1966 to become a fourth-grade teacher at Mitchell Elementary, and we bought a house in the neighborhood, which was in southeast Houston off Telephone Road. Mrs. Emma Boyd, my principal at Hartsfield, had been reassigned to this new school, and she asked me to go with her. By the time I arrived at Mitchell, the school district was working on its second attempt to desegregate. They were beginning to cross over teachers, placing black teachers in white schools and white teachers in predominately black schools. We had extraordinary black teachers, and I observed the students responding to them beautifully. There was Mrs. Barrett in first grade, Mrs. Motley in kindergarten, Mrs. Green in fifth grade, and Mrs. Jones in sixth grade. However, I was deeply concerned because I felt the district was taking the stronger teachers from the black schools and placing them in white schools. I wondered what effect this would have on the black students.

Bertie with 1971 class at Mitchell Elementary.

I absolutely loved teaching third and fourth grade. I had taken art lessons where the black light and phosphorescent chalk were used, and I was captivated by the way it brought the art alive. I believed it would be an effective way to instruct students in the classroom. My assumption was correct, and the students were fascinated by the glowing colors and could hardly wait for the next lesson. It worked extremely well for students who appeared to have attention deficit disorder. Word of this innovation soon spread across HISD, and visitors were flocking to my room to learn the technique.

Mrs. Boyd suggested that I obtain my master's degree so that I might become an administrator. My desire had always been to work with students, but she convinced me that I could affect the lives of more students in an administrative role. It was suggested by many educators with whom I spoke that the best school in the field of education at that time was Sam Houston State in Huntsville, Texas. Because of the distance from Houston, I attended during the summer and in the evenings.

I majored in educational administration and took courses in movement education because of my interest in dance. I also wanted to learn how movement could improve the reading ability of dyslexic students because of how my mother had helped me with my reading difficulties. By this time, I had read Newell Kephart's paper on children's perceptual-motor development and the application of his finding in the classroom. I was fortunate to have a nationally known movement education teacher, Mary Ellen Montague, at Sam Houston.

I graduated from Sam Houston in 1968, and years later I received the Distinguished Friend of Education Award from the College of Education and a Distinguished Alumni Award from the university. My experience at Sam Houston was enlightening and inspirational because I gained so much knowledge in both how to function as an effective administrator and instructional leader. I was particularly interested how the innovative techniques that I had learned could be used to support what were then called "slow learners" in the classroom.

Many of the fathers and a few mothers at Mitchell were employed by NASA, which was in Clear Lake, Texas. The children of these employees and their classmates had a personal interest in NASA's space missions. As a result, the students were extremely interested in learning science and specifically about outer space. In fact, we were all excited about the possibility of landing a man on the moon. This excitement had grown since 1962 when President Kennedy delivered a speech at Rice University in Houston: "We choose to go to the moon in this decade and do other things, not because they are easy, but because they are hard, because that goal will serve to organize and measure the best of our energies and skills, because that challenge is one that we are willing to accept, one we are unwilling to postpone, and one we intend to win."

On July 21, 1969, Neil Armstrong, commander of the Apollo 11 mission, and the pilot, Buzz Aldrin, landed on the moon in the lunar module Eagle. Our students were well-informed because we connected what we were learning in the classroom to the occupations of their parents. We hoped their parents would be able to show the students some of the moon materials the astronauts brought back to earth. The use of the black light and phosphorescent chalk added to the excitement and to the study of science and space travel as the students drew pictures of the planets and moons on the chalkboard. We even drew the astronauts, showing them landing on the moon.

It was during this time that I was informed that I had been recommended by HISD to represent the southwestern United States at Educational Testing Service (ETS) in Princeton, New Jersey. I had never heard of the organization before and did not know that I had been recommended until I received the invitation to participate. Perhaps it was because I had been chosen as one of the top ten teachers in HISD that I was recommended. The letter I received informed me that the ETS was a nonprofit organization and was interested in providing innovative measurement answers to improve teaching and learning while advancing equity and the quality of instruction. ETS had assembled a think tank of educators from across the country to study this issue. I could hardly wait to board a plane and head to Princeton. It was the first time I had been on a plane, and I loved it. I was fascinated by the view of the terrain and being able to see parts of the country I had only read about. At ETS, my job as a part of this distinguished group was to assist in composing writing samples to be used in state and national assessments. I learned much by this experience. I met with other educators from all over the United States and gained many insights from hearing their experiences and their knowledge about the writing process and the needs of students. Each night we met informally and shared ideas over brandy. This was commonplace at Princeton, but it was the first time I had ever drunk brandy. That was quite a change for a girl from the Bible Belt of north Louisiana.

I returned from Princeton after a full week with new insights and new ideas about the way we should approach teaching reading and writing. The method of teaching reading in HISD at that time was grouping students by their ability to read. Group one was composed of students who excelled. Group two was for average students, and group three was for struggling students. The Ginn reading series had been adopted by HISD, and those books and materials were used in reading instruction in intermediate grade levels. Doris Gates, whose stories were in the Ginn series, was commonly known as the favorite author of students in grades four and five. They especially liked her novels *Blue Willow* and *Little Vic*. I worked with student representatives from each grade level to invite the author to visit our school. To our delight, she agreed to come.

Doris Gates with Mitchell students.

We began working to raise funds for her airfare from Carmel, California. The entire community joined in the effort, and her visit to each classroom, where she read to the students, was an inspiration to all. She met with them in small groups and got to know each on a personal level. She and my family became close, and we later visited with her in her home in California. Paula, my daughter, was even able to ride her horse, Little Vic, the one who had inspired her book. We remained friends until she died in 1987.

Paula with Willow.

After teaching at Mitchell for four years, I was recruited to fill a new teacher strategist position that was created to assist white teachers who were crossed over into predominately black schools. This required that I leave my teaching position at Mitchell. I visited the classrooms of those new white teachers and held meetings to give them feedback on my observations. I offered suggestions for building relationships with students and improving classroom instructional strategies. It did not take me long to realize that the white teachers involved in this crossover program were, for the most part, first-year teachers. This experience confirmed my suspicions that the district had again found a way to circumvent the true spirit of desegregation. It became apparent to me that the district had taken the more experienced and capable black teachers and crossed them over to the white schools. Inexperienced white teachers were hired and assigned to teach in black schools. I spoke with my immediate superior about my perceptions and the negative impact this decision would have on the black students. Not only did these teachers lack instructional skills, but they were totally unprepared to meet the academic and socio-emotional needs of students because of their lack of experience as teachers in the classroom.

The white teachers in the crossover schools had great difficulty with student discipline. Even though the district practiced corporal punishment at that time, I personally never believed in that method of discipline. The white teachers in those schools were afraid of the students, and they refused to punish them in any way. They called the parents, who would come to the school wielding what appeared to be vintage ironing cords covered in cloth. The parents took their child into the restroom and whipped the child with the cord. Loud cries of pain echoed up and down the hallways. Many times, the students' legs were bleeding after the punishment. The parents were trying to support the teachers, but it simply was not working. The white teachers in these schools never understood that they were giving away their authority in the eyes of the students. Meanwhile, black teachers in these schools had very few discipline problems. I decided early on that the crossover idea was the wrong approach to school integration unless we were going to place experienced, capable white teachers into the black schools.

After a year as a teacher strategist, I was recruited to participate in the nationally funded Individually Guided Education (IGE) program. This was an educational innovation in individualized instructional approaches that originated at the Wisconsin Research and Development Center for Cognitive Learning. It was one of the few innovations scheduled for national implementation. The program sprang from educational psychology and used a behavioristic approach to learning. It involved the school principal in planning and implementing the evaluation of instruction. The program's major innovations included individualized student instruction, a multi-unit school with differentiated instruction, and an alternative to the age/grade lockstep approach. It required multi-age grouping of students based on need rather than age. IGE also had a strong and sound conceptual base and was a total rather than an add-on program. This was one of the most satisfying and creative opportunities I had in education because I had an opportunity to work with schools on innovative approaches that better met the academic and socio-emotional needs of individual students.

After working with IGE for a year, I became the principal of Mitchell Elementary in 1973, and it became an IGE school. Mitchell had been open only seven years, and it was in a new subdivision called Gulf Meadows. Most of the students were white, but there was a small number of black students who lived in a low-income housing project that had been constructed just outside the Gulf Meadows neighborhood. The integration of the school was peaceful, and there were no racially motivated fights among students. The black students quickly became an integral part of the Mitchell family, as evidenced by their participation in school activities and their parents' involvement in the school.

Bertie as principal of Mitchell Elementary.

I developed strong relationships with all my teachers and included them in leadership positions based on their abilities, not their race. One of the ways I interacted with them was using humor. Mrs. Green was one of the teachers who teased me frequently. She had a delightful sense of humor and accepted my joking with her. Mrs. Green, who was black, was often late to school because she lived in a more remote neighborhood on the other side of a railroad track. If she got to the crossing as a train was passing, she would have to wait for a long period of time until it passed. When I told her she had to start getting to work on time, she responded, "I found a solution to my problem with the train. I will just move into the vacant house next to your house." She smiled mischievously, and her eyes twinkled in anticipation of my response.

I grinned and replied, "That's okay. You can just continue to be a little late." I called her the following morning to get her up a little earlier, so she would beat the train. It felt good to be able to use humor in a conversation about a racially charged subject. Everyone, including the parents, loved Mrs. Green.

**Bertie with teacher, Ola Green,
at Mitchell Elementary.**

Many students were transferring into the school because they had heard that innovative programs were in place and that exciting things were happening. We were required to cap certain grade levels as a consequence. This created a problem for me when I told one student who had just enrolled that I would place her on the wait list and enroll her as soon as space was available. She went home crying and told her mother I had said she was fat and I was going to put her name on the "fat" list. The mother came storming into the school and screamed at me, "What do you mean telling my daughter she is fat? I will have you fired for that!" I finally calmed her down and explained I had put her daughter on the "wait," not "weight," list. We had a big laugh, and her daughter was soon enrolled in the school.

Bertie as principal of Mitchell Elementary.

During my tenure at Mitchell, Mexican American students were labeled as white, so most of the predominately black schools were paired with predominately Mexican American schools as a part of the desegregation plan. In 1970, the Mexican American Education Council (MAEC) organized a school boycott in which large numbers of high school students participated. MAEC pressured HISD to act on several issues, one of which was to cease classifying Mexican American students as white. HISD decided to act upon the issues presented by MAEC and to rezone the schools. Forced busing was tried as a solution for a while. This action caused white flight, as the whites moved to the suburbs because urban schools that had previously been entirely white were being attended by more minorities. This desegregation effort was rather short-lived.

Dianne Littlejohn was in elementary school at that time. She stated, "We moved to Houston from the Rio Grande Valley. My father is Mexican American, and my mother is black. My last name was Hernandez, and we attended the black school in our neighborhood. The students really bullied me because of my last name. They even attacked me, and I had several fights because of that, so whites were not the only ones prejudiced at that time."

Dr. Billy Reagan became the superintendent of HISD in 1974, when there was still much racial unrest resulting from the many failed attempts to desegregate. He worked hard to bring the three factions together peacefully. He made frequent visits to the schools and got to know the communities. It helped that he attended the black churches and was down-to-earth and personable. He was a frequent visitor to Mickey Gilley's club, which featured some of the most famous country western music stars. The club also featured a mechanical bull, and if we were lucky, we could hear our superintendent singing "Blue Eyes Crying in the Rain" on the radio program that was broadcast from Gilley's. Dr. Reagan held annual crawfish festivals that brought all factions of the school community together for one shared spring event.

Dr. Billy Reagan

Dr. Reagan recommended a new significant solution to the integration problem in HISD. He suggested establishing more magnet schools and making them racially balanced. The HISD board approved the solution for voluntary desegregation of the district in 1975. Each magnet was required to be composed of 30 percent black, 30 percent Hispanic, 30 percent white, and 10 percent "other." Transportation was provided, as was additional funding.

In the spring of 1979, I returned from an educational conference to learn that I had been promoted to assistant superintendent of Area V, one of the sub-districts that had been created in a recent restructuring of HISD. When I heard the news, I immediately called Dr. Reagan and told him I did not want the position. I had learned to love the students and parents at Michell, and I was heartbroken that I would have to leave them. He gave me a typical Billy Reagan response: "If you don't want to be promoted, you need to stop going out of town."

CHAPTER 15
Embracing the Joy of Broader Challenges

In 1979, when I became the assistant superintendent of Area V, the east side of Houston was predominately Hispanic. There were several Hispanic barrios with a sprinkling of black neighborhoods, including Pleasantville and Clinton Park. I was responsible for twelve elementary schools that were located mostly in the area around the Houston Ship Channel. Dan Ortiz was the Area V superintendent, and Alys Dore was the other assistant superintendent in our office. We were housed off Telephone Road in the deep East End. While this was a real learning experience for me, it simply was not as rewarding as working with students at Mitchell where I got to know the students and families on a personal level. But as I spent more and more time in the twelve schools, I built rapport with the families in that area. I became increasingly aware of the environmental problems faced by these families due to the pollutants being belched from the petrochemical plants that lined the ship channel, and that gave me cause for concern.

Thelma Garza, Bertie's HR Officer in Area V.

I began to develop strong relationships with the principals in the area. They often joked with me and took me to lunch in their favorite eating places in the deep East End of Houston. Norm Luther and George Smith were both excellent principals and real jokesters. One day they arrived at my office unannounced and began to give me directives.

"Come with us and get in the car. Hurry, we can't keep the judge waiting."

"Judge? What are you talking about? Where are you taking me?"

"Just trust us and get in the car. You just have to trust us," they said.

"I am not sure I do," I mumbled as they pulled my arm and led me out of the Area V office toward the car. "What is this about? Have I done something to upset you?"

"Just come with us, and you'll see. You'll be safe with us."

I had no idea where we were headed as the small, light blue Chevrolet moved from the office parking lot, with me bouncing in the back seat every time George sped over a pot hole in the battered street. We headed into the deep East End, and my mind swirled with questions. We careened down Navigation to 69th Street and suddenly came to a screeching halt in front of a building that resembled a courthouse. Both men sprang from the car, and Norm opened my door and shouted, "Get out! Hurry, because we are a little late!"

"What is going on here? Where are you taking me?"

"Don't ask any questions, and just come with us!" replied George grabbing my arm as we entered the building. "We're looking for the office of Judge Armando V. Rodriquez."

"Why on earth are you taking me to a judge? What crime have I committed?"

Suddenly, I was standing in front of the judge. My heart was pounding and my mind, spinning. Norm was on one side of me, and George was on the other.

The judge in a stern voice asked, "And what are the charges against this young lady?"

"Your honor," George replied. "This is Bertie Simmons, and she has been inhaling in a no-breathing zone."

I could not believe what was happening. I was petrified.

Then Judge Rodriquez smiled and said, "Mrs. Simmons, you can relax. These gentlemen were concerned about you being out and about the East End alone. They are concerned for your safety. Our purpose here today is to swear you in as a constable. Would you please raise your right hand?" With that, he swore me in as a constable and handed me a badge that read Deputy Constable of Harris County for me to wear so that the world would know I was an enforcer of the law in the East End.

Norm and George and I thanked the judge, and they hustled me back to the car and to my office. Clearly, everyone in the office knew what was happening, and they cheered as I entered the room.

Harris County Deputy Constable Badge.

The six years that I spent as assistant superintendent in Area V sped by. My days were spent visiting the schools, getting to know the culture of the community and the district in general, while helping to define the role of the newly formed areas. I was ever seeking opportunities to improve the living conditions of the families who lived in this under-served area of town. At the same time, I was always struggling with overwhelming personal problems.

CHAPTER 16
Love, Loss and
the Spirit of Forgiveness

Claude Austin, Bertie's father.

I had decided many years earlier that I had to work to restore my relationship with my father. I decided to visit with him and my mother and to have them visit me in Houston. After a few days with us, my father loudly proclaimed, "Hell, I'm tired of being here and want to go home. I'm going to go catch me an eighteen-wheeler and head back to Louisiana." We ignored him, and he never followed through. After they visited me in Houston, I purchased a house for them in Eros, Louisiana. It was the same house we had lived in on and off during my youth. I purchased the house from Uncle Keith, my mother's brother. He helped them maintain it, and he checked on them often. Dad continued to drink heavily, mostly in the late evening. He developed severe arthritis but still held on to his athletic build. He also began to treat the entire family with more respect.

I needed a new car, so I visited the Houston Teachers' Credit Union where I requested a loan to purchase a new car. Even though I had savings there, I was refused a loan until Kerry, finally and reluctantly, cosigned for me. I was chagrined because I was, in fact, earning a higher salary than he. It was not until 1974 that the equal credit opportunity act passed allowing women to apply for credit without a man cosigning.

Bertie with her husband, Kerry Simmons.

For years, my relationship with Kerry had been unraveling. He was not happy when my parents spent time with us, and I was becoming more and more liberal while he was growing more conservative. His behavior became extremely abusive toward Paula and me. As I reflected on his growing aggression, I believed that something had happened to him while he was in the navy that affected his behavior and his health. He was always angry. I begged him to go with me to marriage counseling, but he refused to go.

Then one day when Paula was still in high school, I intervened as he was yelling at her and asked him to let me talk to her. He grabbed my head between his hands and began viciously slapping me on the side of my face while clenching the hair on the other side of my head. My head felt like it was in a vice. He dragged me into the bathroom and began beating my head on the side of the bathtub. Paula was screaming for him to stop. He finally dropped me to the floor, turned and charged out the back door, jumped into his car, and sped away.

Paula helped me clean the blood from my face as we planned to protect ourselves. We found some strong ropes in the garage and tied a rope to each outside doorknob. We then tied the other end of the ropes to the piano legs, a metal railing that divided the sunken den, and anything else that we could find. We stayed awake all night, but Kerry didn't return that night. Overnight I had gathered all the silver dollars I had saved, my jewelry, and our silver flatware and hid it between the mattresses in the guest bedroom.

When I returned home after work the next day, I found that he had returned while I was gone and had taken everything from the guest room, including what I had hidden there. The next day I called the bank and found that he had taken all the funds from our joint checking account as well as our savings. Later he called, and we agreed on a no-fault divorce, which was finalized in 1978. Paula and I would get the house, and he would pay one hundred dollars a month child support until Paula graduated from college. I was relieved to end the marriage, but after twenty-one years of marriage, I was back where I had started financially.

I was unable to make the payments on the house, plus the payments for my car and a car we had purchased for Paula. I enrolled in evening classes at Rice University to learn more about how to invest in the stock market and how to manage money. One thing that I learned later was how to buy and flip houses. I owned six rent houses at one time which enabled me to increase my income. Eventually, however, I was forced to sell the house. Paula suggested that a longtime family friend, Sharon Koonce, and I should purchase a house together since she had recently divorced and was unable to afford her own house payments. We bought a house in a Jewish subdivision called Meyerland. Paula and I shared this house with Sharon and her two children. This shared living provided support for both families and developed into a trusting relationship that sustained us through the years. For me personally, it provided a safe haven after many years of physical and emotional abuse. It helped that our parents were friends and they gave us moral support that we needed.

Bertie with her mother.

During one of my visits home, I became concerned about Mother's health. She had lost weight and lacked the high energy she once had. I insisted she see a doctor. The news was devastating. She had ovarian cancer that had metastasized, and when she attempted to roll a window down in the car, she heard a crack in her spine. She was left paralyzed from her chest down. I went to get her to come to Houston. She was treated by a local doctor, and she and my father stayed with me. I placed a small bell on her nightstand so she could wake me during the night if she needed something. She made good use of it, and each time she rang, and I entered her room, she was smiling and quoting Oscar Hammerstein's lyrics about a bell not being a bell until you ring it. She invariably quoted the entire poem which ends with a line about how love is not love until it is given away.

One night she had a bowel movement, and as I took care of her, I had the feces all over my hands and arms. Mother lovingly remarked, "I guess my legacy will be that I am the only person who could shit all over you and get away with it." That was the first time in my life that I had heard her use any off-color word.

I made a major effort to keep my spirits high at work as Mother died right before my eyes. She died in 1982, and I had her body sent home to Louisiana for her funeral services and burial. Two of my principals from Houston attended her funeral: Rick Werlin and Jessie Woods. Jessie sang with the Houston Grand Opera, and Mother had wanted him to sing the Lord's Prayer at her funeral. She had requested that I sing "Don't Cry for Me, Argentina" from the Broadway musical Evita. The song ends with Evita singing about keeping her promises.

While we were waiting for the service to begin, I heard a woman behind me ask, referring to Jessie, "Ain't that the nigger that Bertie likes so much?" I got up and brought Rick and Jessie to sit in the front row with the family. When Jessie sang, there were no dry eyes in the room. Most people had never heard an operatic voice before. They also cried when I sang, but I think it was because my voice was so terrible compared to his. After the service, Rick and Jessie spent the night with my father because there were no motels within miles of the town. Later, my father received threats for having a black person in his home.

My father died of lung cancer two years later. My doctor said I was a "cancer waiting to happen." I was so glad that I had bought them a house so they wouldn't always be moving. I was also happy I had restored all broken relationships with my family.

It was at this time that I learned that Mrs. Ewing had cancer and was not expected to live. I drove to the hospital in Ruston, Louisiana to see her, expecting to be the only former student to be there. To my surprise, when I reached the hospital there was a long line of former students waiting to say goodbye to her. After standing in the hospital hallway for an hour and a half, I finally got to her bedside. She had lost so much weight that she was hardly recognizable, but she still had that beautiful heart and smile. I told her how much she meant to me and how I hoped to be able to help other struggling students the way she had helped me. When I left her room, I felt that I had just spoken with an angel, and I was more determined to continue her work.

Mrs. Ewing

After our divorce, I kept in touch with Kerry because of his relationship with Paula. He had remarried and as he grew older, he had extreme difficulty breathing as a result of asbestosis. He had told me that when he was in the navy, the insulation covering the pipes over his bunk was worn and he was constantly inhaling asbestos as he slept. During the last few years of his life, he required an oxygen tank wherever he went. He was sitting at a blackjack table in Lake Charles, Louisiana when he fell off the stool and immediately died. My aunts were saddened by the fact that he was going to hell because he had died gambling, which was clearly a sin.

CHAPTER 17
Growing Together
in Spirit and Mind

D r. Joan Raymond became superintendent of the HISD in 1986 and immediately reorganized the district into clusters. She explained that we had too much power having offices located in the various areas of town. She moved our offices into central administration, and we became cluster managers. Each cluster manager was responsible for schools spread throughout the district.

When the district was reorganized in 1988 from clusters into sub-districts, I was promoted to superintendent of the new District VIII. I was responsible for twenty-four schools, which included elementary, middle, and high schools. This was also in the East End, which was predominately minority.

Bertie as District Superintendent, District VIII.

My team consisted of three instructional specialists, and we worked to increase the arts in education by collaborating with the numerous arts organizations in the city. We received grants that enabled us to take students to theatrical productions at the Alley Theater and Jones Hall in downtown Houston. We were closely aligned with Young Audiences of Houston as a part of the Arts Partners program. Because of this partnership, I received the Fredell Lack Award for the integration of arts in education. The grants also allowed us to take entire families to local art museums, where they learned about the art of Van Gogh, Munch, and Gauguin. They learned about the emergence of expressionism because of humanity's loss of spirituality and authenticity. They learned how this was a reaction to impressionism. The families were thrilled by the experience and appreciative of the fact the message was delivered in English and in Spanish and made good use of real-life materials.

District VIII Arts Festival.

Another area of focus for us was improving students' writing. It became clear as we worked with the school administrators that, while they were adept at writing memos and letters, they had little knowledge of any other writing. The teachers knew and taught sentence structure and grammar, but they were not teaching students to write about subjects with joy and enthusiasm. There was also a great emphasis on penmanship.

I had often reflected upon an experience I had as a new teacher in Houston. I was teaching a writing class when my supervisor dropped in for a visit. The students were all engaged and excited and were writing about their favorite subject in school. So much learning was occurring with a great deal of enthusiasm, and I thought I had taught the hell out of the lesson—that is, until the supervisor called me outside to speak with me.

"Your penmanship is atrocious!" my supervisor screamed. "How do you expect them to know how to write when you cannot write? Have you ever considered a different profession? If you plan to teach here, I expect you to stay after school and practice making ovals, pushes, and pulls on the lined chalk board until you learn how to make your writing acceptable."

She marched away, and I was left stunned and confused. Where had I learned that writing wasn't penmanship? Perhaps my writing was so bad because I had been teaching in high schools where no one ever judged me on my penmanship. This interaction made me determined to learn to make ovals and to teach students to write with enthusiasm.

Paula, Berlinda Lawson, Melanie Uzzell, and Sharon Koonce preparing for a meeting.

We supported teacher professional development related to writing in other ways, too. We invited administrators and teachers to attend a volunteer writing class in the district office where we studied the works of great writers and poets and worked to improve our own writing, which we shared with our students. We took principals on field trips to local museums where they chose a work of art to study, research, and describe in writing.

Melanie Uzzell, Thelma Garza, and Ella Bisher.

Teachers became enthusiastic about teaching writing, not as penmanship but rather as opportunities for students to write about their own experiences and to express their opinions. One of those teachers shared this piece, "Stuck Together," written by a student who really got into describing vividly and honestly an experience he had:

> Yesterday I went outside to play baseball. I found my dog and another dog stuck together from the behind. Me, Paul, and Monica tried to get them apart every way we could think of. Finally, we gave up and we turned around and they got unstuck together. I chased the other dog away.

One life-changing professional development meeting was held at the Rothko Chapel in Houston. The Rothko Chapel and the Broken Obelisk, which stands at the entrance of the chapel, are real-life examples of the history of our city. The Rothko Chapel, designed by the modern artist Mark Rothko, is octagon-shaped with benches arranged in a circular formation as seating for independent thought and reflection. People of all religions, as well as those who embrace no religion, are welcome in the chapel. Fourteen black-hued paintings by Rothko invite visitors to look deeply into their souls and find peace and understanding in this human rights center. It is a sacred place where seminars are held to develop a shared understanding about issues related to freedom and justice throughout the world. It is also a space for individual meditation, which is open to the public daily.

We were inspired as we learned about how the chapel had become an international symbol of justice. The Rothko Chapel Award was created in 1980 to recognize individuals and organizations who had taken great risks to condemn human rights violations. Nelson Mandela was a recipient of the award and gave the keynote speech at the twentieth anniversary of the chapel in 1991. Sadly, Mark Rothko, who was commissioned by John and Dominque de Menil to design this amazing center for justice, never saw the structure because he committed suicide in 1970 after a long struggle with depression.

The Broken Obelisk is a sculpture designed by Barnett Newman between 1963 and 1967. It rests in the middle of a reflection pool in front of the chapel and appears to float on the surface of the water. Its plaque reads as follows:

Broken Obelisk at Rothko Chapel.

The story of the Broken Obelisk by Barnett Newman and how it came to be at the Rothko Chapel was a controversial one, caught up during the turmoil of the late 1960s. The city of Houston had received a grant to help purchase a work of contemporary sculpture for Houston. In 1969, the de Menils offered to match the grant and chose the Broken Obelisk, specifying that it be placed near City Hall and dedicated to the recently slain civil rights hero, Dr. Martin Luther King, Jr. The city accepted the choice of the sculpture but rejected the dedication. The de Menils withdrew their offer and purchased the sculpture outright, setting it instead in front of the Rothko Chapel and, per Newman's wishes, over a reflecting pool. The Broken Obelisk represents the Rothko Chapel's commitment to human rights and social justice and honors a great man whose life and ministry embodies the values of this sacred institution.

We were so fortunate to have had this opportunity to "touch shoulders" with the amazing Dominique de Menil and to hear her stories of the Rothko Chapel and the Broken Obelisk. We discussed how much injustice still exists. I was moved personally to show more compassion to others, and the entire group expressed how much they were inspired by this experience and planned to go back and improve relationships at school and in their communities.

Bertie receiving the Fredell Lack Award.

CHAPTER 18
I Travel Mostly Alone
and at Night

I should have gone sooner to sell the house and would have but for the insufferable pain I knew it would cause me. I had not been home since the death of my parents. Mother had asked me not to tell anyone there that Kerry and I had divorced. She held on to the belief that getting a divorce was sinful. I decided it was time to make one final visit. It had been almost a year since Dad's funeral. I had lived with the false hope that distancing myself would somehow enable me to pretend my parents were still alive. Tonight, though, I knew I had to face the facts and make the seven-hour journey from Houston to Eros, Louisiana, a "stop in the road" that never quite lived up to the spirit of the Greek god of love for whom it was named.

I made the trip alone and, as I had so often done, at night after work. Mother often worried when I drove home alone and especially at night. She and Dad would take bets as to my expected time of arrival, and Dad's calculation was always later and usually correct. He invariably made the same remark when I pulled into the driveway and they charged out to greet me, rubbing sleep from their eyes.

Smiling a broad, toothless grin, his one good eye sparkling and his blind one squinted shut, he would exclaim, "See? I told you she would come dragging in about this time. You know how she can piddle around. How are you, baby?" Then he would tell me what a hard day he had had and excuse himself. I could always smell liquor on his breath. As he turned to stride up the steps, his still well-toned body resembled that of an athlete, but his gnarled fingers betrayed the truth.

Mother would smile knowingly and begin to help me unload the car as she filled me in on the local gossip. Later she would sit on the edge of my bed and talk for hours. Tonight, too, I somehow felt they were taking bets on my time of arrival.

Heading north on highway 59, once the 5 p.m. traffic had died down, the whir of my tires provided the backdrop for my reverie. I had made this trip so many times and on many special occasions. I could hardly wait twenty-five years ago to show my newborn baby girl, Paula, to my relatives. Each trip home at Christmas had been charged with excitement as I arrived with the car brimming with gaily wrapped packages and enough food to fill the Astrodome. I laughed as I recalled the countless reels of home movies we always took, complete with random shots of the ceiling and floor.

At Woodville in far east Texas, I took a right, and the countryside turned into rolling hills. It was dark now, and the tall, slender pine trees stood along each side, protecting me. The crescent moon was a sliver playing hopscotch in the boughs of the trees. I remembered Dad saying about such a moon, "Well, the moon's holding water, so we're in for a thumping big rain soon. Hell, we could sure use one."

Before I knew it, I was crossing the Sabine River, and my lights captured the outline of the Pelican State, welcoming me to Louisiana. Halfway home, I thought. From now on, I must take care on the winding, two-lane, country roads.

Turning north, I wormed my way through the back woods. I could make good time here since the roads had little traffic this time of night. A light wind had come up, and the branches on the trees waved in rhythm with my heartbeat. A thunderhead lurked ahead, and ominous streaks of light cut jagged lines across the horizon like a dull saw out of control. Clouds now covered the moon, and the night was what Dad described as "pitch black." I turned the radio on, and Johnny Cash blasted forth with a song about keeping a close watch on his heart. He said he kept his eyes wide open all the time. I had grown up with country and western music because Dad once had his own band. I recalled with fondness how he had a radio program where they introduced him as the "Singing Cowboy from Swartz." We all thought that was funny and teased him unmercifully. I smiled as I remembered that he never rode a horse, but he did sound a little like Johnny Cash and even shared some of his vices.

I made my way through Natchitoches, slowing down to glance at the silhouette of Northwestern State University where I had completed my undergraduate studies. Then, there was Cain River, bordered by majestic Victorian homes, weeping willows and black wrought iron benches. The lightning was closer now and reflected in the river, reminding me of the fireworks that greeted the Christmas season there the first weekend in December.

In Winfield, I passed the Huey P. Long Memorial, and was on my last lap. The memorial reminded me of Dad's assessment of politicians in general and specifically those from Louisiana. "They're all a bunch of damn crooks," he would insist, and lift a Budweiser to his pursed lips and drain it.

I decided to take a short cut where battered trucks loaded with logs or pulpwood had beaten away at the asphalt, leaving potholes and loose gravel. The road had sharp curves as it wound through a swamp area with thick-trunked cypress trees, moss hanging from the limbs like gray ghouls. Fog had settled in, but still, I prided myself in being able to predict with accuracy around which curve I would spot a rabbit, or perhaps a deer bounding gracefully into the undergrowth, never knowing I had detected the fear in his eyes.

Finally, there was the sign: Welcome to Eros. The fog dulled the glow from the sparsely placed streetlights, and tiny droplets of water formed a rainbow around each light. Sharp's, the only store in town, had long been closed for the day, and the Eight Ball, where idle boys shot pool for hours, was dark. The town was asleep.

Eros water tower.

Off to the right, I could see the house. It was the one I had bought for them so they could stay in one place. We had also lived in this house from time to time when I was a child. Pulling into the driveway, I studied the landscape. In the flower bed where zinnias once bloomed in profusion, tall, dried blood weeds stood at attention. The yard was overgrown, and paint flaked from the house. No one was there to greet me. Grasping my flashlight, I turned the car lights off, opened the door, and stepped into the yard. I turned the flashlight on and eased up the rickety steps to the weathered porch. Suddenly, there was a burst of wind, setting the weeds at battle with the walls and windows. They seemed to be telling me to go away, that I was a foreigner and unwelcome. I clutched the flashlight tightly and reached for the handle of the rusty screen door. When I pulled it open, it squeaked that old familiar squeak, flooding my mind with memories.

I put the key in the knob of the door and quietly opened it. Sweeping the room with the flashlight, I focused on a clean eight-by-ten-inch rectangle on the faded wallpaper that covered the living room wall. That was where the now missing reproduction of Salvador Dali's *Last Supper* once hung. I had brought the print to Mother from my first trip to the National Art Gallery in Washington, DC. She hung it on the wall as she did the many pictures we drew for her. She didn't seem to mind that I had slipped her into surrealism in my efforts to show her that I could recognize Jesus in his many forms. I never told her that I had heard that Dali covered his body with fish oil to make himself repulsive. She probably had read the same thing since she read everything she could get her hands on and continued to check out books from the mobile library on a weekly basis. I recalled the many dictionaries she had literally worn out as she strove to increase her vocabulary and understanding of all that she read. They were still on the shelf in the living room.

I continued to pan the room with the light beam and settled on two books stacked in the corner. Moving carefully through the dust-laden room, I bent over, swept away the spider webs and picked up the books. The *Book of Mormons* rested there atop the Bible, and it was almost as if Mother had the final say even though she had dropped the Mormon beliefs. The Bible was the one I had given Dad. He had insisted that it be the King James version. "Any other," he declared, "was surely the work of the devil." Returning to the door, I placed the books on the floor, so I could get them as I was leaving.

I followed the flashlight into the hallway and then into the kitchen. I could almost smell bacon frying and taste the wonderfully delicious chocolate meringue pies Mother always had waiting for me. My memory bank sprang open. Mother stood in front of the stove singing, "Sowing in the morning, sowing seeds of kindness, sowing in the noontide and the dewy eve." She was dressed, as usual, in a white oversized man's shirt with the sleeves rolled up to the elbow, and a Kleenex jutting from the pocket. The shirttail covered the top portion of her petite jeans, and that, coupled with her pixie haircut, gave her the appearance of a teenager. Her soft, misty-gray eyes and mischievous grin completed the image.

I inched through the kitchen, studying it with my light. I found the back window and peered through it, over the back porch, into the yard. There it stood. I bounded through the door, across the porch, rushed out to my oak tree and threw my arms around its thick trunk. Its boughs shook feebly. A slab of bark fell to the ground when I removed my arms. This tree knew all my childhood secrets, for it was in its shade that I had contemplated the how and why of life. I remember the long hours Mother and I sat leaning against its powerful trunk as we discussed Thoreau, Emerson, and Whitman. And there was the Sunday I visited the Methodist Church, and the preacher told the story of Zacchaeus. This was the tree I had climbed to its highest branches, so I could get a good view of the Lord and ask him to help our family. The tree groaned and gently swayed. I threw the beams into the tree and washed each branch with light. It was then I realized that it was beginning to decay.

I swung the light across the yard and trudged to the back fence, hoping to gaze beyond it into the open field where I once gathered wildflowers and crammed them lovingly into a mayonnaise jar to present to Mother. To my surprise, this open range where cowboys and Indians once cavorted freely, dodging imaginary arrows, had surrendered to progress and was a sprawling concrete foundation of a never completed structure.

I returned to the house for one last look. My damp feet left wet footprints on the dusty back porch and followed me as I made my way through the kitchen and into the hallway. There was one more room I had to explore. It was almost dawn, and I had planned to leave before sunup. I quickly targeted Mother and Dad's bedroom, scanning the ceiling and walls. Assuming the room would be empty, I turned to leave and felt a soft mass underneath my feet. The light revealed a smashed Sears gift box with papers scattered around it. It appeared that someone had rummaged through the contents and, finding nothing of interest, strewn them on the floor. I knelt and picked up the lid and wiped away the dust with the palm of my sweaty hand. The box was labeled TREASURES, and it was clearly Mother's printing. Curious about what Mother considered a treasure, I randomly selected one of the papers, which read:

October 7, 1941

Dear Mother,

I am lerning to rite. I live

you, do you live me?

Live,

Bertie `

I also found that Mother had kept many of the poems I had written as a child. Gathering the treasures from the floor, I stuffed them into the flattened box and stuck it under my arm. I retraced my footprints to the front door, stooped and placed the treasures on top of the books and clutched them to my breast. I opened the squeaking screen door and held it with my foot while I closed and locked the front door. Stepping onto the porch, I released the screen door, and it slammed shut, closing a chapter in my life and opening another.

As I scrambled down the steps, I spotted a small oak tree nestled among the blood weeds, struggling to reach the sunlight creeping over the horizon. I rushed to the little tree. Kneeling, I placed my treasures on the ground, and cupped the tiny seedling between my palms. Visions of my grandchildren skipping out to play under the tree flooded my mind, and I knew why I traveled mostly alone and at night.

CHAPTER 19
Looming Disaster

After my final trip to my parents' home, I threw myself back into my work. The district was reorganizing again, and District VIII was to become the East District. We were making great progress when I received a phone call from an HISD board member. I was in a staff meeting so I took the call from Mrs. Gallegos. She was not my board member, but I assumed she was going to request action that would include my entire staff.

"I'm aware I am not your board member," she began, "but I have a request of you. I noticed you have an opening at Whittier Elementary, and I want you to place a person in that school as principal." Then she told me who the person was. I knew the individual had been campaigning for her during school hours. I also knew the individual liked neither teachers nor students.

"I can't do that," I replied. "I know she worked on your election campaign, but I also know she doesn't really care for either students or teachers. I cannot place such an individual as principal of a school."

"What do you mean you won't do it? Do you know I am a school board member and you are expected to do as I ask? You had better place her there."

"I am aware you are a board member, but I am also aware that your role is to develop policy. You are not to have any role in personnel assignments."

The conversation went on for about thirty minutes when she finally stated, "You are going to pay for this. You mark my word."

"You do what you want, but I like to sleep at night, so I cannot do as you requested," I replied.

My staff and I were shocked. We knew that the newly appointed superintendent of schools wanted to appease the school board member, who was Hispanic. It was a late Friday afternoon, and before I left work, I received a call informing me that I was to report to the deputy superintendent's office on Sunday morning.

During the meeting, I was informed that, although I had excellent assessments, the East End needed a Hispanic male as district superintendent. I was being moved to the district office in the south part of the city and demoted to assistant superintendent. In addition, my salary would be frozen for the next three years. When I asked why I was being moved, I was told I had always done a great job. It was just that the East End was predominately Hispanic, so they needed a Hispanic male superintendent. When I asked why my salary was being frozen, I was told that was just the way things were done.

Bertie at South Area Arts Festival.

I left the meeting confused and sick over the loss of my staff and the schools that we had all grown to love. I began to receive calls from Hispanic politicians asking me to sue the school district. I explained that I was not the "suing kind" and would not do it. I would just go to the south district office and do the best job I could do, and I did.

The HISD superintendent who had removed me was here today and gone tomorrow. He did not last long as our superintendent. When the newly appointed superintendent, Dr. Rod Paige, was informed by Deputy Superintendent Lloyd Choice that my rights had been violated, he immediately called me in to meet with him. He invited me to a closed session of the board of education, where I was to tell my story. When it came my time to speak, I told the story of my phone call from a board member and subsequent actions taken by the district. The board member who had called me stood and began raving at me. One of the most complimentary statements she made about me was that I was a liar. When she calmed down, I simply remarked that the speaker phone had been on and my entire staff had heard her haranguing and threatening me. They had all agreed to testify on my behalf. She was shocked and immediately sat down. I was dismissed from the meeting. I left the building concerned for the welfare of my daughter and grandchildren. Could she possible do something to them? I wondered…

Students of the South Area.

I was promoted to a central office position as an assistant superintendent of campus management. I was assigned the duty of investigating two schools that had been identified by the Texas Education Agency for possible cheating on the state test. An individual from the testing department accompanied me. We found clear evidence of inappropriate actions, which I documented and provided to the superintendent's office. I never knew whether he received the findings, but the two principals of the schools were presented at the next board of education meeting as exemplary principals.

The following day, I retired. I didn't wish to be a part of the organization anymore. I was aware of its politics and the influence its leaders wielded.

I had earlier had job offers, and I accepted one from Kid's Now, whose mission was to raise funds for public schools. I became the representative for the southwestern states, which included Texas, Arizona, Tennessee, Missouri, and Kansas. I worked with the schools to raise funds and had the opportunity to work with many star athletes in the National Basketball Association and the National Football League. I worked with Clyde Drexler, Peyton Manning, and others. One of the most outstanding individuals with whom I worked was former First Lady, Barbara Bush. That lady was a class act and worked diligently to assist students in public schools to improve their reading skills as well as to raise funds for schools. Her heart was the size of the Astrodome, and her generosity was unsurpassed. She became a new role model for me.

Bertie receiving the Kids Now Award.

Ashley

She came to us on cotton feet.
No drumroll, no fanfare.
Wise beyond her years, she took
A page from Nostradamus's playbook
And began to fill our hearts and souls with love
and possibilities.

She traveled widely in her short life,
Seeking knowledge and inspiration,
Enjoying Broadway and searching for Seasons of Love
And gold in Alaska.
Ever seeking – seeking for a way to
Make the world a better place for all people.

A thoughtful young lady who smiles down on us
from her Wyeth's Window,
Sending her quiet, unassuming strength to her followers,
All of us, her loves,
Charging our weary hearts and souls to activism and determination,
To unwavering commitment, to hope.

She was my first grandchild
But much, much more.
She was my anchor in a turbulent, restless sea of life.
She is now my memory mentor fueling me with strength
to make the world a better place for all people,
just as she had predicted.

-Bertie Simmons
2017

Bertie with Ashley.

CHAPTER 20
The Unbelievable

"When are we going snow skiing?" Ashley pleaded. "I'm sixteen, and all my friends have done it."

"Why not?" I replied, remembering Ashley had never had that experience and forgetting what I had read about left-handed people not being able to handle skis. Ashley was left-handed.

Our family decided to make the trip to Ruidoso, New Mexico, and go snow skiing over spring break. Sharon Koonce and her son, David, and daughter, Melinda, and their spouses joined us on the expedition. My granddaughters, Ashley and Brooke, were giddy as they prepared for the trip. Austin, their fifteen-month-old brother, could not have cared less.

Bertie's granddaughter, Ashley Fendley.

Several days before our departure, my Aunt Orell, the one who checked on me when I was four, called.

"I wish you wouldn't go on your ski trip. I have a strange feeling about it, and it involves Ashley," she said. "Would you just think about it?"

I had that same uneasy feeling but hadn't told anyone. How could I throw cold water on everyone's excitement? So, we boarded the plane for Ruidoso and a fun-filled week of skiing.

Ashley as a jazz dancer.

Ashley wanted to practice on the bunny trails on the first day and then go bobsledding the following day. Brooke and Ashley convinced their father, Terry, to take them to the bunny trails for their first runs. The women decided to remain at the cabin and relax for the day.

Ashley kissed me good-bye saying, "We will have a ball tomorrow on the bobsleds."

"Please have fun and be careful," I whispered to her as she prepared her face for the intense sun. "I love you."

Several hours later, there was a frantic pounding at the front door. We rushed to open it, and there stood Terry and Brooke, crying. The two ski patrols stood beside them on the front porch.

"What happened?" screamed Paula. "Where is Ashley?"

"There was an accident," one of the ski troopers replied. "Ashley was injured and has been taken to the hospital." He handed Paula a card. "You can call this number to check on her."

Paula rushed to the phone. "How badly is she injured?" she asked, shaking and crying uncontrollably.

"The accident was really bad," the voice replied.

"Is she dead?" screamed Paula.

"Yes," was the reply. "I am so sorry."

We all fell apart physically, mentally, and emotionally. I ran to

Paula and held her as she groaned and convulsed with sobs. How could that be? What had happened?

Ashley as a ballerina.

The three skiers had moved from the bunny trails to a longer beginner slope for the last run of the day. Brooke, who was only eleven years old at the time, fell after a short distance and was too afraid to keep going. As Terry moved toward his younger daughter who was sitting on the slope, he heard Ashley call out as she glided down the slope, "Look, Brooke! It's easy." A few moments later as he helped Brooke to her feet, he heard someone scream, "Medic!" When he turned to look, he did not see Ashley anywhere. Fear swept over him, and he screamed for Ashley. There was no response. He screamed again and again, and then saw where another skier was pointing.

Ashley's skis had struck something in the snow, catapulting her through the air until her head hit a tree. Terry forgot Brooke, who was still sitting at the top of the slope, and ran to Ashley, lying at the foot of the tree.

After the accident, despite the fact she had witnessed the tragedy while sitting alone at the top of the ski slope, Brooke somehow pushed through it all and lifted our spirits. She reached deep inside herself and found the strength to continue to give us hope and a degree of peace which none of us ever thought we would find. When Austin would wake up during the night, he would slip out of his bed and climb in bed with Brooke. When Paula was inconsolable, Brooke would hold her and comfort her. Brooke had a clever sense of humor that kept us laughing in spite of our grief. She later described how many people who had witnessed the accident came to her. "I learned there are many caring people in the world," she said. "I want to grow up to be a caring person."

Bertie's granddaughter, Brooke Fendley, as a dancer.

121

Bertie's grandson, Austin Fendley, as a "tough guy."

Austin, on the other hand, completely stopped talking after Ashley's death. When he began to talk again, his first words were, "I saw Ashley. She was flying in the air." We were overjoyed when he overcame his trauma and began to verbally express himself. He often spoke of Ashley.

We all attended numerous therapy sessions, but it never worked well for me. I was especially concerned about Paula, and her pain multiplied mine. She was working as a counselor at Bellaire High School and had recently returned from a week-long training about grief counseling. She and I had discussed how helpful the training had been. Somehow, I knew it would not help her personally as she dealt with her own tragedy. I ached as I heard her guttural sounds as the pain ripped at her soul. She responded better to the therapy and survived by throwing her energy into helping others. She had graduated summa cum laude when she completed college and went on to receive her doctorate in educational administration. She later became the principal of an award-winning high school on the east side of town with a predominately Hispanic student population. She loved the students and parents, but after five years of working at the school, she felt called to do something more. After over thirty years of a highly successful career in education as a teacher, counselor, assistant principal, and principal, she retired to pursue other interests and is now flourishing as an educational consultant and life coach. This dream job enabled her to assist others in living the life they desired. I have always taken such pride in her.

**Bertie at Brooke's graduation from
the University of Houston.**

Brooke grew from a shy eleven-year-old girl to a strong young woman who has touched the lives of many people with her love of life, creativity, and compassion. She graduated from FIDM (Fashion Institute of Design and Merchandising) in Los Angeles and then cum laude from the University of Houston with a bachelor's degree in retail and consumer science. She later completed her teacher certification through an alternative certification program. Brooke married Tim Conley, the love of her life, and became a distinguished teacher of mathematics. She created a math wonderland of creativity and excitement for her students. She moved from teaching to her first love, interior design, when her child, Hank, was born. That made me a great-grandmother, and I was happy to hold little Hank in my arms. I hoped he would possess the compassion, creativity, and imagination of his mother.

Hank the Tank.

Austin became a little boy with an insatiable thirst for knowledge and an unusual ability to make friends with diverse groups of people, adults and children alike. He never met a stranger and was quick to express empathy if he sensed that someone was sad or upset. As he grew older, he developed a deep interest in environmental issues and demonstrated unusual skills in music and athletics. Austin had always excelled in school and received honors for his academic achievement. When he entered public school after having been enrolled in Montessori classes, he was placed in a grade level one year above his peers. He played the tenor saxophone and made all-city band as a sixth grader and was first chair in his middle school band.

When Austin was in the fifth grade, he demonstrated a strong social awareness by working with the City of Houston to address a safety issue in his neighborhood. As a result, four-way stop signs were erected at an intersection where numerous accidents had occurred. Later in that same year, Austin made a presentation to the HISD Board of Education, admonishing the board about the environmental and health hazards related to the use of Styrofoam trays in school cafeterias. He quoted Drew Dellinger's poem "What Did You Do Once You Knew?" He then looked directly at the board members and asked, "What will you do?" At the following meeting, the board approved funds to replace the Styrofoam trays with environmentally friendly ones in the elementary schools. Austin brought joy into our lives. However, I often threatened to give him a humility shot when he was asleep.

Austin, University of Texas graduate, 2019.

Before we left Ruidoso that March of 1999, I had called Tarrant Fendley, Ashley's grandfather and Terry's father, and asked him to establish a scholarship foundation in her name. The funds would be used to provide college scholarships for deserving students in two areas: one would be a humanitarian scholarship and the other a fine arts scholarship. These were both areas Ashley valued. So far, the funds have enabled us to help over ninety students attain their goal of attending college.

Ashley and I had been writing a book for high school seniors entitled *Wind for New Wings*. The book was about half finished when she died. I completed the book, and it was published in 2000. We presented the book as a gift to graduating seniors who attended our *Wind for New Wings* conference, which was held yearly for three years after her death. The proceeds from the sale of the book were donated to the Ashley Fendley Scholarship Foundation. Perhaps Ashley was continuing to make the world a better place for all people.

As so often happens when such a devastating event occurs, Paula and Terry separated and eventually divorced. They remain good friends, and both continue to love and support the children.

Terry Fendley and Bertie autographing
Wind for New Wings.

125

PART II

Instructions to the Artist

Reflections after two years as the
Furr High School Principal Houston, Texas:

I wish my body to look like Venus
One arm chopped off from days at Furr.
The other one just a whisper of what once was.
My face should be without
Wrinkles and the color
Of freshly gathered honey,
While my eyes are azure peeking
Out from long, long lashes.
Place me in a garden of flowers
With a harpist strumming a
Brahms melody – Songbirds flitting
Through the air and the
Wind playing tag with
The weeping willow.
If a horse is included
Let it be a donkey
Placed strategically near my
Foot for when I need to kick
Ass (just in case I need to do it).
Place a setting sun in the
Distance and a rainbow
Over my right shoulder
Which supports a pot of golden pigeon eggs.
Then run like hell!

-Bertie Simmons
February 10, 2003

CHAPTER 21
The Struggle to Maintain Ethics

School principals in general, but specifically high school principals, are expected to be single-handedly accountable for the varied and near-overwhelming responsibilities they face daily. They are instructed to practice zero tolerance and decrease the dropout rate at the same time. They are reminded daily by central administration that the district is decentralized, and yet control and punishment are delivered from on high. When it is mandated that ninth graders must pass all core courses in order to be classified as a tenth grader, how can the principal convince those students held back that graduation is a reality for them, especially if they have been retained twice before they reach the ninth grade? What about the ninth graders who are nineteen or twenty years old? How long will they hold on to hope? All principals want to be held accountable, but does that accountability model necessitate that they receive little support from the district? Clearly, there is a need to create a caring school climate in the high school, and there must be high expectations for school personnel and students. It is a given that a rigorous academic program is essential to prepare students for a future we cannot even ourselves imagine.

The question is, How does one reinvent a high school while operating in an oppressive school system driven by high-stakes test scores? What do high school principals do when, on one hand, emphasis is placed on innovative approaches, such as breaking up large schools to create smaller personalized learning communities, while, on the other hand, they are told the only things that really matter are raising scores on the state-mandated test, reducing the dropout rate, increasing the graduation and completion rates, and furthering individual student growth, which is measured by an elusive, confusing assessment that no one understands? How do principals meet all requirements without compromising their principles? Or perhaps a more fundamental and frightening question is, Do principles really matter in today's fast-paced society? Have we substituted looking good to the public for hard work, honesty, and integrity and for doing whatever it takes to meet the needs, both personal and academic, of each student who enters the doorway of the school? Have we sold out to a business model that calculates our gains and losses by hiding the debt—which in the case of our work is the student? Do we use questionable accounting techniques to show inflated gains in test scores while treading water in a cesspool of immoral and unethical maneuvers? Can we then with a clear conscience present ourselves as a system that has found the silver bullet? How many lost students will it take before someone declares, "The emperor has on no clothes?"

When principals' jobs are dependent upon their school having high scores on mandated tests, to what levels will they stoop in order to keep food on the table? Is that practice contributing significantly to the moral decay that abounds at all levels in our present society? In the name of "leaving no child behind," are we ignoring all research indicating the negative impact that repeated failure has on students? Will that senseless slogan with its abusive results require that principals, with even more desperation, search for ways to hide the loss? How many effective and caring principals can survive the demands of such requirements that fly in the face of all we know about human needs and the human spirit? Do not these outside controls strip the school community of its soul, leaving it to function as a mindless, uncaring machine? Finally, when cash bonuses are meted out to principals, teachers, district superintendents, and the general superintendent as a result of these tests, does that blast open the door to fraud even wider?

This is the story of one principal's attempt to face these challenges. It is not intended to be a model for others but rather a story of one individual's struggle to find her way while attempting to hold on to a principled anchor lest she become adrift in a sea of propaganda and incalculable loss of human potential. This experience led to the unimaginable end of my story.

CHAPTER 22
A Return to the East End

As I left my home in West University Place, in the year of 2000, I was having second thoughts about accepting the role as hourly principal at Furr High School. It was a troubled school located in the deep East End, and I knew the school had widespread gang activity, a high dropout rate, and low student attendance and graduation rates. I knew the achievement scores on the state-mandated test were expected to improve but primarily because the school had obtained a waiver from the district that permitted them to maintain the ninth-grade classification for those students who had not passed all ninth-grade core courses. Only tenth-grade scores counted toward state accountability. I knew it was a predominately Hispanic school with a significant number of black students and a few whites. I was unsure whether the students would accept me, a sixty-six-year-old Anglo. I knew many of the teachers would not. They wanted no supervisor, and certainly not me. I had known many of the teachers when I served as their district superintendent and knew some of them to be an arrogant, disrespectful group who screamed for "academic freedom," which to them meant Let me do what I want to do, and leave me alone!

The district superintendent had called three times asking me to take over the school. I refused the job twice, and after the third request, I agreed to come out of retirement and take on the task for just three months until the school year ended. It had been a year since Ashley's death. Her expressed goal in life had been to make the world a better place by ensuring that all people were treated fairly and had equal opportunities. Somehow in my warped state of mind, I felt I might be able to do that during my short stay at Furr. At that time, a retired administrator in the state of Texas could return to work as an administrator only on an hourly basis, working a limited number of hours at a greatly reduced salary. I took on the task of hourly principal at Furr in the hopes of leaving a legacy for Ashley. It was a daring adventure that was to change my life forever. It was spring break week in March, so traffic was lighter than usual, and I made exceptional time as I made my way north on highway 59 and turned onto I-45 South. It had been years since I had followed that route, and I noted how much the East End had changed. I was happy to see that Garcia Realty was still there in spite of the weak economy, and a new community college stood off to the left, a symbol of progress and hope. In contrast, the shops in Gulfgate, the shopping center that once was the hub of the East Side, were closed and boarded up to ward off vandals and the homeless.

Turning north on 610, I approached the bridge that crossed the Houston Ship Channel. That is when the old ache tore at my heart and flooded my mind with memories. Ten years earlier I had served for several years as district superintendent over much of the East End. During that time, I grew fond of the diverse groups of hard-working people who choose this location as their home, even though I was unceremoniously removed from that position for political reasons. I had worked tirelessly to create a choir of the community singing as one voice. These were my children! I knew them by name and by need. They were still a part of me. Could I once again be a part of them? I wondered...

The tires on the eighteen-wheelers provided a backdrop for my reverie, and I was once again with the people I had long ago learned to respect and love. I was quite surprised that I still had such a strong feeling for the students of the East End. I was surprised that I had any feelings at all since I had been in a robot state of mind since the devastating spring break of the previous year. Heavy toxic smog hung menacingly over the water and wrapped its smelly arms around the chemical plants and oil refineries lining the ship channel. I thought of the children still fast asleep in tiny beds in tidy, wood-framed houses, unaware of the unwelcome intruder that was their nightly visitor.

To the southwest of the ship channel sprawled the Hispanic barrio known as Magnolia, which had produced many strong political leaders. To the northwest was the El Dorado barrio, and to the west was Denver Harbor. Many of the prominent Hispanic business people who were beginning to have an influential voice in local and state government came from that last neighborhood.

Nestled in the middle of these three Hispanic communities was Pleasantville, a black neighborhood and one of the most powerful voting precincts in Houston. Pleasantville was made up of well-kept wood-framed houses with manicured lawns. Almost without exception, the houses had a covered carport jutting out from the front, and the cleanliness of the neighborhood spoke to the pride the residents took in the enclave. The community voted as a block and was therefore heavily and universally courted by local politicos, who made empty promises in exchange for their vote.

Just off to the right of the ship channel lay Clinton Park, a small black community composed of shotgun houses and a few larger, white framed houses that leaned like the tower in Pisa. It was as if a fierce wind from the Gulf of Mexico had repeatedly blown through the neighborhood, tilting the houses toward the north. A few churches dotted the area where known crack houses abounded. This community was comprised primarily of grandparents who took care of the one hundred fifty or so African American students who marched dutifully to Clinton Park Elementary School every day. The school was always underfunded due to low enrollment, and the residents were constantly on guard because of unceasing rumors that the spotless little school would be closed, and the students would be transported across the 610 freeway to Pleasantville.

The angry driver of a battered, faded-blue pickup truck was intolerant of my memory walk, and it was his sudden blast that snatched me back to reality. I was already turning onto I-10 East. I drove with purpose for a block and took a left on Mercury. Two blocks later, I was approaching the school along a street of middle-class homes and well-kept lawns. This neighborhood, which surrounded Furr High on three sides, was deceiving. I was soon to learn that few students lived in the immediate vicinity of the school. They instead came to Furr on nineteen school buses from apartments further down I-10 and from the neighborhoods of the East Side. This fact contributed to the thirteen gangs on campus and the lack of school spirit.

I approached the school and, with an uneasy feeling, parked my car in the space marked Principal. When I arrived at the front door, it was locked, and I realized I did not have a key. I wandered around the campus in search of a member of the custodial staff. As I walked, I noted the once army green color of the ironwork had faded into an anemic gray. The drab posts that supported the tired roofs of the covered walkways matched the iron fence separating the courtyard from the entrance of the school. The entire scene would have been one of hopelessness but for the immaculate, manicured grounds.

"Hello, hello!" I shouted as I continued to walk. Just as I approached a huge graffiti-covered rock between the main building and the rows of temporary buildings, George, the plant operator rescued me. His friendly smile coupled with a twinkle in his eye told me right off I was in good hands. We introduced ourselves, and he welcomed me to the school.

"What is this hideous thing?" I asked, pointing to the rock. "And how on earth did you ever get it here?"

George smiled as he told me how the former principal had it moved there using a big truck and a crane. "It was put here so students could write on it and not the walls. It may have helped some, but we still have students who still write on the walls."

As he opened the door and walked me to my office, I knew I had found a friend in this handsome, neat, young Hispanic man. The terrazzo floors in the hallway glistened.

"These floors are so clean you could eat off them," I remarked, impressed by the pride he took in his work. "The employees and students here are fortunate to have you and your team."

"We do the best we can," he replied modestly. "If you need anything else, you just let me know." He let me into my office and returned to his task of cleaning.

When I opened my office door and turned on the light, I could hardly believe my eyes. The fancy furnishings I had seen in the office the Friday before when the superintendent brought me to the school to introduce me were gone. Someone had worked all weekend to remove the furniture and replace it with a much-used teacher's desk and a cheap, broken-down, armless secretary's chair with a faded blue padded back that tilted to the left. Dingy cotton stuffing hung limply from the chair's split back and waved sadly when the air conditioner came on with a jolt. Beware, it seemed to be saying. Just you beware!

136

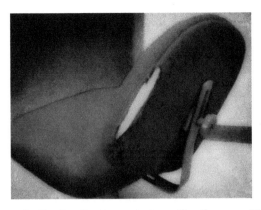

Bertie's desk chair waiting for her at Furr.

I pulled the cotton stuffing, and it immediately came loose revealing a yellow foam padding. I forced my eyes from the questionable rollers on the bottom of the chair and scanned the dingy gray walls. A pale rectangle was the only break in the drab wall, covered in a dull residue from years of critical decision-making in a smoke-filled room behind closed doors. I wondered what the now-missing picture had been privy to during the gatherings of this exclusive club and what stories it could tell. I also wondered when HISD board policy had changed to permit smoking within the school. I picked up the phone to call the district office and inhaled the stale smoke that had permeated the mouthpiece. I left the office in search of rubbing alcohol to clean the phone.

In the outer office, I bumped into a slightly built black man who introduced himself as Erskine Vanderbilt. He said he was the technologist at Furr and a twelve-month employee. There were other twelve-month employees, but they had chosen not to come to work and were taking vacation days. The implication was that they did not want to be there when I arrived.

When I asked why he had come to work, he replied, "I don't believe all the things folks have said about you. They said stuff was gonna hit the fan with you here 'cause you don't take no mess off nobody! I'm here to support you any way I can. I sure am!"

Now, I liked that because I clearly was going to need all the support I could muster. I asked for Erskine's help in locating some rubbing alcohol. "Why don't you come into my office and tell me about the school while I clean the phone?" I asked. "I need to learn as much as I can—as quickly as I can."

He followed me into the office. As I removed the mouthpiece, cleaned it, and poured alcohol into any hole I could find on it, Erskine gave me his account of a troubled school in need of help. It was not a pretty picture.

"All this is a part of the plan, as I'm sure you know by now," he said. "They're trying to tell you that you're not welcome here. We have some really mean-spirited folks here at Furr, but I bet you'll be able to handle them."

He stood uneasily, shifting from one foot to the other. The sweat that had collected on his brow from the manual labor he had been performing made its way down the sides of his cheeks, creating river maps that made me think of the uncharted waterways I was now sailing. He excused himself nervously and escaped to more comfortable quarters. As he made his exit, I thanked him for being there and told him I knew it took courage, because the others would accuse him of "sucking up." He just smiled shyly, and I felt better that he had decided to come to work.

I had listened with great interest to Erskine, but nothing he said bothered me or made me question my ability to overcome any obstacles. I could take anything for three months—and I kept reminding myself that was all I had agreed to do. Later, I realized that the numbness I was still feeling from the death of my granddaughter was what would sustain me during the weeks and months ahead.

All the alcohol in the world could not remove the acrid odor of stale tobacco from the phone. Finally, I gave up trying and began to search for any records that might help me to learn more about the school. I found nothing. I did discover, though, that the drawers of my desk would not open. That meant any paperwork that I might have must be stacked on its top. I sat on the broken chair and contemplated what the next three months would be like. One thing I knew for sure was that I would never complain about the furnishings in my office. I was sure it would give someone great pleasure if I did, and I was not into feeding their sadistic needs.

A sudden ring of the phone startled me out of my contemplation, and I sprang to answer it, anxious for contact with the outside world. I was pleasantly surprised when the voice on the other end of the line was a student.

"Miss," he began with the confidence of an attorney. "I have checked you out, and word on the street is that you really care about students and you listened to them when you were superintendent of this part of town. I'm just checking you out for myself and was wondering if I could come in to talk with you about Furr?"

Badly needing a break from the dejected mood of the office and eager to hear his story, I invited him to come immediately and visit with me in my office. I was interested in any student with such initiative, and I went out and stood in front of the school, waiting for his arrival.

When Vincent arrived, he gave the appearance of an athlete, tall, slim with perfect muscle tone. He was dressed in a clean, white, starched shirt and heavily starched and pressed jeans that, if he stepped out of them, would stand alone. His straight, white teeth accented his broad smile. His Afro was neatly trimmed, and it was clear that Vincent believed it when he was told "cleanliness is next to godliness." I was immediately charmed by this good-natured, young gentleman.

Pointing to the chairs in the outer office, I said, "Let's just sit out here and chat. So, tell me about yourself, Vincent, and about Furr."

"Well, to tell you the truth, Furr sucks," he blurted out. "Some students here have taken the same class three times and passed it all three times. This school is for the teachers, not for the students. We have no science labs, and the teachers don't really teach. They just tell us to read the chapter and answer the questions at the end. I don't really think the teachers know the subject matter at all. If they do, they sure keep it to themselves. I want a good education 'cause I want to go to college. I don't really think the teachers think we can learn. This is a throwaway school, Miss. We need help. So—do you think you can help make Furr a good school for students? I'll be a senior next year, and I don't have much time left at this school. From what I hear, I think you'd be good for this school." I told Vincent I planned to be at the school three months and would do all I could to make it a better place for students. I was shocked at his response.

"My God, Miss! Jesus Christ himself couldn't clean up this mess in three months! Couldn't you just stay through next year 'cause that's when I'll graduate? Promise me you'll think about it. Okay?"

I believed that students in general want to learn. In fact, they hunger to learn, and their behavior often communicates that fact. How could I not promise this serious young man I would think about it? It must have been important to him—he wouldn't have given up this vacation time to come in and talk with me about it otherwise. I liked his desire to learn in a rigorous instructional environment with teachers who care about him and believe he can learn. I liked him.

When he was gone, I felt a charge of excitement and hope. A fresh, gentle breeze had blown through the school, sweeping away all traces of unpleasantness.

I decided to walk through the school and check out the classrooms. George let me in each room, and I got to know him a little better. He shared his hobbies, which included building furniture. The more I learned about him, the better I liked him.

The classrooms were drab, with no student work displayed. Bulletin boards begged to be covered. Stacks of ungraded student work and musty newspapers reached lazily out to me as I moved from room to room. It appeared the graffiti stone in front of the school had failed to measure up to expectations: graffiti spilled over from tables and desktops onto the walls in some classrooms. In one of those rooms, I was encouraged to find several novels on the teacher's desk. Later, I learned to my dismay that they belonged to the teacher who was reading them while the students answered the questions at the end of the textbook chapter on their own. I saw no evidence that teaching and learning were going on in the school.

Then, we entered the magnet hall. I felt as if I had suddenly entered another world. A colorful sign read The International Studies Magnet School. Hallway bulletin boards proudly displayed student work, which was tastefully mounted on colored paper. Interspersed among the student papers were pictures of students and teachers taken on a recent field trip to a local theater. The sea of smiling faces was the counterpart to the lack of any indication of student involvement I had seen in the "irregular regular program." Student work sang from every wall of the magnet classrooms and spilled over into the hallways.

"Look at me," this school seemed to be gleefully singing. "I am proud of the work I do."

I felt like Alice in Wonderland and expected any minute to see a huge, white rabbit with a clock hanging around his neck scurrying down the hallway because he was overdue and might wind up in a rabbit stew. It suddenly dawned on me that was exactly where I was. I was in a rabbit stew. Or could it be I was overdue?

CHAPTER 23
Identifying Problems and Seeking Solutions

HISD's magnet school plan had been designed to integrate the schools and to have an enrollment that mirrored Houston's ethnic population. In 1974 there were 104 magnet schools, some stand-alone and some as a school within a school. Many minorities opposed the plan because they believed that although the students in the magnet schools would receive a quality education, the majority would be left with an inferior one. The magnet schools would receive additional funding, which would provide them with more educational opportunities for their students, while the students in the regular program would not be afforded the same opportunities.

In the case of Furr, the International Studies School was a magnet school within a school. While race was no longer used as a basis for acceptance into the school, high academic standing was required, and extra funds were allocated to the school budget earmarked specifically for the magnet program. The dramatic difference in the appearance of the classrooms in the magnet hall at Furr and those in the regular school was clear evidence that, at least at this school, the fears of inequality were well founded. I envisioned a sign over the magnet hall that read "Haves" and a contrasting one over the regular school that read "Have Nots."

I immediately returned to my office after visiting the magnet hall and asked Erskine for the name and phone number of the PTO president and set up a meeting with her executive board the following day. Perhaps I could learn something from them that would enable me to better understand the inner workings at Furr. I spent the remainder of the day cleaning the office and hunting down additional chairs in anticipation of the meeting with the parents.

When I left Furr that afternoon, eager to get home and wash away the odor of smoke that seemed to permeate my body, I seriously questioned whether I could make a difference during the three months I planned to be there. I was looking forward to meeting with the parents to see Furr through their lenses and attempt to gain their support.

The Furr High School PTO Executive Board that greeted me the following morning surprised me. The parents, who were all black, were eager to get the best education possible for their children and clearly and eloquently articulated that desire. The spokesperson, a well-dressed woman who appeared to be in her late thirties, began by informing me that Furr High School was structured for the teachers, not kids!

"Very little real instruction goes on here," she said. "Few students have an opportunity to take the PSAT and SAT tests. There are no prep classes for those tests, and it's as if the teachers don't think our kids want to go to college. Furr has a high dropout rate, and the student and teacher attendance is down right disgraceful." Ms. White continued, "We have been to the school district office and spoken to the district superintendent about our concerns, and she assured us you could make things right. I think you would have to be a miracle worker to do that, if you want to know what I think!" She looked at me with her clear, light brown eyes and announced: "We're all hoping you are a miracle worker."

A rather heavy-set young woman, Ms. Walker, had been shifting from one cheek of her buttocks to the other since she arrived. She sighed loudly, rolled her eyes at each remark, and supported the spokesperson with a loud and determined, "Yeah! Yeah! I know that's right!" She suddenly came into her own as if she had, without warning, received the Holy Ghost. She sprang to her feet and bellowed, "We want teachers here who know their subject matter and who don't cuss our kids!" Her eyes burned with anger. "These teachers cuss each other all the time—and cuss our kids when the kids ask for help! We've been trying to get science labs in this school for almost two years, and we still don't have any. This school district is full of empty excuses. The district superintendent gave some money for the labs, but the district always has excuses for why they're not complete. We're ready to call the television stations about the problem. That's the only way we can get anyone in the district to listen to us. What happens in this school would not be tolerated in a school 'cross town!" She was breathing hard, glaring at me and flailing her arms as she finished.

Ms. White, encouraged by this explosion, added, "And the food in the Furr cafeteria is just awful! We met with the food service provider who made promises that have not been kept. What was the superintendent thinking about when he outsourced food services? I think some hanky-panky is going on, if you ask me!"

I thanked the ladies for all the useful information and promised I would do what I could to address their concerns. When they were gone, I called and made an appointment with representatives from our food service provider for the following week.

I was deeply troubled that both the student, Vincent, and the parents had expressed the belief that the school was organized for teachers, not students. Although I had been retired from education for five years, I had kept up with educational research. I knew that educators were being encouraged to reexamine old ideas about schools and the people they are meant to serve. The consensus was that schools are primarily designed to serve students, but they must also serve others within the school community. But at Furr, it sounded as if the only needs being met were the teachers.

I vowed I would make it my business to give voice to all members of the school community. I would work to create a school climate conducive to teaching and learning. This meant that the principal and everyone responsible for the high school would create a climate favorable to education, even if it occurred outside the school.

The following day, I obtained the Furr data from the central office. The demographics showed the school was 76 percent Hispanic, 21 percent African American, and 3 percent white. Furr High School had the highest dropout rate in the school district and was identified by the state as a dropout factory. It was a pipeline from high school to prison. It also had the lowest student attendance rate. It had been identified as a location for all special education programs offered by the East District, and many special education students attended from outside the school zone. The results on the Texas Assessment of

Academic Skills (TAAS), which was the state-mandated test, were expected to show that at least 80 percent of the tenth graders had met state standards. This expectation was possible only because of the waiver from the district. More than 50 percent of the 1,450 students at Furr were in the ninth grade. Some of them were nineteen years old. The whole system appeared to me to be an unethical, political ploy to give the appearance of higher scores on the state-mandated test because the only students who were tested were those likely to pass. Furr also had much gang violence on campus, and I was told a student had recently been shot there. A staff member had reported that she had looked out her window one day and spied snipers on top of the building housing the auditorium.

I was disturbed as I studied the data. I was especially concerned about the violence and about the TAAS score being the single determinant of whether a student graduated from high school. The data contained a note that one gang had a contract on the life of the former principal.

I left the school at the end of my first work week with evidence that the system had carefully crafted a plan that would present the appearance of high student achievement while vast numbers of students, eager for a good education, quietly gave up and slipped away. I questioned whether I could change that. As I contemplated my odds of making a change at Furr, I thought back to my departure from the District VIII superintendent position several years earlier, when I had been removed at the request of a school board member. Here I was again, still white and still working in a predominately Hispanic school. Would they permit me to do the things that must be done to provide an effective teacher in each classroom? They must have known I would still do what I believed to be right, regardless of the consequences. Only time would tell. I wondered...

I flipped on the radio as I made my way back over the ship channel bridge in the heavy 5 p.m. traffic toward home. My grandson had changed the station, and a female singer was wailing an old country western song about a cheating heart and how it would keep you awake at night and eventually catch up with you. I considered the irony of those lyrics being sung at that moment. I remembered that I had originally retired from HISD because of what appeared to me to be questionable decisions around test results on the TAAS. I wondered how many HISD administrators slept well at night. I wondered if I would be able to sleep well and if my insomnia would be worth it if I could somehow change things. Was this song a metaphor for my stay at Furr? Only time would tell. I wondered...

CHAPTER 24
The Struggle Begins

It was storming that morning, and aggressive sheets of rain swept across my car as a gale-force wind attacked with a vengeance, causing the car to sway to the left. I was on my way to Furr High School to meet the students and staff for the first day of school after spring break. My enthusiasm for the occasion was somewhat diminished by the battle with the unexpected storm. Lightning shot daggers at the earth, followed by loud bursts of thunder that shattered the heavens and rumbled off into the distance. The ship channel bridge, which was to become a symbol for my crossing over to the biggest challenge I had ever undertaken, was completely enveloped in driving rain. I struggled to keep my eyes on the line separating my lane from the one where speedsters, honking loudly, forcefully slap-bathed my car with grimy street water, apparently determined to force me into the guardrail. Perhaps this battle was a precursor to my term as hourly principal of Furr High School.

The storm had subsided by the time I reached the school, and I noted there were few cars in the teacher parking lot. I stood in the outer office awaiting the arrival of the students and staff. My intent was to welcome each and express my joy at the opportunity to be there. Some staff members arrived early, and my attempts to make conversation with them were received with a cool indifference. The individual who was to be my personal secretary, Darrow Ward, had been at the school many years, and her body language mumbled to me around her faint smile and limp handshake. Clearly, she was uncertain of my motives, but over time she became a supporter and a lifesaver to me. She was extremely capable and an ethical, decent human being. A few old-timers with whom I had worked when I was the District VIII superintendent chatted with me and held me upright against the onslaught of suspicion and outright disdain.

When the bell rang, I noticed that many teachers had not arrived. I asked where they were and was told it was not necessary for them to come in because their first two periods were a planning period and a support period. That meant they would be in two hours later. I also found many teachers were leaving two hours early for the same reason. "This school is progressive," I was told. "The school is broken down into five houses, and each member of the house has a period called 'support.' The teachers meet and plan." I assumed they were doing their planning off campus since many of them were not at school. I was later to learn this was a reform effort implemented in 1995 to personalize the learning environment. I was aware Furr had moved into small schools because as assistant superintendent of campus management, I had received calls from parents about the problems at Furr.

I realized I needed to learn quickly about the school if I planned to make any improvements during the three months I would be there. I ask the dean of instruction, Carol Harris, a pleasant, unassuming, middle-aged, black woman who I liked right off, to schedule separate meetings with teachers in each house, each group of elective teachers by departments, all clerks and office workers, all administrators, all counselors, and all members of the custodial staff. I wanted to hear from the staff about the good things going on at Furr, as well, as their concerns. I sincerely wanted to understand the problems and as much about the individuals as possible, though I doubted they would ever understand me.

I conducted walk-throughs in classrooms where the teachers' eyes shot anger bullets at me, even as I found something positive to say to each. I spoke to students about their learning as I made my way around the school.

Juan, a rather heavy-set Hispanic young man stated, "Miss, I'm not learning nothing. This is a throw-away school, Miss. Why would you drive all the way 'cross town to come to a throw-away school?"

I asked Juan to come to my office to talk with me at lunch. I continued my classroom visits with him on my mind and wondered if he would really follow through on my request. Juan did not let me down. He entered my office so quietly I would not have known he was there but for the fact I sensed someone's eyes on me. I looked up from the work I was doing, and Juan was standing awkwardly in front of my desk.

He spoke in a forced whisper, "Miss, did you really want to see me?"

I sprang from my chair and moved around the desk, hugged him and sat next to him. I asked him to tell me what he meant when he said Furr was a throwaway school.

Juan glued his eyes to his hands, which he folded and unfolded repeatedly in his lap. He said in a haltering voice, "Miss, nobody cares about this school. Just look at it! Does it look like a school where anybody cares? The teachers don't care about us. They just put us out of class. I want to learn, Miss, but I'm not learning. And another thing, Miss," he continued unemotionally, "I'm real embarrassed 'cause we have to pack our shirttails in our pants. I'm real fat, miss, and I feel bad 'bout myself with my shirt packed in like this, Miss," and he pointed to a large roll of fat pouring over the top of his pants and resting in his lap. I swallowed hard as he looked up at me and said, "See, Miss? If I could wear my shirttail outside, you wouldn't even see my fat so much!"

I later learned that twenty to thirty students were suspended daily for not having their shirt tails tucked into their pants. In north Louisiana where I grew up, they would say we were "gagging at gnats and swallowing elephants."

I obtained a list of students who were suspended more than twice for not having their shirts tucked inside their pants. While this seemed to be a minor problem to many of the teachers, it was a major problem to the students involved. The instructional time they lost was even more compelling and damaging to their school success than the possible negative impacts on diminished funding. I suspected that a large part of the absenteeism that caused Furr to have a student attendance rate of 87 percent the previous year was attributable to the fact that students were counted absent every time they were suspended.

I called the repeat offenders to come in to see me. As the students entered my office, the problem was clear. Twelve of the girls were pregnant, and it was impossible to tuck in their shirts. The students who were not pregnant were obese and were embarrassed to tuck their shirts in because it exaggerated their weight problem. I knew we had to correct this practice if we were to ensure student success and improve the student attendance rate.

I presented the data I had collected on repeated shirttail violators to the Shared Decision-Making Committee and asked them to talk with all staff members so a decision could be made at their next meeting. The Shared Decision-Making Committee was an advisory group mandated by the state of Texas and made up of members of the community and school staff. These educators and community members were reasonable people, and they voted unanimously at the next meeting to amend the student uniform policy and drop the requirement for shirts to be tucked inside pants or skirts. Hallelujah!

After this, the focus of the teacher complaints suddenly changed. Rumors abounded that I was a student advocate, not a teacher advocate as the Houston Federation of Teachers (HFT) executive director, Gayle Fallon, had assured them. "I have known this lady for many years, and she is the only superintendent in the district who, as a hearing officer, ruled in favor of a teacher rather than an administrator if she thought the teacher was right," Gayle had told the Furr HFT union representative, Dan Beier. He had proudly passed that message to the teachers. As it turned out, Dan was a loyal supporter of mine during my entire tenure at Furr until he retired.

Now the kids are running the school. This line replaced the derogatory comments in the lounge about students. The teachers had a field day with the subject and often made the comment within my earshot. It had never occurred to me that teacher advocate and student advocate were mutually exclusive positions.

I attempted to eat lunch in the cafeteria, but the food seemed to swell in my mouth and become a boulder in my throat. I listened to the students and teachers as they told me how bad the food was, and I agreed with them. It was then that I learned that Furr had an open campus and most of the students and teachers left campus for lunch. I recalled that a Furr student had recently been mortally wounded from a gunshot at a nearby fast food restaurant where he had gone for lunch. I was concerned when I learned that over twelve hundred of our students left Furr each day at noon to go wherever they chose. I thought about my own grandchildren. Would I want them to have such freedom under the conditions that existed in the Furr community? I decided to use this in negotiating with the food service provider the following week.

At the meeting with the food service provider and the PTO Executive Committee, I promised to create a closed campus so that more students would eat in the cafeteria in exchange for better food and service. They agreed to the plan, and things began to improve in the cafeteria. The food was tastier and was served more attractively; the selections were expanded to include a snack bar with sandwiches and pizza. The parents were pleased with the changes, and I was pleased that Furr students were remaining on campus during the lunch period.

My mind wandered back to a situation that had led to an upheaval at Furr when I was the district superintendent over that area. An African American student had called and reported to me that he had not been permitted to enroll at Furr because all the classes were full. I knew the enrollment was down and that there should have been room for him. When I called the school and questioned why the student could not enroll, I was told the school was at capacity. I met the young man and went with him and his parents to Furr to enroll. That day, a mushroom cloud rose over the school as a result of my visit, and I made many enemies at "Furr Independent High School," as it was facetiously called by the HISD employees outside the school.

Many of the staff members who were there then still bore the scars of my visit and were now determined to make me pay for my unprecedented actions. As more and more minorities enrolled in the school during that period of white flight to the suburbs, even the International Studies Magnet School could not prevent the mass exodus, and Furr quickly became a minority school. Now, from what I was being told, the school was hanging by a thread, a blight on the east edge of an ever-growing school district.

I wanted to meet with the teachers to get input from them regarding the needs of the school and changes they would like to see made, but they were reluctant to meet with me. Rumor had it that I had been sent to Furr by the East District Office as a spy to report back to the district superintendent. They also remarked snidely that I had been a superintendent and did not know anything about running a high school. My enemies fanned the flames of discontent with complaints such as "I can't believe they sent that woman out here!" Those remarks always got back to me. I overheard one say, "She's a rich bitch who lives in West University Place. What could she possibility know about how to work with minority kids?" I chose not to add dignity to such remarks and ignored them as I maneuvered daily through a field of land mines.

I did have the support of the students, however, even though we could not have assemblies or after-school activities because of gang violence. I often worked late, and it was frequently dark outside when I left the school. Some of the male students always stayed and walked me to my car. On one such occasion, they told me some of the teachers were trying to pay them to "key" my car. I smiled and responded that they could not key my car because I kept my keys in my purse. They were surprised to learn I did not know what "keying a car" meant.

"Miss, you need to learn some street smarts if you plan to work here," Juan said with concern. "They told us they would pay us to run a key down the side of your car to scratch it and ruin the paint job," he continued.

I thanked them for not going along with the teachers' request and assured them that was not a normal request from adults who had principles. I quickly learned it was not the gang members I had heard so much about that I had to fear. It was some members of the faculty.

CHAPTER 25
Making Sense of Small Schools

Carol, the dean of instruction, had tried to schedule a meeting with the school staff for several weeks and was finally successful in arranging meetings. I spent days listening to complaints. I heard there was no support from the parents and that the students were poor and didn't want to learn. I heard that the students did not come to class on time and were not prepared when they did come. I heard that the school received no support from anywhere in the school district. I learned that all new ninth graders were required to take boot camp, taught by the ROTC instructors—a requirement designed to teach the students discipline. I heard that the elective teachers felt alienated. I learned the coaches felt their athletic program had been destroyed when all ninth graders were required to take ROTC as their elective. That meant they did not take physical education. The list went on and on, but it was clear the teachers felt they were victims of bad decisions made by others.

Only one teacher, Sheila Whitford, spoke positively about the students and about instruction. She spoke of the school's work with Critical Friends groups that allowed individuals the opportunity to give and receive feedback on their work. This work was a result of a grant the school had received from the Annenberg Foundation in support of breaking large schools into smaller learning communities. I knew Sheila and knew she cared about students. I remembered her as one of only two teachers in HISD who had passed the State Master Teacher examination several years earlier. I liked her and hoped she could help me make the necessary changes at the school. Sheila Whitford was a buoy in the turbulent Disconsolate Sea at Furr.

I was alarmed when I learned that no one was being held accountable to make sure teaching and learning met the needs of students. Each of the school's five houses made its own discipline policy, had its own attendance rules and committee, and did or did not enforce the student dress code, depending upon the whims of the teachers within the house. No house was following the state-mandated and local policies on discipline and excessive absences. No one spoke of using data to improve student achievement and to inform instruction.

The idea of small schools was a good one. The creation of small schools was a recommendation made by the Carnegie Foundation for the Advancement of Teaching to banish the anonymity that plagued students at large schools. If these efforts were to improve student learning, it was essential for everyone to stay focused on the learning opportunities that are made possible by "small."

Efforts were being made to create small learning communities while the school itself was beginning to look like a city dump. The trash I had noticed in some classrooms in the small learning communities spilled over into the courtyard where the students ate lunch. After lunch, the campus was a sea of trash. I walked among the students while they were eating and encouraged them to keep the area clean. The following day during the opening exercises, I made a positive announcement about the need to keep our school grounds neat. I told the students I would be checking the courtyard that day after lunch and was sure they would throw their trash in the garbage cans.

One member of the administration stormed into my office following the announcement and reprimanded me, snapping, "These are young men and women. You are treating them as if they are elementary kids. They will never respond to that kind of talk!" I smiled. I told the individual it might take me a while to understand that, but I would certainly work on it. And I did, though not very hard.

At the end of the lunch period, the courtyard was much cleaner. One administrator assured me it would never last. So what? It was clean that day! Thought birds flitted through my head bearing the chorus of an old country western song, and it gushed right out my mouth as I sang about taking one day at a time, sweet Jesus. The individual looked at me as if I had lost my mind, turned on an angry heel, and stormed from the office. I never heard any more about my announcements.

I started dropping in on the nonexistent house support meetings. When I saw members who should have been present but were not, I told them how much I had missed them at the meeting. Slowly, teachers began coming to school in the morning on time and remaining in the afternoon until the end of school. All house teachers began to meet, albeit with much ado about nothing. At least they were meeting.

It was in late March that the East District superintendent came by to take me to lunch. "I think you are crazy for taking this job," she said. "But would you consider staying on next year?" I made no promise because I was meeting so much resistance from the teachers and the students were fighting daily, but I told her I would consider her request.

I mingled with the students to get to know them, and teachers continued to warn me I was being too friendly with them. "They will take advantage of you. You have just been a superintendent and you don't know how high school kids act. They will lie to you, especially Ernesto. He is no good and should be sent away. You need to get rid of him as quickly as possible. He is trouble," they would say. I continued to mingle and talk to students throughout my tenure and was not taken advantage of by them—well, perhaps a bit. At least I was aware when they were doing it.

Many teachers approached me, turned their bodies to the side and moved in a cautious manner, keeping their distance and never taking their eyes off me. I had decided what I needed was a whip to complete my role as lion tamer. But I was pleased when one day some of them began to speak to me as a normal human being. Progress was being made, bit by painstaking bit, sweet Jesus.

It was mid-May when I told the superintendent I would return to Furr High School for the following school year. I announced that decision to the faculty and staff amid groans and outright sounds of disgust. Immediately, rumors ran rampant that everyone was leaving. I continued to behave as usual and even felt a tinge of excitement that we might be able to make Furr an even better place for all members of the school community. The question was, Would I be doing that with an entirely new staff because of their disdain for me?

My heart skipped a beat as a frightening ticker tape moved slowly through my head reporting the huge drop in my market value. It reminded me of a 1972 hit song about being left alone in an hour of need.

CHAPTER 26
Once More with Feeling

S trange things began to happen as soon as the teachers learned I would be returning the following school year. They began to flood me with students they considered disruptive. The attitude among the teachers was that since I was a student advocate, I could just handle all the discipline problems. I could not have been happier! I listened to each student who was brought to me—really listened! There were usually long lines outside my door where the students patiently waited until their turn. I was learning so much about the lack of instruction in the classrooms. The chatter now intensified among the teachers that I really believed what the kids were saying. "Maybe this isn't such a good idea after all," they were reported to have been saying. "If she's going to believe them, then the stuff is really going to hit the fan." Suddenly, the flood of students dwindled to a mere trickle and finally ran dry.

Teachers were being encouraged to leave the school by some administrators who criticized my poor leadership to them. Just when I had reconciled myself to the fact I would be hiring a new staff of teachers, a group came to me because they were concerned that Furr needed a new small school. I was surprised by their initiative after getting nothing but resistance for months, but I sent several teachers to visit other schools and asked them to bring back suggestions for organizing a ninth-grade academy. Even if they left, I would have the information. They came back excited and began making plans to present to me for my consideration. They then announced their intent to return to Furr the following year. As it turned out, only one teacher left after that first year. He met with me and explained that he did not share my philosophy and requested my help in getting a position in one of the top schools in the HISD. I did assist him and told him that I appreciated his candor.

I felt uneasy as I carefully made my way into the inner workings of the school, ever in search of solid ground to place my foot for the next step. As many of the hidden secrets were revealed to me, they were as dark and complex as a Rothko painting. So I trusted no one and fought against paranoia.

There was one day when I even questioned whether the superintendent might have had an ulterior motive for placing me at Furr. I had called the district office to inform them I would be off campus at a meeting in central administration. "Oh, no," the clerk remarked with an urgency in her voice. "We're expecting one of the refineries on the ship channel to 'blow,' and we want you to be there if it happens!" I chuckled to myself. She had no idea how that sounded to me considering that most of the people at Furr would be happy to see me "blow" with the refinery. The "blow" did not occur.

Things were slowly changing. I was excited about the possibility of starting a ninth-grade academy, and one day Thelma Garza, the area superintendent, visited and told me to order new furniture for my office. I had been perfectly happy with my battered desk and chair with the stuffing hanging out the back. I had returned the stuffing to its rightful place and hand sewed the edge to keep it intact. She thought it was a bad reflection on the school, but I viewed it as my ability to overcome obstacles, persevere, and exercise fiscal responsibility. I ordered new furniture.

Immediately after her visit, as I rolled around my relic desk to sit next to a parent for a conference, the chair I was sitting in collapsed like Little Pig's straw house. The wheels went east, and the seat and back split from each other and went west. I hit the floor with a clunk. I had never been known for my grace, but dignity flew out the window as I struggled to pull my dress down to cover my exposed undergarments. I was starring in my own *I Love Lucy* show! Once I had regained my composure, the parent and I had a big laugh, and it released the tension that had emanated from her when she had come into the office. A clerk brought in a chair, the one she herself had been using, telling me she was sorry I had fallen. That was the first kind remark anyone had made to me during my two months at Furr High School.

At the end of the school year, I was invited to the ROTC formal banquet and, to my surprise, was made to feel welcome by all present. The events of the evening followed the military tradition and were done with such class and the adults and students displayed such grace and charm, I felt proud to be a part of the whole affair. Their behavior was so foreign to the Furr I knew, and I took great joy in discovering a wholesome, polished side of the school I had not seen. The male students, who appeared confident in their military uniforms, treated the young ladies, who were beautiful in their long evening dresses, with refreshing respect. Captain Trege, dressed in full regalia, had planned an evening for students and their parents they would never forget. It was the first evidence of excellence I had witnessed at Furr, and it gave me hope.

Senior prom night was another end-of-year activity that I was eager to attend. It had been years since I had been to a prom, and I was anxious to see how things had changed. I was not, however, prepared for the changes I witnessed at the Furr senior prom. I attempted to make conversation with everyone. Some staff members received me coolly, while others struggled to avoid me. Students were unhappy and told me they did not like the location of the event, which was held at a restaurant in the East End. They explained they had wanted a more upscale place because the evening was so special to them. The prom sponsor made all the decisions, and the students told me they had no input on the location, which they felt was unfair since it was their prom. I made a mental note of that and determined to give voice to students in the future. I soon learned why my presence was not welcomed. Several staff members were drinking alcoholic drinks, and they were afraid I would object to such actions. I did, of course, but kept it to myself until later when I told them I thought it was inappropriate and took steps to make sure it did not happen again. I had kicked over another stone and made a new discovery about Furr.

With the school year coming to an end, we needed to plan for teacher training at the opening of the new year. I called the HISD professional development department to request training for the first professional development day of the next school year and was politely told no one in that department would ever come to Furr High School to conduct professional development. They described how they were treated so rudely in the past that some of them had been reduced to tears. "That school has the meanest group of teachers I have ever seen," one told me. "They act as if they know everything." Carol Harris had told me she had had the same experience. I decided she and I would conduct the training. She was not sure that was a good idea, but I assured her we would work during the summer to plan, including actions to be taken if the teachers rebelled and behaved in a rude manner. Stone, after stone, after stone.

In May, the results of the TAAS arrived. The teachers made a mad rush to the office to obtain the test results. I looked on in amazement as they, hands shaking and face muscles twitching, reviewed the results. All test results had improved significantly. That called for a celebration, and teachers ran up and down the halls, announcing the good news. Furr had finally moved from acceptable to recognized on the state accountability rating scale. This meant money to many employees. Hourly principals could receive no bonuses, but all other professionals could. Jubilation was the word of the day, and joy filled the hearts of the teachers! All, that is, except one social studies teacher in the International Studies Magnet hall. He freely dumped ice water on the celebrants, expressing his disgust at celebrating inflated test scores because ninth-grade students who were likely to fail the test had been kept from advancing a year. Only tenth graders were included in accountability. He felt, as did I, that the scores were a lie and were a political ploy to fool an unsuspecting public.

As I studied the joyful revelry over the fake test results, the excruciating pain in my chest warned of an impending heart quake. How would I ever change the practice that resulted in such a feeling of euphoria on the part of the staff? And since the district approved, could it be that I was wrong? Who did I think I was, anyway? Michael Jackson's "Man in the Mirror" was spinning in my mind on a 45 disc. I wondered...

CHAPTER 27
Being in the Arena

In early June, after graduation, Furr had an opportunity to present a proposal for a small school grant from the United States Department of Education. I called together several administrators and teachers to solicit their input and assistance. I needed to depend upon them to do the bulk of the writing because of commitments I had made prior to assuming the position of hourly principal at Furr. I would be gone the last two weeks of June to present at a seminar and then again in early July to attend a curriculum mapping conference in Park City, Utah, at the request of my district superintendent. I was counting on them to care enough about the grant to complete it by July 10, when the proposal was due to the HISD grant office.

Each person working on the proposal assured me it would be ready when I returned at the end of June and that it could be submitted before I left for Park City. It did not happen. The committee had done some work on it, but it was not ready to be presented to the HISD grant department. I engaged my friends outside Furr High School to assist me in completing the proposal and, by working forty-eight hours straight, we had it ready to submit the day I was to leave town for the curriculum conference in July. The last step in the process before submitting it to the grant department was to acquire the appropriate district-level signatures and those of cooperating organizations and agencies. I was able to accomplish that and left the proposal with one of the administrators to deliver to the grant department. I left town bound for Park City, confident she would follow through with my request.

Park City, Utah, was not a place I would have chosen to visit since ski lifts and ski slopes were in every vista. T-shirts and billboards screamed invitations to Ski Park City, while others advertised the upcoming Winter Olympics. The whole scene tore at my viscera and triggered an explosion of visions of my granddaughter's deadly accident on just such a slope. Flashbacks pulsated in my mind like strobe lights, creating a disjointed illusion of reality. I struggled to follow through with my commitment to bring back to Houston ideas that we might use in mapping the curriculum.

I attended several sessions at the conference and tried hard to concentrate. Dr. Heidi Hayes Jacobs, the guru of curriculum mapping, was her usual wonderful and informative self, but I was somehow not able to concentrate. I had already decided to leave the conference early when I dropped in on a session being conducted by Dr. Bena Kallick, who was speaking on the work she had done on Habits of Mind with Dr. Art Costa. For some inexplicable reason, she struck a chord within me, and I came alive and vitally interested in pursuing some of the suggestions and activities she offered. I had studied Art Costa's work and had a high regard for the contribution he made in the area of cognitive coaching. Bena Kallick talked about her work with him on Habits of Mind, which are sixteen problem-solving, life-related dispositions necessary to operate successfully in society. They promote strategic reasoning, insightfulness, perseverance, creativity, and craftsmanship. That sounded interesting to me and like something that would be helpful for the entire learning community at Furr. When I left her session, I had several ideas I could implement in the fall. I even felt that I might be able to truly make a difference at the school and was inspired to give it my best. This was the first time that I became aware that I had not been giving my full attention to Furr and likely would not be able to for some time. I felt guilty at my inability to put aside my grief and do my best for the Furr learning community. The words of Theodore Roosevelt, when he spoke of the credit belonging to those who are in the arena, appeared from my memory like a Morse code, tapping out my role and responsibilities:

> It is not the critic who counts; not the man who points out how the strong man stumbles or where the doer of deeds could have done better. The credit belongs to the man who is actually in the arena, whose face is marred by dust and sweat and blood, who strives valiantly, who errs and comes up short again and again, because there is no effort without error or shortcoming, but who knows the

great enthusiasms, the great devotions, who spends himself for a worthy cause; who, at the best, knows, in the end, the triumph of high achievement, and who, at the worst, if he fails, at least he fails while daring greatly, so that his place shall never be with those cold and timid souls who knew neither victory nor defeat.

I made a commitment to myself to do everything within my power to be more in the arena and to dare greatly. I would know either victory or defeat. Little did I know what was in my future.

I decided to stay through the end of the conference, and on the last day, as I was about to leave Park City, I bumped into Dr. Bena Kallick and asked if, by chance, she could come to Houston and help me at Furr High School. She was kind but informed me she was booked for the entire year. Though I was disappointed, I left with a determination to do whatever it took to bring her to Houston. I wanted to work with her to create a community of learners at Furr High School and a vibrant learning environment for the knowledge-thirsty students on the far east side of HISD. We would change blight into a shining example of hope and success. She did not let me down.

When I arrived home from Park City, there was a message on my answering machine from the grant department of the HISD. The material that had been hand delivered to that office was not the proposal. The administrator who was responsible for delivering the information was on vacation the following day, but we were able to locate the official document in her office and submit it for consideration. The grant department had generously extended our deadline because the administrator had worked with me before I retired and knew I had been out of the city.

I was deeply concerned about the lifeless and anemic appearance of the campus. My district superintendent came to my rescue and gave me thirty thousand dollars to use as I saw fit at the school. I decided to have the school painted before school began in August, to let the school community know things were going to change with the new academic year. When I informed the superintendent I was using the school colors, red and black, she was shocked. Once I explained I was only painting the trim, she calmed down somewhat, but she still did not like my taste. I put new red and black tile in both cafeteria entrances and had the word Furr embedded in the middle of each. The school suddenly took on a new, vibrant personality. Red posts replaced the dull gray ones, and the repaired roofs no longer sagged and were painted white with a black trim. I walked to the front of the school and pretended to be a student seeing the changes for the first time. I hoped they and the staff would feel the pride I felt as I made my way between the shiny red posts covered with clean white roofs trimmed in black. It all looked and smelled so fresh and clean; much like a freshly mowed meadow after a soft shower announcing the arrival of spring. This scene heralded our new, daring beginning. As I made my way back into my office an imaginary choir sang with great conviction in my head the old hymn "The Gospel Train":

> Get on board little children,
> Get on board little children,
> Get on board little children.
> There's room for many more.

> The fare is cheap, and all can go,
> The right and poor are there,
> No second class upon this train,
> No difference in the fare.

> So get on board little children,
> Get on board little children,
> Get on board little children,
> There's room for many more.

CHAPTER 28
Hope Reigns Eternal

When I thought I was prepared for the opening of school, my carefully sewn plan began to split wide open at the seams, and I again was forced into crisis management. It was in late July when I learned the master schedule with all assigned students had been deleted from the computer files, and I had to recreate the entire file before the students arrived in the middle of August.

Before I left for Utah, I had asked the technologist to keep everyone off the computers while I was gone. I had heard rumors that an attempt would be made to sabotage the schedule and "throw me into a tailspin." When I returned, he told me a counselor, who just happened to be the husband of an individual I had once refused to place in a principal position, was working on his computer, and the technologist was unaware that he was changing the schedule until he saw him shut it down as he was about to leave his office. I was far from being computer literate, and no one present in the building knew how to create a master schedule. I called an individual in the professional development department, and she came out to teach us how to create the schedule and assign students. The task was doubly difficult because we had to schedule by house. We worked all that day and late into the night and the following day and night to complete the scheduling task. I was eternally grateful to all for working tirelessly to have the schedule ready for the opening of school. I never really learned who the culprit was who committed such an egregious act.

I was beginning to believe that somewhere deep inside my soul lived a phantom masochist. Otherwise, why would I continue to endure such abuse while trying to maintain a positive attitude, while staying determined to find solutions to a string of never-ending, intentionally created problems? Then I remembered my reason for being at Furr. I tied a knot on the end of my goal and wrapped my mind tightly around it so I would never let go until it had been reached. I continued to work to create a better world even if it had to be done one person at a time.

Would I ever empty that Furr Pandora's box of its mean-spirited and unbelievably corrupt contents and create a wholesome, caring environment where the focus was on student achievement? Clearly, it would be an uphill battle, with the enemy often dressed in the uniform of my army, while marching to the beat of their own drummer—a drummer of dissent. I recalled my mother teaching me the words of Thoreau. I was beginning to question the wisdom of one of my former idols and his statements about being a majority of one, though I strongly embraced his belief in the significance of the individual in society. It appeared that some of the teachers had read and bought into Thoreau's ideas as outlined in *On the Duty of Civil Disobedience*. However, I was convinced they had taken his beliefs out of context, since several of them were obviously not civil. Their behavior begged the question, When do individual rights end and group norms prevail? It occurred to me that the question had not been clearly answered in their minds, and it was now my responsibility to assist them in working through it to its logical conclusion if we were ever to work toward a common goal at Furr.

It was clear to me that someone outside the school could provide an unbiased and human-centered approach to the cultural change that was necessary at Furr High School. When I accepted the position of hourly principal at Furr, I brought with me considerable baggage left over from my experiences with the school's teachers as their former district superintendent. Despite my desire to dump that baggage from the ship channel bridge into the murky water below, some of the teachers clung to their own baggage like barnacles attached to the sides of the ships moving slowly down the channel. Even those ships required cleaning after so many barnacles collected on their hulls.

I had decided Dr. Bena Kallick was just the person to inspire our minds and cleanse our souls. Not only did she project a real understanding of human nature, but she also had a wealth of ideas and instructional strategies, which were needed at the school. I had been flooding her with email since I returned from Utah and hoped she could wring out at least one day from her busy schedule to come to Houston during the school year. In retrospect, I suspect she could easily have concluded from my frequent communication that I was a desperate, despondent deviant who preyed upon innocent victims kind enough to respond to perpetual professional pleadings.

I spent much time in introspection attempting to understand why the things she had said during the conference were so energizing and inspiring to me and why they remained crystal clear to me long after I returned to Houston. Why did my mind keep returning to that inspiration? It was then that I realized Bena was that rare type teacher who had opened my eyes to a new way of doing things and had helped me to see life as I had always seen it prior to Ashley's death. I had never been so uplifted and enlightened in all my years as an educator. I felt a real kinship with her and was convinced that if anyone could rebuild Furr High School, she and I could do it. I was determined to bring her to Houston!

Our hope for the future:
Dr. Kallick and Dr. Art Costa.

One might have expected that I would receive the inspiration I needed to begin the school year at the HISD administrators' annual meeting, held at the beginning of each school year. It was there that the superintendent addressed all principals concerning the core values of the school district. I could hardly sit through the meeting as he talked about common decency being one of the core values. Clearly, that value was given mere lip service. The number of employees who had been removed from their administrative positions in a way that stripped them of their dignity and left them to pick up the pieces was evidence enough. Remarkably, some of those individuals were among the best and the brightest in the district. The business model used to replace employees required no reason for removal other than "in the best interest of the district."

Questions flooded my mind as I made my way back to Furr. Are high expectations all that is required to improve student achievement? Does this notion reflect our governor's thinking? I had heard him state at a recent luncheon that all children in Texas would read by the time they were in third grade. Can we simply mandate that students read by a given grade level and cause it to happen? Can we mandate high student achievement, and it will miraculously occur? If so, my job would be an easy one. Do these erudite decision makers know about individual differences?

It was time for Carol Harris and me to plan the professional development for the beginning of school. I wanted to include teachers but was not sure they would be interested. The first task was to work on civilizing the group. We both agreed we must communicate through the training that this was not business as usual. We were conscious of the need to create a training that would be meaningful to the teachers and likely would not create a hostile atmosphere that would invite an attack on us by them. I thought about Gandhi's belief that we should be the change we wanted to see and decided we would model the change we wanted to see at Furr.

We started the planning by reflecting on the teachers' attitudes when school had ended in June. Many of the middle-aged and younger teachers had no respect for the well-seasoned teachers and, in fact, openly called them dinosaurs. I preferred to think of them as vintage wine, especially since I had been around longer than they had. But after several weeks at Furr, I had begun to view myself more as lukewarm beer. The teachers who had been "insiders" with the former principal were self-proclaimed intellectuals, and they often made disparaging remarks about any teacher who was not a part of the "in" crowd. The minorities were excluded along with the older teachers, except for one English teacher who was still "hip," meaning he fit their description of "with it." He was an aging "hippie" whom I later learned to appreciate for his vast knowledge of literature, which he sought to pass on to his students. These arrogant teachers were anti-establishment and appeared to consider anyone in administration to be a buffoon, especially those in the East District office and in central administration. They insisted upon academic freedom and refused to teach the district curriculum. They were the ones who usually attacked the in-service presenters and reduced them to whimpering puddles of helplessness. Most human beings do not expect to be attacked, and these presenters were unprepared for the rude and insensitive treatment and were at a loss as to how to handle the situation. I knew I must always be prepared for such an attack.

Carol and I decided to take the teachers out of their comfort zone, which would possibly make the "intellectuals" less likely to attack. We rented space at the Museum of Natural Science and planned for a guided tour of the museum as a part of the training. The museum would supply materials that could be used with students and invite the teachers to bring their students to the educational programs there. We agreed an introduction to the Habits of Mind would be valuable for us all and possibly begin the process to behave in a more civil manner. We decided that a historical timeline would be a non-threatening way of giving credence to all faculty members. We would have them describe the educational program, student population, and school environment in fifteen-year chunks beginning with 1961, the year the school opened. We would end the day by walking across the street to the Museum of Health and Medical Science in the hope that teachers would become more aware of educational opportunities available for their students. We would make the day a positive, enjoyable, productive experience for all.

We arrived at the museum early, and placed large footprints inscribed with the Habits of Mind on the floor, leading from the parking garage to the meeting room. Chart paper was available for the teachers to work in groups on the Habits of Mind. We hung additional chart paper on the walls with the appropriate date chunks and put on a Kenny G CD. Who could be hostile while listening to smooth jazz? Assistant principals were ready to act as facilitators. Breakfast arrived, and we anxiously awaited the onslaught, poised as novice matadors ready to receive the bulls. As we waited, I looked at Carol, a quiet, gentle soul, who had so willingly joined me on this perilous journey, and I sensed her ambivalence. I winked at her, and her face broke into that disarming smile by which I will always remember her. "It will be okay," I assured her. "We have covered all the bases, including having breakfast for them. What more could they ask?"

As it turned out, we learned much from each small group as they reported to the larger group about what Furr was like during the period when they were first hired. The older teachers had much to tell that no one else knew about the school. They described in vivid detail how Furr had begun as a junior/senior high school in 1961 with the central focus on agriculture. Students were responsible for keeping livestock and exhibiting them in school as well as participating in district and state competitions. Once a year, a parade was held in nearby Jacinto City, and local politicians, school board members, and school superintendents rode on a flatbed trailer containing bales of hay and pulled by a pickup truck. I had once ridden in the parade as district superintendent, though I never quite understood the purpose of the event. The student population was predominately white at the time the school opened but began to see more and more black students as the HISD integrated the schools. Teachers were expected to teach the district curriculum and did so. This group described how race riots broke out on the campus as the population at Furr continued to shift. This led to a shooting at the school and a student being shot to death at the nearby fast food restaurant. The group described the period between 1961 and 1976 as the best and the worst times at Furr. The school became a high school in 1970. More and more whites moved to the suburbs, and there was no holding back the tide of integration.

All teachers, except for several in the magnet house, listened with interest as each group presented. Some of the magnet group continued to make jokes and sarcastic remarks. Their presentation was by far the weakest and only showed their inability to work as a vital part of the Furr learning community. I learned a great deal as I listened and watched the reactions of various teachers. I had always respected the older teachers, having worked with them when I was District VIII superintendent. But I gained even more respect for them as they took their task seriously and added so much to our knowledge of the school's history. At the close of the formal activities, I stressed the importance of each group's contributions and the richness of the Furr patchwork quilt that they had created. When we asked for reflections, we received many positive comments.

Later, during the debriefing session with Carol, it was clear she and I shared the same desire and believed in the possibility of a positive change happening in the culture at Furr. We had made it through an entire day without any confrontations. The minor rudeness displayed by a few could be overcome in a positive way over time, and we were committed to taking the steps necessary to accomplish that task. The events of that day resulted in one giant step for Furrkind! We were looking forward to many more giant steps, realizing that there would be obstacles in our pathway as we continued to move forward.

Over the summer, some houses had been relocated. Some teachers had expressed concern about where individual houses were located when I first arrived at Furr in the spring. Teachers in one house had always been in the temporary buildings, and they requested a move into the main school building. This seemed a reasonable concern and request, and I discussed this with a group of teachers who had always been inside the building. When I asked them to move to the temporary buildings in the interest of fair play, they were angry. They insisted there was no need for the move. We pushed ahead anyway, moving some teachers from the third floor of the main building to temporary buildings.

Afterwards, I could not turn off their complaint button. They often came to talk to me, but always together, threatening to leave. They were also upset that they were not permitted to schedule their own students. They accused me of being a dictator, controlling and discriminatory. "She just thinks we're trailer trash, so she moved us into temporary buildings," they complained. "Trailer trash! Trailer trash! That's what she thinks of us and our students!" When students came to ask why I considered them trailer trash, I thought the teachers had gone too far, and I told them so. They were friends of the former principal and were all too eager to find fault with everything I did. I listened with empathy and understanding and found them to be rather amusing. More accurately, I liked them: they had come to school early in August and were working in their rooms as they complained. They slowly warmed up to me, but they still hated being housed in their new location.

I had not realized the move from inside out and outside in would be such a big issue until several teachers came to me and expressed their surprise that I would do such a thing. "I never thought I'd see the day those people would be moved outside," one remarked.

Another teacher playfully warned, "Watch your back, baby, 'cause you've gone to meddling with the 'in crowd.' Just watch out, you hear?"

"Everyone's in the 'in crowd' now," I replied. "How does it feel to be in?"

"Real good," she grinned, her eyes sparkling. "Yes, indeed! Real good!"

CHAPTER 29
Beyond Bartering

News came in August 2000 that Furr had received the small schools grant from the United States Department of Education, the grant whose deadline we had nearly missed earlier that summer. That meant we would be getting one hundred thousand dollars per year for the next three years to create smaller learning communities. Some of the teachers who had worked so hard to create the house system in 1995 were energized (though not enough to work with me to plan the use of the funds). Carol Harris and I made the decision to use the funds for staff development and a leadership conference for students. We would continue to work with teachers to make them a part of the change process and to establish an internal locus of control.

I was eager to establish internal control regarding campus decisions rather than always being forced to respond to external mandates. Just as individuals play a significant role in society and have needs that must be given consideration, so it is with individual schools. Each school possesses its own culture, its own set of mores, and its own traditions. For real change to occur at Furr, it must be born from the minds and hearts of the individuals within the school community. Their natural talents must be set free to enthusiastically create or reinvent an organization perceived to be better than the existing one. Furthermore, we must be ever mindful of those forces that would, inevitably, work against us to impede our progress. It was clear in my mind that I would not be the leader who would "save" Furr High School. If Furr High School were to be "saved," it would be driven by all the people in the Furr arena: students, teachers, administrators, and community people working collaboratively to bring about sustainable change. What I would provide was the moral order and leadership that would bind us together around a common goal and belief system.

It is common knowledge that most change efforts fail. My years in public education have convinced me most of those failures are the result of an individual at the top propelling the change with very little input from the people on the front line. The research is replete with failed change initiatives. Furr High School was a perfect example. It had adopted the small schools model in 1995, at least five years before any other school in Houston. The change was dictated from one or two individuals at the top, and staff who did not want to be a part of the initiative were told they could just find another school. As a central office administrator, I responded to the calls from resisters, and I knew which teachers had dug in their heels and yawned nonchalantly, "This, too, shall pass." That change initiative, initiated with such energy and enthusiasm, failed—not because it was a bad idea but rather because no one stopped to consider what might impede and eventually kill the effort.

In the case of Furr, there were numerous forces that contributed to the demise of their hard-fought effort. Clearly, one was the assumption that simply changing the structure would result in the more substantial changes that were needed. The structural change did little to change the climate, student advocacy, the instructional program, or the curriculum. Another force was a lack of planning to ensure that what they wanted to have happen did, in fact, happen. Even with the best-laid plans, members of the organization must take stock at certain times and then decide whether to continue the same course or make changes. A third force that impeded progress at Furr was that teachers were assigned to the houses by the principal, under the assumption that simply assigning individuals to groups would create fully functioning teams. I was aware of how all of these had handicapped Furr in the past and was committed to being ever mindful of those pitfalls. I wanted to guard against making the same mistakes, realizing that mistakes would be made despite careful planning.

Before we could form an internal locus of control, we had to work to civilize the environment. I had to gain the teachers' trust and involve them in the change process. I had always been intrigued with the work of Thomas Sergiovanni on value-added leadership. I had attempted to use his moral leadership model when I was a principal and superintendent. Furr begged for moral leadership.

Certain assumptions apply to this model: emotions and beliefs are important; and what is good and right is as important as what is effective. Commitments are made around shared values and beliefs, and the professional learning community believes that collegiality is necessary. Moral authority arises from the felt obligations and responsibilities that spring from shared community ideals, values, and thinking. We would function not because of a contract with the community but rather because we have a covenant with the community. The creation of such a covenant would be difficult in a school district and state driven by high-stakes tests, but I believed it could be done. Furr High School's distance from my vision could best be described as infinity.

In Sergiovanni's model, Furr was not even at the bartering level: they were not even fulfilling their contractual agreement with the district. They were not giving a day's work for a day's pay. We must begin at that level and, hopefully, move onto the building, bonding, and banking levels.

Bertie feeling positive.

CHAPTER 30
Running for Safety

O ver the summer, there had been increasing warfare between two neighborhoods that fed into Furr, and there had been several drive-by shootings and gang-related fights in the streets. That warfare erupted on the campus on the first day of the new school year, before the school day began. A member of one gang grabbed a chain from the neck of a member of another gang. The two began a fight that resulted in one student being thrown through a plate glass window. He lay sprawled on the shiny, glass-spattered terrazzo entryway of Furr, with a huge gash across his forehead, as we waited for the ambulance to arrive. His sweat-covered face resembled a shiny black pin cushion with tiny shards of glass releasing miniscule streams of blood that trickled down his cheeks and pooled on the floor. A punctured pressure point on his neck pumped blood like a newly blown oil well as a staff member frantically worked to stop the bleeding. I stood in silence, praying this young man would not die.

Several days later, the student who had thrown the young man through the glass window was shot to death in front of the Pleasantville Community Center. A full-fledged war erupted after the shooting and, naturally, spilled over into the school. Many of the students were seething with anger, and no amount of counseling would extinguish that fire in their bellies. They were after revenge, and nobody was going to stop them.

"Miss, my homeboy's been killed, and we just can't cut it loose. Somebody's got to pay," one student told me. I attempted to reason with him, but my attempts fell on deaf ears.

Furr had two police officers who were regularly on campus. One was part-time from the Houston Police Department (HPD), and the other was an HISD police officer. The HPD officers often made demeaning remarks about the HISD officers, calling them "play" cops and never taking them seriously. I later decided that attitude was because the HISD officers had a more tolerant approach to students than many of the HPD officers had.

Peaceful Furr courtyard.

I was not fond of the idea of police on a school campus, but it was clear to me that we needed additional assistance in controlling the gang problem at Furr. In desperation, I called for the gang task force to come and attempt to quell the violence that would not cease.

They responded immediately and appeared to relish the idea of slamming students. They grabbed disruptive students, pushed them against the side of a brick wall, and handcuffed them. Then they grabbed some of our better students, called them "thugs," and manhandled them if they looked like they "had an attitude." One HPD officer threw a student to the floor in the cafeteria and handcuffed him, causing a revolt by the other students and concern on the part of the teachers who witnessed the event. A teacher approached the officer and suggested such rough treatment of the student was not necessary. The police officer, in the presence of the students, threatened to arrest the teacher if he did not "back off." I cringed when I saw an officer grab a student who had accidentally bumped into him and throw the student to the ground. I was told the officers loudly cursed the students, called them names and treated them as if they were criminals. Parents, teachers, and students complained about the brutality and the explosive atmosphere that resulted.

At the request of teachers, and out of my own concern, I spoke with the officers and suggested they were behaving in violent ways that only exacerbated the problem. They told me to stay out of their business because once they became involved, the principal had no say in the actions taken against students. I was not aware that zero tolerance now meant I had no control and the school was a police state. Besides, in my experience as area superintendent, I had never embraced the idea of zero tolerance since it was highly ineffective in getting at the root cause of violence. No students were rehabilitated as a result of the action, and they often returned to school with more sophisticated ideas for disruption. It was much later when I learned the officers had misinformed me and had, in fact, exceeded their authority on the Furr campus.

The violence began to impact all students and staff. Word began to spread around the district that I was soft on discipline. This was the result of students asking the police officers if they could talk to me when the police officers were manhandling them. I was anything but soft on discipline, but I believed that students had rights and should be given the opportunity to be heard. I also believed that violent behavior on the part of adults on campus only encouraged students to act in violent ways. I believed in intense counseling of students and the opportunity to identify and treat the causes of the violent behavior. I was still convinced that if each student had one caring adult on campus to go to with their problems, then the violence would diminish. I believed that even the tough gang members would respond to sincere concern.

We became aware the gang task force members appeared to take pride in pushing the students around. They appeared to thrive on physical intensity, and there was no sign that they wanted the violence to decrease. I finally had enough and called the police captain to describe what I thought was unusually violent behavior on the part of the officers and requested that he remove the gang task force from Furr High School.

On September 1, 2000, prior to the removal of the gang task force, a teacher ran up to me as I was exiting a classroom where I had been teaching a class in the history of music. She told me I needed to go right away to the school's front office, where a female police officer had lost it and was "jacking a male student around and was in his face." When I entered the front office, I saw students, teachers, parents, and school personnel watching in shock as the police officer, who was in a rage, grabbed the student and shouted threats at him. Her face was immediately in front of his, as she continued to call him names and threaten him. I recognized the officer and knew the student was a special needs student.

I placed my hand on the officer's shoulder and calmly requested that she bring the student into my office to talk with him. She jerked herself around to face me and thrust her left hand in my face as she shouted, "No! You are not in charge of this! I am!" Her face was scarlet, and her eyelids had surrendered to her bulging eyes, which were about to pop right out of their sockets. It was clear she was out of control. I again requested that she bring the student into my office to take care of the problem. She again yelled that she was in charge and would take him to her police car. I replied, "Please do."

When I turned to walk into my office, she followed me, yelling at the top of her voice about the fact the student had on a muscle shirt, and I had done nothing about it. I later learned when the student's mother came in, demanding to file a lawsuit against the officer, that the student had gone to the doctor that day and had not attended classes. He had come on campus in his street clothes with his mother who wanted to speak with the nurse. That explained why he was out of dress code.

Bertie driving students home in her convertible.

178

Once in my office, the officer stood inches from my face, yelling that I needed to be trained in how to run a school. She called me incompetent and accused me of discrediting her gang task force by requesting their removal from the school. Any attempt I made to calm her down only resulted in the intensification of her rage. She told me I had asked for zero tolerance and I was getting zero tolerance. She then began yelling about my "little angels who wear muscle shirts to show off their tattoos." Her fury-purpled face and bursting, blood-shot eyes screamed of insanity. I looked at the revolver strapped to her waist and realized she was dangerous as she screamed, "Your school is going to implode, and the blood is going to be on your hands!"

I calmly replied, "It almost feels as if you want the school to implode."

She barked, "Your school is going to implode, and when you call us, we are not coming!" She turned and stomped from my office, slamming the door loudly behind her. I sat down and wrote a letter requesting that she never return to Furr. I never saw her again, the gang task force was removed, and the climate improved significantly.

None of my actions made me popular with the police officers. I frequently received reports of statements they had spread around the school district and city. It was said that I was too old to run a school and too soft on discipline. It was said that I tied the hands of my assistant principals and would not permit them to discipline the students. It was said that I should go to the house or, better yet, to "the home." That idea was sounding better and better to me.

One of the officers who criticized me most vehemently was the HPD officer who threw the student to the floor in the cafeteria. He was also the one I caught sitting in his office, feet propped in another chair, reading the *Weekly World News* tabloid. He immediately took his feet from the chair and stood when I entered and asked to see what he was reading. The headlines read "MINI-MERMAID FOUND IN TUNA SANDWICH!" The adjacent picture was of a man with a mouthful of sandwich, holding a small, shapely mermaid upside down by the tail. "'I asked for extra mayo & got THIS,' says Iowa man" was the caption.

I kept the paper and said to him, "I may appear soft on discipline, but you are trashy on literature." Then I asked, "Is this what tough men with a revolver strapped to their waists read?" For some reason, he never, ever liked me after that, and I cannot say I cared.

Still, the police responded one day when one of my gang member informers told me an adult rival gang would be in front of the school at dismissal time that afternoon, with the intent to shoot down every student who wore a red shirt symbolizing the Little Reds gang. The police arrived immediately and foiled the attempt. I wondered if I could ever make a difference at Furr High School. I wondered...

CHAPTER 31
Heartbreak

I was about to learn another example of Furr being a "have not" school. It was time for the football homecoming game, and I was to play a major role. All week, the school had been involved in activities leading up to our big game with Davis High School, a rival school in another low income area in north Houston. The pep rally set the stage for a victory on the field that night. I arrived at the game early, but I had obviously misunderstood the weather forecast because I was dressed for winter. It was an unusually warm, muggy night in late October 2000, and the chill that I had expected came from staff, not from tlhe weather.

"Dr. Simmons go now!" an assistant principal shouted. I sprang to my feet, and without a hitch, made my way gracefully to the spot on the field that had been marked for me. I watched in admiration as the Davis marching band, complete with drum major, plumes, boots, and beautiful uniforms made their way off the field.

This was Furr's big moment, and the excitement mounted with wild cheering from the stands. When we struck up our band, it was made up of three drums and two guitars. No marching band, no plumes, no boots, and no marchers. Several young female students dressed in T-shirts and skirts danced to the music. After the ceremony, I returned to my seat, still perspiring but with a heart full of warmth for our students who were forced to face such indignity in front of our supporters and the fans from Davis. I cannot tell you what happened after that and whether we won or lost. In my mind, our school had already lost. I didn't know if I could do anything about the problem, but I planned to try.

I vaguely remembered new band uniforms being delivered to the school right after I had arrived in the spring. I checked it out the day after the homecoming game, and sure enough, hanging in the band room closet were beautiful black and red uniforms. I called central administration and asked why Furr had received these obviously expensive uniforms when we had no band. I was told it was Furr's year to receive band uniforms, and we received them whether we needed them or not. I was shocked at such outright inefficiency and downright waste of taxpayer money. What a foolish practice! What Furr needed was money for band instruments so we could have a band.

I chatted with the students the following week about the homecoming game. They seemed to take it for granted that Furr didn't have a marching band and never would have one. Maybe I was making too much of it or maybe their expectations were too low, as often happens in under-served minority schools. But it didn't seem right to me, and I still wanted to do something about it. It would be difficult, though, because there were no music programs in most of the feeder schools and no band programs in the middle schools. This would clearly take time to achieve, but I felt it was worth the effort. For about a week I could not shake from my head the haunting voice of Billie Holiday singing about the fact that those who have will get and those who don't will lose. How much loss would these students have to endure? It was ten years later that we had a marching band, and the crowd cheered wildly when they proudly marched across the football field.

CHAPTER 32
A Magical Experience

Bertie and a student decorating the campus.

Try as I might, it seemed impossible to make significant progress toward changing the climate at Furr. I would take a baby step forward and two giant leaps backward. A major problem that impeded our progress was the inordinate amount of time I spent in the fall of 2000 working through problems with individual teachers. It seemed never-ending.

That fall, we had established the new ninth-grade academy. I was feeling good about this step forward until one day, Carol and I were invited to attend a ninth-grade support meeting. Sarah, the house leader and a second-year teacher, attacked me as soon as I sat down because I did not permit the teachers in the house to track the students. That meant putting all the below-grade-level students in one track. George, an algebra teacher, had asked my permission to regroup his students by ability. I was shocked at his request since he was concerned about only twelve students in the class. Earlier, I had given the teachers an article to read about a successful ninth-grade academy, which I referred to as I discussed other research on homogeneous grouping and differentiated instruction. The academy leader went into a rage, and with her face red, voice quivering, and eyes bulging, she screamed, "We don't want to hear what the so-called experts say. We are the experts!" I stood and very calmly told her she was being rude and insubordinate, and they, in fact, were not the experts. I informed her

I would not tolerate her subjecting us to such treatment and I would set a time for her to see me in my office about the unprofessional act. With that, we left the meeting.

Later that day, I called Sarah in and talked with her about her behavior. I also told her I was aware she was friends with some of the teachers who did not want me at Furr, and I suggested she not be influenced by their behavior. She replied that she resented my statement to which I countered, "I understand, but you have such great potential and I want you to be successful. Please don't be influenced by others' perceptions of me and know that I will help you to grow in any way possible, but you can't continue to be rude and expect to succeed." She wept, hugged my neck, and apologized. I never had any more problems with Sarah. She was a Teach for America teacher, who left after fulfilling her two-year obligation. This was a pattern for Teach for America teachers.

When I visited classrooms, there were times when I was angered because of the laid-back attitude of the teachers and lack of instruction. Still, I maintained a professional demeanor and attempted to model the behavior I wanted to see in others. As I began to have conversations with teachers about their work, more and more of them began to stop me in the hallway or come into my office to chat. Some of them responded well to the reflective questions, and on occasion, I would see a glimmer of hope. But then a dark cloud would suddenly block the sun, and I would be convinced I had witnessed a mirage. Any change for the better that might be occurring was moving at the pace of a wounded snail, and gang fights were omnipresent.

I was becoming discouraged and thought it would take a miracle to bring long-term civility to Furr High School. I had walked into a world I had not known existed. If someone had told me such things went on in schools, I would not have believed it. When I agreed to stay an additional year at Furr, I believed I could make a difference. So far, all I had done was struggle to partially empty the Furr Pandora box and deal with its contents. I could find very little evidence of growth within the school community, and I had been there nine months. Every time I scratched the surface of my goal to provide moral leadership at Furr, vile behaviors and attitudes spewed forth like the geysers in Yellowstone National Park and sprayed over my consciousness.

My spirit was drenched, and I longed to escape this stream of evil. I welcomed the Thanksgiving holidays with my family. And then I hid away to regroup. Bobby Rydell's song "A World Without Love" spun in my mind like a record stuck on replay. Reflecting on the lyrics of that song reminded me that I needed to look inside myself for the answers. I had hired a vocal music teacher in the fall, and the voices of the students always uplifted me. We had been unable to hold assemblies because of the threat of gang fights. Also, the auditorium was so small that for all students to participate required that we have two assemblies, which increased the chance of warfare. Despite this danger, I decided to have the choir perform for the school at two assemblies. Their voices were heavenly, and many teachers told me how much they had enjoyed the music and thanked me for inviting them to the assembly. This was the first time we were able to have an assembly with no gang fights. Perhaps the tide was turning. I wondered...

Just before the winter break a few weeks later, I decided to invite the faculty and staff to my home for a party. They could get to know me better, and I could thank them for their efforts. What better time to spread the true spirit of caring? I invited all 130 of them, and most of them came. Something magical happened that evening as we gathered around the piano and sang Christmas carols and later sat in front of an open fire and shared special remembrances of the season. The staff members who attended seemed to be comfortable and made themselves at home. When the last guests had gone, exhausted though I was, I realized that Furr High School would never, ever be the same. If the spirit that was present in my home that evening could be made to spill over into and fill all the days of our lives, our goal would be realized. My soul was renewed, and I was even more determined to see it through. I hoped...

Austin at the Furr
Christmas party.

Darrow sharing secrets with
Ms. Wiggins and April Turner.

Carol Harris, Angela
Borzon, and Debbie Kubiak
at Christmas party.

Astrid Wich piling it on.

Watch Darrow Ward's
finger!

Gloria Lemond
munching out.

Go for it, Mrs. Lavina!

Darrow and Sheila Whitford
sharing secrets.

CHAPTER 33
Spring Came, but Not Forever

It was the first day of school in January 2001, and as I made my way toward the rising sun, I retrieved the memories of the last eleven months at Furr High School from my brain vault, where I had stored them as slides. I placed them into my View-Master and, one by one, clicked the trigger to observe each in the light of a new day. Golden rays of sunlight were awakening and stretching like giant streamers over the horizon and jutting into the heavens, adding brilliance to each memory view. The yellow smog that usually clung to the ship channel had been swept away by a welcome north wind, leaving a crisp, clear, clean panorama. On this glorious, cloudless day, I could see for miles in each direction as I crossed the ship channel bridge. This was quite a contrast to my first trek over the bridge to Furr High School. Perhaps I was beginning to see my way more clearly and was more focused on my goal. Perhaps this refreshing scene really did announce a new beginning.

The holiday party with the Furr staff in my home had reminded me of what I already knew but had permitted to float around only in the periphery of my mind. Much that happened at Furr High School was dependent upon my own attitude and enthusiasm about the job. If I expected a new beginning, one that would endure, then I would have to embed that positive attitude and enthusiasm within my psyche. I would have to let it drive my actions while I steadfastly kept my eye on the goal: to reinvent the school in a way that would produce successful and moral students and teachers. I must be omnipresent, even while fighting the unexpected plunges into the stygian depths I still experienced at the thought of Ashley's death. A thought about her could so easily be triggered by something as simple as a fragrance, a melody, a dancer, a beautiful sunset. I resolved to keep in mind my purpose of being at Furr, knowing I would at times fall short in my efforts.

Most of the staff were excited to be back at school, as were the students. More and more, teachers consulted with me and hung out in my office after school. They planned and implemented an after-school program to enable students to recover courses they had failed. They used data to identify students who needed tutoring for the upcoming TAAS test and arranged tutorial classes. I brought consultants in from the Writers in the Schools project to work with selected students to improve their writing skills. Teacher participation saw a sudden spurt, and most teachers seemed to share my enthusiasm: they were clearly willing to assist and work to prepare the students academically. I believed in my head and heart we were on our way.

The teachers, while more excited about their work, were still not providing rigorous instruction. A few of them were engaging the students, but the instruction was generally shallow and lacked real meaning. And although most teachers were pleasant, some were still disengaged. There were the "intellectuals" who would not speak to me unless I spoke first. I continued to support the magnet program, although some of the teachers distanced themselves from me, and we were recruiting small numbers of students from outside Furr into the program. The culture of the regular school remained one of mediocrity, and it lacked urgency. The instructional abyss into which the teachers had fallen was so deep it would require an educational Geiger counter to locate their presence and a shared Herculean effort to lift them to a higher level.

The students were what made it easy for me to maintain a positive attitude and enthusiasm for my work, despite the external mandates and the challenges with the teachers. They dropped into my office often and put their arms around me when they saw me in the hallways. They kept me up to date on gang-related activity and gave me a heads up when something was about to "go down." I was thrilled that they trusted me and really began to care about the school. They greeted me with a "What's up?" and a high five and were never disrespectful when I corrected them. They told me I had really "turned the corner" when I participated in a Mexican dance during an assembly program. I knew I was in solid with them when they invited me to "chill." Now, if I could just get them to be academically successful!

Shattered Dreams Day.

One deep concern I had with the students was their raging use of drugs. Alcohol was a growing drug of choice, so I was glad when it was time to implement the Shattered Dreams program we had planned with the Coalition of Behavioral and Health Services representatives. Our entire student body was released to the front of the school to witness the event. All local law enforcement agencies and hospitals worked with us to carry out the plan. The program required that a terrible mock automobile accident be staged on the street in front of the school. The driver of the car was to have been drinking alcohol on his way to school. Some of our students were in the crushed auto, and they required removal by cutting away the side of the car. One student was flown by helicopter to a hospital in the medical center.

Twenty students spent the night in a local hospital where they received counseling and a workshop on drug prevention. During the entire school day, a student dressed as the Grim Reaper, complete with scythe, removed a student from a classroom every twenty-six minutes. This was to point out that one teenager died every twenty-six minutes from drunk driving. The entire community had been prepared for the event and came out in droves to watch the realistic representation of a disaster. I informed the parents of the girl who had been airlifted, and they were taken to the hospital by Furr staff. When they arrived at the hospital, they were informed by a physician their daughter had died. (They were part of the plan and knew it was not true.)

191

The following day, parents and students talked to the entire student body in an assembly about the impact the event had on them. The students took the event seriously and asked meaningful and thoughtful questions. As a result of our participation in the program, twenty of our students received an all-expenses paid trip to San Antonio for one week in the summer where they were trained in peer mentoring. Furr also received a counselor to work with the peer mentors the following school year at no cost to the school. The program continued for years and was one of the most powerful tools available to assist students at Furr with peer mentoring and counseling.

I had been at the school for one year. A friend of mine brought Mae Jemison, the first black female astronaut, to Furr. The students were so excited to meet a real astronaut, especially when they learned she was a chemical engineer, scientist, and physician who not only spoke English but also Russian, Japanese, and Swahili, and she looked as if she was about nineteen years old! They had insightful questions for her, and she stole their hearts and left them with hope. She gave them posters and autographed copies of her book, and for days after her appearance, every girl who talked to me assured me she was going to be an astronaut.

Mae's visit was followed by a visit from Dr. Bena Kallick. Yes, she did make time for us after all. I had continued to communicate with her throughout the year and had encouraged my friend Sharon Koonce, assistant superintendent of professional development for HISD, to invite her to be a speaker at a local conference. Bena had agreed to speak, and she came to Furr the following day. She shadowed me all day long, and we had an opportunity to talk about my goals for the school. She fit right in with the teachers, and it was clear they liked her. I knew we would make a good team, and I was thrilled when she agreed to work with our school.

We made plans for her to come back to Houston in early June to meet with the Furr Instructional Council, which I had established to make plans for the following school year. I never knew what convinced her that we needed her help, but my spirits soared when she agreed, and I had no doubt we could reinvent the struggling Furr High School. After dropping Bena off at the airport, my mind swirled like a tornado with images of what the school would look like after the transformation. New energy had been breathed into my soul, and I was eager to move toward that light at the end of the treacherous funnel cloud.

Wind for New Wings **conference.**

The book I had been writing with Ashley, *Wind for New Wings*, was written to highlight Houston leaders and was intended to be used with high school students who would become the leaders of the new millennium. We held a *Wind for New Wings* conference for all juniors at Furr, and students chose noted Houstonians from the book who were invited to be presenters and tell their stories. The conference was absolutely one of the best things we had done. Although two Nobel Prize winners were in the book, students chose individuals with whom they felt they could relate. Linda Lorell, a local news anchor, was the MC, and all the keynote speakers and those in breakout sessions were down-to-earth and related well to the students. One of the keynote speakers was a young rabbi, and the students thought what she said was thought provoking and wonderful. They had never heard a rabbi speak before and never knew a rabbi could be young and female. The entire day was enlightening and enjoyable. What a wonderful way to end the school year!

By the end of that first full school year, the school was again recognized by the state, I had been able to counsel two teachers into more appropriate teaching positions, two assistant principals had retired, I had made friends with many of the teachers, and I had fallen in love with the students. I hired a band to play at graduation exercises and had spent so much time talking to the graduating seniors about appropriate audience behavior that we headed off the spiritual revival of the previous year's graduation when the audience hooped and hollered the entire time. The exercise went off without a hitch, and I was so proud of the graduates and their behavior. The school year had ended on a positive note. As the teachers checked out for the summer, I called them in one at a time to review the year and express my appreciation for something that each teacher had personally done.

CHAPTER 34
Stormy Weather

D
r. Bena Kallick came back to Houston on June 7, 2001, a few days after my second graduation at Furr. She was to meet the following day with the Furr Instructional Council. I had also arranged for her to meet with all school principals in the Furr feeder pattern at a brunch in my home. She planned to talk with them about the possibility of implementing curriculum mapping across the feeder pattern. I had been discussing that need with them throughout the school year in order to identify gaps and redundancies in the curriculum and encourage vertical planning.

It was the evening before the brunch, and according to weather reports, Houston had been spared the brunt of Tropical Storm Allison, which had been churning in the Gulf of Mexico for several days. It had been raining all day, and the wind twisted the treetops as if attempting to unscrew them from the ground. The eye of the storm was to hit land miles south of Houston, so I had no concern about our plans with Bena. Sharon Koonce and I were busily planning for the principals' brunch the following day, sure the rain would subside by then. We were about to call it a day when I heard a gurgling sound. I went into my sunken den to determine the source of the noise, and to my amazement, the den was a two-feet-deep sea of rushing water! Startled, I waded through the icy, swirling liquid and started grasping at my valuables spinning on the surface of the unwelcome indoor pool. I yelled for help, and we began moving furniture and placing it on concrete blocks for protection. I, having never experienced such a thing, began frantically scooping water with a bucket and running to the bathroom to pour it into the basin. Despite my efforts, the water continued to rise. The designs on my beloved rug became an eerie Jackson Pollock painting, and a letter from my deceased mother floated up and lodged against my leg as a voice whispered in my ear, Don't panic. Everything will be alright.

Suddenly, the water was sucked from the room as if a huge vacuum had reclaimed this wayward sea and sent it back into the ocean that rumbled down my driveway and into the street. I stood in awe as I observed the water being suctioned out underneath the doors, leaving only puddles here and there in the room. I could only think of the biblical story of the parting of the Red Sea as I began to mop the remnants of the flood and wash the walls and floor with disinfectant. My soaked rug had to be dragged outside, never to be used again. It was well into the wee hours of the morning before I went to bed, fretting about the brunch the following day. Lyrics from the Alice Cooper song "Hurricane Years" were my lullaby.

The following morning, the entire city of Houston was flooded, but I was able to pick Bena up from her hotel and bring her to my house. I prepared the brunch on the chance that some principals would swim over to hear Bena. Only two individuals were brave enough to navigate the city along the one dry labyrinth that led to my house. Bena met with them while my neighbors, wearing tall rubber boots, stopped in for brunch. The rain continued throughout the day, and all airports were closed. Bena had no choice but to stay another night, and I worried whether she would ever return after this harrowing experience.

After I dropped Bena off at the airport the following day, I cautiously made my way to Furr to check for flood damage. In some spots on I-10, eighteen-wheelers were completely submerged in water, and the entire neighborhood around the school was under water. Furr stood high and dry, but many of the Furr families had lost everything.

When the water subsided the following week, many of our students were still homeless. We organized a food and clothing drive for them, and many were forced to relocate outside the Furr school zone. Houston was declared a disaster area by President George W. Bush, and it was many months before our Furr family's lives returned to normal.

We were ready for something positive to happen at Furr, and just as we were closing the school for the school year, we learned about an opportunity to submit a proposal for a grant from the Carnegie Foundation to reform the school. I worked with teachers to prepare to present the proposal by August. Things were looking up for the next school year, especially since Dr. Bena Kallick would be working with us every other month, and her friend, Marian Leibowitz, would work with us the months Bena was not there.

CHAPTER 35
Not to Be Believed

It was in early August. It was a beautiful sunshiny day with an unusually cool summer breeze. There was a lack of the humidity that usually reduced Houstonians to limp, wrung-out dishcloths. I had been working with the parent coordinator, Ms. Maria Victoria Aguirre, to prepare for a parent conference on that day. She had held daily and evening classes for parents at Furr during the school year and knew the parents well. In preparation for the conference, we had passed out flyers in the neighborhoods served by the school, and we had visited churches in the area to invite parents to attend the conference. We had also emphasized the importance of parents bringing their high school students with them to the conference.

**An amazing parent coordinator and human being,
Maria Victoria Aguirre.**

Consuelo Castillo Kickbusch, the first Hispanic woman to be named lieutenant colonel in the United States Army, had been invited as keynote speaker. Representatives from community organizations were invited to lead breakout sessions. Fortunately, we had been able to obtain refreshments and buses for transportation, as well as a babysitting service provided by Furr students. We did everything we knew to do to make the conference a success. Teachers had repeatedly warned me that parents would not come to school during the school year, much less in the dead of summer. I remained unconvinced, despite their repeated warnings.

The morning of the conference, I attended the HISD administrative meeting where Consuelo Kickbusch was also the keynote speaker. The event ended at noon, and I rushed to Furr to await the arrival of Lieutenant Colonel Kickbusch and our parents for the first annual Furr Parent Conference, which was to begin at 1:00 p.m. Ms. Aguirre was waiting and, as usual, had a beautifully presented table of refreshments in the Furr living room for our keynote speaker and a few honored guests, who had already arrived from the central office. I chatted briefly with them and then moved anxiously to the window to watch for the arrival of the parents.

Droplets of perspiration formed on my brow, and my heart began to pound, pumping streams of hot blood to my temples and flushing my face when I saw no parents. That tiny voice in my head kept whispering, These parents won't come to school during the school year, much less in the dead of summer. I started to fidget as if I had suddenly developed Saint Vitas Dance, and I repeatedly shifted my eyes from the window to my watch and back again. It was 12:45 p.m., and not only had the parents not arrived but neither had Consuelo Castillo Kickbusch.

At 12:50 p.m., I saw Consuelo approaching the front door, but there was not one parent present. I greeted her as she entered the room and expressed my concern about the fact we might not have an audience. She just laughed and said she would simply address those of us in the room if no parent showed up for this rare opportunity. I returned to the window to watch while my other guests entertained her.

It was exactly 12:57 p.m. when I spotted a lone parent approaching the front door of the school with her high school–aged son and a baby in a stroller in tow. And then there was another and another. In no time, a caravan of parents was making its way to the door. Many of them had babies in strollers and were in search of babysitters. My heart danced on a musical note as I rushed out to greet them, just as a bus pulled up in front of the school and an endless stream of parents and students flowed from the open bus door. The parking lot was suddenly overflowing with automobiles, and entire families made their way into the auditorium to hear Consuelo speak.

At once, the auditorium had standing room only, and the remaining guests spilled over into the courtyard. My amazement turned to sheer joy as I watched the parents and listened to Consuelo, whose message vacillated between Spanish and English. She was a bona fide showstopper with her dramatic, heart-wrenching stories and humor. The audience interrupted her often with wild applause, and it was apparent they related to her in a sincere way. At the end of her speech, she called me to the front. She told the parents how fortunate they were to have me as principal and asked for their help in working to make Furr the best place possible for their children.

Standing in front of the sea of parents, I began, "Estimados amigos. Estamos contentos aquí en esta gran ocasión. La escuela es para los estudiantes. Es necesario que ustedes se envolucren en la escuela. Los Latinos son muy buena gente." I had memorized a few Spanish phrases, and I hoped they would not ask me any questions because I had about emptied my memory bank.

Many of our students were present, and they started the standing ovation I received. I was overwhelmed and a bit misty-eyed at such a genuine show of support. Later, the parents rushed to me and asked me to bring Consuelo to work with the school. I promised I would try but warned them we had limited funds and might not be financially able to afford inviting her back to the school.

When the day ended, we had registered over six hundred parents and students! The breakout sessions were a great success, and of course, the food was enjoyed by all. The mothers told me how good it felt to be able to enjoy the conference without having to take care of their babies, and the fathers liked being there with their families.

All in all, it was a wonderfully exciting day and one that convinced me that minority parents will come to school when there is a good reason to do so. I took no credit for the success of the day. The credit belonged to Ms. Aguirre, our parent coordinator. I explained that to the parents and told them to thank her for the event. She was as proud as I was when we reported the results to the nay-sayers, who could not hide their disbelief.

As I reflected on the parent conference day, I realized it was simply the beginning. Just to get that many parents to attend was quite an accomplishment, but we must do much more if we were to have long-term, meaningful involvement of parents in the education of their children. We needed to find a mechanism to open communication between the school and home and among members of the Furr family. The more we learned about each student, the more likely we were to ensure that student's success. Furthermore, we needed, in many cases, to help parents understand their role as parents, within the home and within the school. We needed to develop trust within the family and between family and school. We needed to work together to build self-esteem and a sense of belonging within the school community. This was just another in a long series of tasks that we had to accomplish if we were to reinvent Furr High School. And then there were the disconnected youth who had no home and no family. What must we do for them? This was an essential question that we had to answer.

Maria Victoria Aguirre had accomplished what I wanted all staff to do. I had created an opportunity for her to perform, and she had applied her talents to the opportunity and run with it. Many authorities in education speak of great school principals as "transforming" a school. I have never found that to be the case. I have found that leaders transform neither organizations nor individuals, and they do not "empower" people. Leaders create an empowering environment that encourages people to act in powerful ways. The opportunity to go where no one at Furr had ever gone was all Maria Aguirre needed to create a miracle. At the beginning, she asked me how we could get parents to come to Furr in August, and I quickly told her I did not know. We brainstormed some ideas, and then the project was all hers. I gave her permission to figure it out for herself, and her only other questions concerned funds for buses and food. A month later, she had come to me with a plan. She was determined to prove it could be done, and she did it.

My view of leadership was quite different from most school administrators I had known. I often told the teachers I was there to "grow people," but not to spoon-feed them. I was at Furr to create a climate that would foster an institution of learning, and I could not do it by directing the actions of the staff. Besides, I was never well-known as a performer. I could create an environment where others could become better and better at performing, but my stage presence had always been questionable. I could inspire, but I was not a noted director. I could have a vision, but without the help of the staff, my vision would be in shambles. I thrived on uncertainty and never had any certainty about whether what I did would work. I knew only that if it didn't work, I would simply try something else.

My major strength was in practicing the Jessie Jackson slogan "Keep hope alive!" Will Rogers, the great humorist, once summed it up by saying, "You've got to know what's cooking, you've got to believe in what's cooking, 'cause you can't heat an oven with snowballs."

CHAPTER 36
In Search of Compassion

In early September 2001, I was in a staff meeting with my assistant principals when a clerk came to tell us an airplane had crashed into one of the World Trade Center towers in New York City. I flipped on the television just in time to see another plane fly into the second tower. At that moment, our whole world changed forever. The word terrorists clung to our lips like a vampire, sucking from us our security and infusing us with a fear like none we had ever known. We watched the devastation and death with horror and felt helpless and confused.

Rumors abounded that the refinery-lined ship channel might be the site of a second terrorist attack, and many of our parents, with panic in their eyes, rushed to get their children to take them home, somehow feeling safer when the family was intact. They drove miles to avoid crossing over the ship channel bridge. We all suddenly realized we were not safe anywhere anymore. The safety we had so long taken for granted had faded like a whisper in the wind.

The few students who attended my music class that afternoon, a class that I taught to show the teachers I would not ask them to do anything I was not willing to do, appeared unmoved by the tragedy, and I was shocked at their indifference. I could not believe what I was hearing.

Robert asked, "Miss, them folks in New York don't care 'bout us; so why should we care 'bout them?"

"They are all probably rich or else they wouldn't have been working in them big buildings," remarked Angela.

Marcus added, "Miss, we have our own problems in the 'hood to worry 'bout. We don't have time to worry 'bout other folks miles from here."

"Miss, New York is way over yonder from here, so why should we be bothered? It ain't none of our business. We don't need to go meddling in other people's business," offered Madison. "Besides, I don't really believe it happened."

They went on and on, confirming my suspicions that we had all failed these students in so many ways, not the least of which was in making them more humane, in making them more sensitive to others, more compassionate, more loving, and more understanding. Perhaps it was because many of the sixty-nine students who had been assigned to my class were all gang members. But regardless, was that not an area of accountability for us as educators? Or had we become so possessed by the almighty TAAS test that we had no time to provide lessons that lift the human spirit to a level that transcends the self and encourages a worldview that embraces all human beings as our brothers and sisters? I would find a way to do that, or I would leave the school district again. I was uncertain how long I would last if I did not devote all our instructional time to preparing for the TAAS. Quite frankly, my dear, I did not care.

Project Clear (our HISD curriculum) required the class syllabus of my music class to relate the history of music to the history of literature. I took that a step further and related the early literature and music to the present, to today. I worked with the students to analyze the John Donne poem "No Man Is an Island":

No man is an island, entire of itself;
Every man is a piece of the continent, a part of the main;
If a clod be washed away by the sea, Europe is the less,
As well as if a promontory were,
As well as if a manor of thy friends or of thine own were;
Any man's death diminishes me, because I am involved in mankind;
And therefore, never send to know for whom the bell tolls;
It tolls for thee.

We talked about how one person's actions impact others. We talked about gang fights and the impact they have on others. We dropped a pebble into a pool of water and discussed the impact of the resulting ripples. We had wonderfully exciting lessons on cause and effect and related it to the TAAS as best we could. In the end, we related the poem to the once popular song "No Man Is an Island" and learned to sing it.

Later, I told the students of my having visited the restaurant Windows on the World, which had been in one of the twin towers of the World Trade Center. I discussed the individuals associated with the restaurant who had lost their lives. Then I played and discussed the thought-provoking song "The Windows of the World," with lyrics by Hal David and music by Burt Bacharach, and sung by Dionne Warwick.

Captain Trege and Bertie at ROTC banquet.

During the opening exercises each morning, Captain Trege, the ROTC instructor profiled an individual who had lost his or her life in the World Trade Center tragedy, and one morning I played the "Windows of the World." Captain Trege put together a moving PowerPoint presentation concerning the tragedy and shared it with all students in an assembly complete with the presentation of colors and playing of taps. An unusual silence fell upon the crowd, and many of the students wept openly. We could only hope that this time taken away from preparing for the TAAS taught an even more important lesson in character development. Little did we know then that very soon some of our best and brightest would be fighting a war in Iraq.

As a culminating activity for the class I was teaching, I decided to use the one thousand dollars I had received from a grant I had won for integrating arts into education. We had been studying hip-hop, and I would take the class, all sixty-nine of them, to The Great Caruso, a dinner theater on the west side of Houston where they had a program on that subject. I taught the students table manners, the difference between a salad fork and a dinner fork, and so forth. As it turned out, only about half the class could attend because many worked at night. I ordered a limousine party bus, and students were served soft drinks as we made our way to the theater. One of the activities at the theater involved starting a song with a name and then adding to it to make a rhyme. One of the students yelled, "Use Bertie. That is our principal's name." The musical group started with my name and created an entire song. One of the students stated, "Where in the world is this place? Do you think they have a map? This would be a great place to bring a date, but I don't know where in the hell we are." He was given a map. We all had a glorious evening.

CHAPTER 37
They Came from
the East Bearing Hope

While we were still in the throes of 9/11 and our attempts to diminish gang activity, a ray of hope and encouragement came to us. It came in the form of outside consultants, Dr. Bena Kallick from Connecticut and Marian Leibowitz from New Jersey, who continued to work with us on a monthly basis to effect change at Furr. They had worked together for years and could offer the consistent support and guidance we so desperately needed. Bena provided staff development activities for the entire staff. We welcomed her with "Bena, You're Our Angel," a rendition that would have made Shaggy weep. A friend rapped the personalized lyrics, and I was thrilled that teachers were willing to provide backup. Bena took it good-naturedly, and it appeared we were beginning to come together as a school community.

Although Bena had worked with the staff before, they now showed a greater readiness to assess where we were as a community of learners at Furr and to identify steps needed to reform the school and improve teaching and learning. Bena had clearly been profoundly touched by the happenings on 9/11, and its emotional impact was clear in her every action. The incident was all too close for her—her children and grandchildren lived in New York City, and she and her husband, Charles, lived in nearby Newport, Connecticut. She wept as she talked with us about the impact that unforgettable day had on her family and friends. Yet the resolve in her steel-gray eyes coupled with her silver hair commanded an uncommon respect and a call to action. She carried her tall, thin, statuesque body in a more upright and determined manner that added seriousness and insistence to her presence.

As she worked with groups of teachers in each small learning community, Bena had the teachers set individual and group goals. She discussed Habits of Mind and helped begin to build the disposition for higher-level thinking. She instructed us on the concept of planning from assessment to instruction by using a thought process that would prepare teachers for using curriculum mapping. Her examples of project-based learning, which ranged from small to elaborate, made the approach easy to understand. She addressed the essential questions of how to plan for student success and how project-based learning connected with what the teachers were attempting to accomplish. It was fascinating to watch her at work and to see how she used questions with underlying positive presuppositions to shift our thinking. When she left to return home, we embraced her ideas and claimed them as our own, believing that we had thought of them. Her way of conveying the information had maintained each teacher's sense of personal worth and had encouraged each to move forward with implementation. Bena Kallick should have been awarded The World's Best Questioner and Listener Award! We were the phoenix rising from the ashes.

I struggled with giving follow-up support and made empty promises to do better next time. The secret of how that could be done effectively was not revealed to me until two years later when Sheila Whitford became a literacy coach at Furr. Her drive, tireless work ethic, attention to detail, and need for immediate closure were the mechanisms for efficient and effective staff development follow-through. It also helped that she was not an administrator. This was a lesson for all those who believe in career paths for teachers. I learned the hard way that elevating the right teacher to a higher level is far more effectual and cost-effective than adding administrators.

By this time, we had replaced the many teachers who did not believe in our students with those who did. I was determined to have an effective teacher in each classroom and often told the applicants when I interviewed them that they should take the risks and I would take the blame. Sheila provided the missing link between teacher training and teacher evaluation. Teachers could implement new strategies and ideas in a risk-free environment and get objective feedback for improvement without fear of the information being used to negatively impact their annual summative evaluation. She coached teachers, planned lessons with them, and team-taught with them. She opened discussions around teaching strategies and student work and provided a safety net for the teacher. Even though Carol did not conduct summative evaluations of teachers, the fact that she was an administrative staff member clung to her in the minds of the teachers as tightly as a spore clings to the back of a fern leaf.

It was helpful when Marian Leibowitz, mother of Jon Stewart (then the host of Comedy Central's *The Daily Show*), came to Furr to provide teacher training. She and Bena planned together to ensure seamless training delivery from consultant to consultant. I had never met Marian, but she came so highly recommended by Bena that I had no reservations about her ability to assist us in our endeavors. As I awaited her arrival at the airport, I was charged with excitement and high expectations. All Bena had told me about her physical appearance was "she looks a lot like you," that is, silver haired and with a short stature. As I observed the passengers deplane, a dancing silver aurora borealis created a luminous stream of gray light as one silver-haired passenger after the other exited the plane and moved slowly toward the baggage area. How would I ever recognize Marian when silver hair was the hair color of choice on this flight? And then I saw her! I knew it without a doubt. I ran to introduce myself and help. As we chatted, I caught a glimpse of mischief crouching behind her tiny, hexagon-shaped, wire-rimmed eyeglasses.

As we drove to the hotel, Marian told me of her plans for the teachers. I liked her right off, although it was clear her approach was quite different from Bena's. She was much more verbal than Bena and did not mince words. Marian Leibowitz told it like it was! As it turned out, her direct approach worked well with many of the teachers, especially those who wanted to be told what to do. Marian had once been a special education teacher and a public school administrator. The special education teachers particularly liked her and felt they had found a true friend who could make them a critical part of the Furr community. Marian continued the work begun by Bena and obtained commitments from each small school and department regarding what each would do in preparation for Bena's next visit. Slowly, instruction was improving.

As these two consultants worked with Furr each month, teachers began to focus more and more on student needs and less and less on their own desires. A survey was conducted in early May, nine months after Bena and Marian began their visits, to determine the effectiveness of their work. Most of the responses indicated teachers considered their presence helpful and productive. Not surprisingly, there were teachers who complained just for the sake of complaining.

When Marian came to provide training in cooperative learning, we met at the Houston City Club. Most of the teachers expressed their appreciation that I was treating them as true professionals by providing training in what they called a "classy" venue. As expected, some of the "intellectuals" called in sick and did not attend. This became a common practice and one that would continue for some time until they all left the school for other jobs.

One off-campus staff development day was spent at the water wall, which was in a picturesque, peaceful park in the midst of the famous, upscale Galleria shopping center. One teacher planned not to attend because she was afraid she might be bitten by a mosquito and get West Nile virus. Another complained that the traffic was so bad that he would not be able to negotiate it. They called the Houston Federation of Teachers to see if I had violated any rule by planning the professional development at this location. But they all showed up for the event as did several invited students.

It was a sweater morning and the slight wind sprayed us with tiny droplets from the water wall. I explained to the group it was simply our baptism into a new beginning. We seemed to have so many new beginnings. The sun broke through around mid-morning and all felt toasty warm. Everyone appeared to be enjoying the experience. The place had grown on the teachers by this time, and they were hard at work on the learning activities. Bena worked with us on capturing the best within each of us and naming it so we could not only share with each other, but also with the students. Most of us had not even taken a sideways glance into our inner self for years, and it was a new and exciting experience, albeit a bit scary.

I had prepared box lunches for each participant and delivered them in my now-famous decorated shoe boxes, depicting what I thought of each of them. I had also hired a student violinist from Bellaire High School to serenade them during lunch. I was surprised as I watched each teacher comparing the boxes and making remarks such as, "I didn't know she thought this about me! Can you imagine the time it took her to do this?" The ultimate was when I overheard the basketball coach, Coach Glenn, say, "I'm going to put this in my office to remind me when I get down that someone thinks I'm great!"

I was truly amazed when at the end of the day some teachers had created wonderful pictures of the water wall and surrounding area, while others had written extraordinary poems and compositions describing their surroundings. One such picture presented a line of bare trees with naked arms reaching for the sky. The sturdy, unoccupied park bench underneath them added a restful mood to the desolate rendering. Below the picture was written:

> Like trees that we planted, we grow cover and shade
> for a season;
>
> So often our students pause under our branches for
> nourishment.
>
> What will we feed them?

An eventful day at Houston's water wall.

Despite the fact the teachers said all the right things during the discussion that day, only a small number of them had that degree of student engagement in their classrooms in the following weeks. I was baffled as to why and asked several of them to help me understand. What they told me was something I already knew but too often forgot. When one has done something one way for so long, it is difficult to change. They were using the same lesson plans they had used for years, and to write new plans not only necessitated looking at teaching and learning in a different way, but it also was a lot of hard work. We still had much work to do.

One of the complaints of the "intellectuals" was that professional development should be based on teachers' individual needs. I agreed with them in general, and those opportunities were made available. However, I was also aware we would never establish a sense of community if we never had common learning experiences.

The year ended, and there was still an absence of rigorous teaching and learning. It was then that Sharon Koonce made me aware of an opportunity to unite the staff while working across the feeder pattern. We were in for a life-changing experience.

CHAPTER 38
Looking for the Summit

W hat? Surely you jest! Why can't we go to Estes Park in Colorado for seven days to develop a plan for Furr and our feeder-pattern schools? Texaco had generously provided a grant to the HISD professional development department for leadership development that was intensive, innovative, and more than a one-shot experience. Texaco had viewed the School of Innovation trip led by Rolf Smith of the Office of Strategic Innovation as one that met their criteria for the grant. Rolf had developed this program after he retired as a colonel from the United States Air Force. The program was designed to encourage individuals in business and industry to innovate and think differently and creatively. This trip would include working in teams as we climbed Colorado mountains and created a vision for Furr. Furr faculty and teachers within our feeder pattern were electric with excitement that a seven-day mountain-climbing expedition would build teamwork and be an experience of a lifetime.

A New Beginning.

Then the news came to us that the feeder-pattern schools were required to drop out. The administration did not think it was a good idea. I was shocked and more than disappointed. I began making calls to find out what was going on that would kill such a once-in-a-lifetime opportunity. I was told by my district superintendent it was not something we should be involved in and none of us were to go. I stressed it was being done in the summer when we were all on vacation. Still, I was met with resistance. Since we had already made the arrangements and met with Rolf Smith and several others from the Office of Strategic Innovation that would conduct the training, we had passed the point of no return, so I continued to plan for Furr staff and one teacher from a feeder school to participate in the program on our personal vacation time in June. We continued to work with Roth Smith to identify our strategic exploration and discovery areas:

- School system reform and transformation
- Academically stimulating environments
- Innovative teaching techniques, concepts, and strategies
- Thinking styles
- Teaching styles
- Learning styles
- Curriculum mapping in the Furr feeder pattern
- Different training for teachers in the feeder pattern
- Interdependency

Identifying Our "Mess."

As we worked with Rolf in afternoon planning meetings, we learned about positive energy and how important it is in reaching a personal goal or working with a team. He led us to realize that when we release positive energy toward someone, it comes back to us. The same is true when we release negative energy. We practiced reducing the negative and "growing" the positive, and we continued to identify our "mess," as Rolf Smith called the work we would be doing on the mountaintop in Colorado.

We all took the Kirton Adaption-Innovation Inventory (KAI) and the Myers-Briggs Type Indicator (MBTI). The KAI helps to clarify the differing perceptions that people have on change. It identifies individual scores on a continuum from highly adaptive to highly innovative. Those individuals who are more in the adaptive range tend to solve problems within the organization, while those who score on the innovative range are those who tend to solve problems by challenging the norms of the organization. As Rolf gave us feedback on the KAI, we learned that an effective and efficient organization requires individuals from all points along the continuum. As an example, when I became aware that I scored off the chart on the highly innovative range, I realized how desperately I needed the other members of the team who scored highly adaptive to make our plan functional at the highest level.

The MBTI complements the KAI. It provides insights into people's attitudes and the way they function. It is based on Jung's theory of human personality and is based on certain patterns of behavior. We looked forward to getting in-depth feedback on our MBTI scores during the School for Innovators in Estes Park.

Every member of Furr's teaching community spent extensive time in self-reflecting and learning to understand and appreciate the strengths of others, which the KAI and MBTI had helped us identify. To be sure, only one of the "intellectuals" elected to go on the "expedition," and as a result, the others laughed and poked fun at those who participated. None of their remarks mattered to the enthusiastic team of thirty who had made the commitment to participate in the pre-planning sessions and to the extended adventure in Estes Park. At least we had a critical mass.

As we continued to work on the "mess," we identified one goal after another that would define our expedition. The goals included a comprehensive plan to reform Furr based around curriculum mapping, which would result in a positive change in the school culture. We also came to realize that we would need a plan to keep the momentum going once we returned to the everyday challenges of Furr High School. We anticipated this would involve establishing a base camp, identifying roles people would play, and defining methods of communication. Ultimately, the last goal or summit was for the

Furr staff to become a team to improve instruction and thus student achievement by creating, implementing, and supporting the use of curriculum mapping to align learning standards and teaching.

Finally, at the last meeting before we embarked for Estes Park, participants were given the opportunity to generate questions about our experience on the expedition. They included the following:

- What will be the outcome, and how will we measure our success?
- Will I survive?
- What is the daily routine?
- How many miles a day will we hike?
- Are the bathrooms inside?
- Are there dangerous animals in the region?
- What should I bring and what should I wear?

The list got longer and longer until everyone had an opportunity to ask questions, express concerns, and define the results to bring back to the school. Then we were ready to depart on the expedition that truly would transform Furr High School. We were all confident that after the School for Innovators, Furr High School would never be the same again.

On the day of our departure, we met at the airport at 5 a.m. where all participants were given expedition vests and thinking caps. We had a brief meeting to set the stage for the experience. When we landed in Denver, we received passports that gave us permission to participate and that we were to use as a journal throughout the expedition. We were expected to share ideas on the bus ride from the airport to the lodge in Estes Park and to enter them in our journals. We were required to write a given number of entries in the journal, with each signed by another participant. The purpose was not only to generate new ideas but also to provide an opportunity to get to know each other better as we discussed our own personal summit. When we arrived at our destination, eager to get started, we were surprised that the Elk Horn Lodge and Guest Ranch where we would spend the next seven days was only a step up from a bunk house! There was no television, no clocks, no telephone, and no Starbucks! At that point we were all required to give up our watches and cell phones. This caused great consternation for the Js (judging) folks. The Fs (feeling) and Ss (sensing) found it amusing, and they began to tease the Js. Teachers had embraced the MBTI so much that it was even the source of our jokes.

We quickly settled into our pristine rooms and rushed to our first meeting. The rules we were to live by were laid out in no uncertain terms. We were told we would work long hours, there would be no trips into town for Starbucks coffee, all meals would be eaten on site, we would never know what time it was, and we would work until the work was done. Participants asked, "How will we know when to wake up in the morning?" The answer was that someone would come to our rooms and wake us.

The first day, we were put into groups based on our scores on the KAI and MBTI inventories. The leaders of the expedition led us up treacherous paths into the woods, and we did not return to boot camp until dark. They made sure we drank bottles of water to prevent headaches and to help us acclimate to the new environment and to the altitude. The intent also was to take us out of our comfort zone—not that we were not already out of our comfort zone!

Bertie at 68 years old.

Once we returned to the lodge, exhausted and hungry, we ate and jumped right into the work of identifying our summit and continued to work late into the night. The intensive work continued throughout our seven days there. We always worked very late, even though we never knew exactly what time it was except by our exhausted brains and bodies.

On one of the most exciting days, we had the rare opportunity of visiting Eagle Rock, a school in the mountains designed for students who did not fit into the regular school program. This was a most enlightening trip where we were able, not only, to meet with the founders of the school, but also to visit classrooms where we spoke with the students and teachers. We attended a "gathering," which was how they began each day. This meeting included students and teachers and was led by either a student or a teacher on any given day. The day we attended, the "gathering" was led by a student who was extraordinarily talented in composing music and playing the guitar. He talked with the group about where he found his inspiration for the lyrics and how he then put those lyrics to music. He played and sang the song he had written and then opened the session for questions. This event, high in the mountains on a cold day, as we sat in front of an open fire, moved all of us so deeply that we began having "gatherings" once a week at Furr when we returned. Many of them were led by our very own talented students and parents.

By the time we returned to Furr, we had clearly identified our Furr summit and steps to be taken to reach that summit. With our plans in hand and a renewed spirit of determination to succeed, we anxiously awaited the opening of the 2001–2002 school year to continue our quest for a common summit for all teachers and staff at the school. My heart was filled with hope and joy, not only because I, at sixty-eight years of age, had climbed a mountain and successfully reached the peak in rock climbing, but also because I had a strong core of teachers who were eager to work together to make Furr High School a school that could make us all proud! We learned that it was not necessary to be an extraordinary individual to accomplish great things. One only needs to be highly motivated. Even an ordinary person can accomplish great things. That was what we planned to do.

Summit reached!

CHAPTER 39
A Few Ordinary, Motivated Individuals

Eager to begin our Furr summit work, the expedition participants scheduled meetings over the summer with teachers and community members to report on the work that we had done and to involve them in decisions concerning implementation of the plan we had developed at Estes Park. I was pleasantly surprised to find how quickly they bought into the plan and made major contributions. The leadership team at Furr had been studying the work of Thomas Sergiovanni, who suggests that a covenant be established between the school and community. He believed that in a school, the social structure bonds people together in oneness. In order to make this idea work, according to Sergiovanni, the community must accept two principles. One is the principle of justice, which means that every member of the school community must be treated with equality, dignity, and fair play. The other is the principle of beneficence, which means that every member is viewed as an interdependent member of the school and the community. Everything done in the school must work for the good of the community.

It was immediately determined that the group needed to establish a covenant with the community. They began working tirelessly on defining exactly what our beliefs in the Furr community are and how they should be stated in the covenant. While not every teacher was convinced and some ridiculed those who strongly believed we could make it happen, the working group members were determined to see it through. We were on a roll now, and many of the teachers, staff members, students, and community members approached the task with enthusiasm and determination. Once the covenant was written, it was shared with all community members including ministers of local churches, district administrators, parents, teachers, students, staff, and area politicians. A covenant signing was held at a special meeting convened solely for that purpose. Several copies were printed at an enlarged size to enable all who were interested to sign it. Our district superintendent, Thelma Garza, attended the meeting and signed the document to indicate a commitment to follow the principles and terms of the covenant. The evening was a memorable one, although some of the teachers refused to sign.

This act of not signing the covenant separated those who refused to sign from most of the parents, students, teachers, administrators, and staff. The covenant clearly sent a message about the direction the school would be taking, with or without them. Those opposed to our reform efforts continued to ridicule those who signed the document. The believers, though, began to practice the terms of the covenant. The remarks of the nonbelievers were now falling on deaf ears. Some of the teachers who supported the covenant told the others outright to get lost. It was amusing to watch them squirm when their fellow teachers refused to be intimidated by their childish and unprofessional remarks. Eventually the nonbelievers were all gone, either by their choice or by my choice.

Now that we had a covenant to guide how we would operate, we had to build capacity within the school community. "Coffee with the Principal" was held twice a month to keep parents informed about what was happening at the district and school levels and to get their input on school issues. In addition, we started classes, held during the day and in the evening, where parents could learn computer skills, English for non-English speakers, and Spanish for English speakers. We adopted as the Furr High School mantra the Margaret Mead quote about how a small group of committed citizens could change the world.

PART III

CHAPTER 40
The Rumble

The unbelievable was happening! Despite all the hard work by so many individuals over the preceding two years, we clearly had not adequately dealt with the gang problem on campus. We had a dress code that did not include colors of any of the thirteen gangs on the campus at Furr, and we were listening to them more often. That did not prevent a school riot that erupted in the fall of 2002 when street gangs from outside the campus came on campus to attack several of the Furr gangsters. When I arrived from an off-campus meeting and parked my car in front of the school, I witnessed a riot in the true sense of the word. Metal garbage cans were sailing through the air and hitting students on the head. Students were fighting each other and outsiders that I did not recognize. Adults on campus were attempting to control the madness, but the courtyard resembled a war zone filled with screaming, fighting individuals throwing gang signs and beating each other to a pulp in a sea of trash. Extra security had been called, and police officers were assisting in gaining and maintaining order, as ambulances were carrying injured individuals away. I was aghast!

When the melee ended and the outsiders had escaped, I learned that the assistant principals had decided to send thirty-two of our students, gang members all, to an alternative school. This was the action always taken in such cases but was never effective. I decided to take a risk and insisted upon a different approach. I spoke to the assistant principals and asked them to let me work with these students. I wanted to determine if we might take actions that would result in an end to the violence on campus and perhaps change the behavior of the gang members permanently, at least at school. They explained to me that the district's established guidelines required that the students be removed from the campus and placed in an alternative setting. I explained to them that I understood the policy. The question was whether such action changed student behavior. We all agreed that it did not. Still, they would not commit to breaking the rules. I promised I would assume responsibility for any consequences and that they would not be held accountable. They then reluctantly agreed to hold off on sending the students away.

Even though the school had been complying with district rules and had, for years, been removing students who engaged in gang violence, it was still impossible to hold assemblies or student activities on campus during or after school without fear of gang fights. At this point, having allowed the school culture to be dictated by a fear of gang activity for years, we clearly saw that some other action had to be taken to create a safe and student-centered environment.

I did not know exactly what I was going to do or whether whatever strategy I decided on would work. I knew all the culprits by name and the personal history of each one. Most had been in my history of music class. I had a feeling that I could reach them and change their behavior if I had the chance. It seemed worth a try. The worst that could happen to me was that they would send me back to my house, or as my daughter always suggested, to "the home."

I decided to call all the identified students in and have a discussion with them. I told them the action that we had decided to take in response to their involvement in the riot. They were obviously surprised and thanked me for not sending them to an alternative school. That response opened the door for me to inform them that they had to take responsibility for their clearly inappropriate actions and that before the meeting could end, each would be required to sign a behavior contract. I knew them all to be individuals of their word, and I believed that they would adhere to the contract. Although they were reluctant to answer me for a while, I probed them with questions. Finally, they began to talk, and their remarks were remarkably revealing about their beliefs and lifestyles. When I asked if they felt empathy for others, they said they did not know the meaning of the word. I realized how important it was that we effectively implement the Habits of Mind that Bena Kallick was working to make a part of our school culture.

The students informed me that they trusted no one outside

their families and other gang members. They said, "We really don't trust public officials because they don't give a damn about us. The government is against us because we're minority and poor. They think we're dumb." I was shocked and amazed when they explained that they believed 9/11 never happened and the government was using a movie with an ulterior motive to attempt to fool them.

After much discussion and honest discourse, I informed them that I knew for a fact that 9/11 did happen and how our entire nation was changed as a result of the disaster. While I admitted that I had deep concerns about the state of some political decisions, I emphasized that they were very mistaken about the events of 9/11. When I asked what actions could be taken to bring peace into their lives and peace to the Furr campus, they fell quiet and into deep thought. Eventually they all agreed that if they could see Ground Zero with their own eyes, then they would have more faith in others and especially in the government. Without hesitation, I agreed to take all thirty-two of them to New York City if there were no more gang fights at Furr during the 2002–2003 school year. This discussion happened in August, and I agreed to take the trip the following June. We drew up a contract, and the thirty-two of them signed it.

Once we had signed the contract, I had no doubt that I would be able to obtain the funds for the trip. After all, didn't everyone want to contribute to a trip to New York City for a group of gang members? Right? Wrong! When I approached the individuals in the HISD Office of Strategic Management about the possibility of obtaining corporate donations to take thirty-two gang members to see Ground Zero, they were appalled. One replied in hushed tones, "I would keep that agreement you have with the students very quiet because people will think you are crazy!"

Since I clearly would get no support from the school district, I approached corporations on my own. None were willing to help. We tried fund raising, but in a community where no one has money, there was no chance of raising the funds in that manner.

It was now April, there had been no gang fights on campus, and I had no funds to take the trip. Did I need to encourage the gangs to have a baby fight so I could save face? Suddenly, money began pouring in from all over and from as far away at Hawaii. Bena,

Marian, and Art Costa believed in what I was trying to do, and not only did they contribute but their families, friends, and celebrities contributed. Before I knew it, we had the funds and were eagerly making plans for the trip. It helped that Marian Leibowitz's son was Jon Stewart of Comedy Central.

Paula, who was a counselor, and I had been meeting with the gangsters all year on a monthly basis to prepare them for the excursions we would take in New York. We had worked hard with them to prepare them for the trip to the United Nations. All the work paid off when we made the visit.

The gang members were terrified when they learned that we would be flying to New York City. They had never flown in an airplane and were certain the plane would crash.

"Couldn't you please drive us, Miss," they begged. "Please, Miss!"

I was amused when I realized that despite their rough exterior and all the tattoos, they were still young children inside. I also realized the courage it took to admit they were afraid. It made me love them more. Not only had they kept their word, they had also shown their insecurities.

"I am an old woman," I told them. "I am not about to drive a group of thugs to New York!"

The "gangsters" laughed heartily and continued to beg. I stuck with my original reply.

The teachers really pounced on the fact that I was rewarding inappropriate student behavior. "She must be as crazy as we thought she was," they were reported to say. "I can't wait to see when they have a gang fight in New York City. It's going to be all over the news."

I did not let any of their snide comments deter me as we excitedly made our plans. Only one teacher agreed to help chaperone on the trip, so Sharon Koonce, my daughter, and my grandchildren, Brooke and Austin, accompanied us. Nothing was going to stop us.

We decided to also take all members of the National Honor Society so that we rewarded them as well. There were only nine members. Can you imagine what it would be like to have thirty-two gangsters and nine National Honor Society members on the same trip to New York? Actually, it was wonderful!

On the day of the trip, a bus was to leave the school at 5:00 a.m. to take us to the airport. I worried that none of the gang members would be there, either because they couldn't get up that early or because they had decided not to go. I arrived and found them all seated on the bus, just waiting for me. They were more dependable than I had anticipated.

Once they boarded the plane, several of the gang members begged me to change seats with someone so I could sit next to them. Because they were afraid to fly, a few weeks before the trip, I arranged with Continental Airlines for a field trip to the airport where they all had an opportunity to explore the inside of a plane so they would know what it would be like. This trip had clearly relieved them only to a degree. I told them if one "thug" goes down, all thugs would go down. Fortunately, all our seats were in proximity, and I could talk with them as they sat quivering with fear while the plane ascended into the heavens. I do not believe they relaxed until the plane landed.

Once we were settled into our hotel rooms, we boarded a tour bus that took us to Chinatown. While walking down the street in Chinatown, I turned around and saw our boys taking off their shirts. I knew this is what they did when they were about to fight. Fortunately, they looked up and saw me looking, put their shirts back on, and rushed up to me. One of them said to me, "No disrespect, Miss, but could you get us the f--- out of here before we have a gang fight in New York City?" A street gang in New York had recognized them as gangsters and accused one of our boys of making a pass at one of their girls, and they were threatening a fight. We got on the bus quickly and headed to our next destination.

While in the city, we visited the Empire State Building, the Statue of Liberty, Central Park, and the United Nations. After our visit to the United Nations, one of the docents remarked that this was the most informed group of students that had ever visited there.

One of the experiences the students enjoyed most in New York City was when we took in a Broadway musical, *42nd Street*. Before we went to the performance, the students asked if there would be mariachi music or hip-hop. When I told them there would be neither, they were unsure they wanted to attend. But once they were in the theater and the musical began, they were spellbound and begged me to take them back the next night.

Then there was the day when we finally visited Ground Zero. Afterwards, I entered St. Paul's Chapel, which miraculously suffered no damage when the World Trade Center collapsed across the street. I saw all our gang members on their knees at the altar of the church. Later they came to the back of the church, and one remarked to me, "Miss, I bet you didn't know we prayed, did you?"

"Sure, I knew you prayed," I said. "I'm sure you were praying for the people who lost their families and friends in the Twin Towers on 9/11."

"No, Miss," he replied. "We were praying that our plane won't crash on the way back to Houston."

The four days that we spent in New York City with Furr students was a life-changing experience for them and enlightening to all of us. We had no trouble with any of the students, and when we returned to Houston and held our debriefing session, one of the National Honor Society students, who was also a magnet student, remarked, "One important thing I learned is that gang members and magnet students are really no different. It's just that we have had different experiences. Now, I consider some of the gang members my friends."

As long as these gang members were students at Furr High School, there were no gang fights on campus. Most of them graduated, and I still hear from some of them even today. One sent me a picture of him in uniform and informed me he was on his way to Iraq. Even after these students graduated, it became rare to have a student fight on campus. A district supervisor of our campus police officers kept insisting that the officers must not be reporting all the disruptive behavior at Furr because he remembered the history of our campus from years ago. I give Furr's officers, Officers Danny Avalos and Craig Davis, credit for having relationships with the students that built trust and mutual respect.

I am still uncertain about why the behavior of these students and other gang members on campus was changed in a positive way. Perhaps respect, relationships, and trust between and among individuals have a greater impact on student behavior than threats and punitive measures. There are no threats that we could make toward our students that would be worse than the violence they experienced every day in their neighborhoods. Our students did, however, respond to respect, kindness, and love expressed toward them by the adults on our campus. The staff of Furr continued this practice of dealing with students in a positive way and providing numerous opportunities for them to experience the world outside their neighborhoods and the city of Houston.

This culture of caring was the result of our covenant and our study of the Habits of Mind, and they became a way of life on the campus and in the school community. Is it possible there is a message here to be learned about the need to teach the "whole child" rather than using a power test to determine who graduates and who doesn't?

Furr students at Ground Zero memorial fence.

Bertie and a student at
Ground Zero.

Bertie, teacher Charles Meisgeier,
and students at Ground Zero.

The memorial fence.

Making contact.

Charles instructing the group.

The whole Furr gang and Austin
in New York City.

CHAPTER 41
Stitching the Pieces Together

One of the most exciting field trips our students took was the one to the Quilts of Gee's Bend Exhibit at the Houston Museum of Fine Arts in September 2002. We had learned that getting them out of their neighborhoods tended to open their eyes to view life in a different way. I chaperoned a group of our students to view the exhibit. Their eyes and mine were opened in a way that helped us to artistically patch together the historical story of Gee's Bend. The exhibit told the story of a tiny black community in a remote area of Alabama surrounded on three sides by the Alabama River. The quilts were true works of art that had been a cultural tradition, born of necessity, for generations to provide warmth for the families.

A traditional design by Leola Pettway.

The women who were at the exhibit from Gee's Bend were friendly country folks who loved to tell the stories of their struggles as poor, hard-working people who worked in the cotton fields and were descendants of slaves. They worked on the Pettway Plantation and took the name of the plantation owner. Therefore, most of them were named Pettway.

I was so moved by their stories that I wanted to take my grandchildren to Gee's Bend so they could have a profound cultural experience. Leola Pettway gave me her phone number and told me to call at any time. She invited my family and me to visit with her.

I spoke to my daughter, Paula, and Sharon Koonce about how extraordinary the exhibit was and how we all fell in love with the Gee's Bend women. I told them I would call Ms. Pettway and see if we might visit with her over spring break of 2003. They were on board and were excited when Ms. Pettway said she would love to have us. She said, "Now it is really hard to find Gee's Bend. You have to take highway 41 out of Selma. After you go a little while down the road, you'll see a big pole. You turn there on the road to Gee's Bend. Do you know where that big pole is?" she asked.

"No, I don't know where the big pole is because I have never been there," I replied. "But we will find it because we are eager to visit with you in Gee's Bend."

So, in the spring of 2003, we boarded the plane bound for Birmingham, Alabama. The group included Paula, Brooke, Austin, Sharon, Anh Truong, Brooke's friend, and me. We could hardly wait to get to Gee's Bend.

We rented a car in Birmingham and drove the ninety miles to Selma. The following day we eagerly drove down highway 41 in search of "the pole." We had difficulty locating the pole, so we stopped to get directions. When we reached Gee's Bend, we stopped several times in search of Ms. Pettway's house. It appeared that every resident in the tiny settlement in the bend of the Alabama River was named Pettway, and we kept being sent to the wrong house. We did finally arrive at the home of Leola. We had passed dozens of houses where clotheslines displayed the quilts made through the years. We experienced our own art exhibit of recycled clothes, feed sacks, and fabric remnants sewn together into geometric improvisational designs that broadcast the artistic ability of the women of Gee's Bend.

Leola Pettway was standing on the porch of her tiny, blue wood-framed house. She hugged each of us as we made introductions and, then she asked us into the front room of her house. The aroma of fried chicken and collard greens awakened our olfactory senses in a way that only home cooking could do. She had prepared a mouth-watering lunch for us complete with peach cobbler.

After lunch, some local women joined us as Leola excitedly announced to us that she and the women were about to be on television. We were all thrilled at the possibility of seeing them on television when they made their trip to New York City. She turned the television on, and nothing happened. "I know how to get this thing to work," Leola said. She walked over to the TV, kicked it hard twice, and suddenly there the women were on national television. Their quilts were on exhibit at the Whitney Museum, and they were being interviewed. We all sat spellbound as these black women from the tiny Gee's Bend settlement talked about their lives and how they never thought they would ever be on TV.

Leola Pettway's starburst quilt.

After the program was over, they talked about their trip to Houston, the location of their first exhibition. They said they got to stay in a hotel. They were shocked when someone came in and made up their beds, cleaned the rooms and left little candies on the pillows at night. Leola said, "I never knew them quilts was that important. I started making quilts when I was eleven and we didn't have nothing to make them from. I just used feed sacks and old worn out clothes. Sometimes I found old clothes on the road and used that. I started out just cutting out blocks. After I pieced it, my auntie Deborah Young teached me to quilt it. We were all poor 'round here. I used to go to school when I was sixteen. That's when I started. The school was down the hill a piece and up there in the woods. I just went a day or two a week. I had to plant and pick cotton, and when they put the cotton on the porch, we rolled around in it 'cause we ain't got nothing to do. We couldn't go nowhere. We just worked. I learned good and taught my children. We had nothing." Leola told us she had eleven kids, but one died. She said she was doing pretty well for her age.

Suddenly the women began singing gospel hymns acapella. Brooke had been videoing, but she stopped when they began singing. She said she was afraid she was invading their privacy. They appeared to have received the Holy Ghost and began shouting. When it ended, we had witnessed a spiritual awakening.

Sharon and I each purchased a Leola quilt. Leola had hand-quilted both, so she signed and dated each. We paid $125 for each of the quilts. We both treasure our purchases. We left Gee's Bend with a heart full of love for the wonderfully talented women there and their works of art.

We drove back to Selma where we spent the night. We were filled with warmth from our trip to Gee's Bend and were anticipating lessons to be learned the next day as we walked across the Edmund Pettus Bridge and visited the Rosa Parks Museum. I had tutored my grandchildren, so they were fully aware that we were in the midst of significant events in the history of civil rights. I had taught them about the three protest marches over the bridge in support of voting rights.

Civil Rights Memorial in Selma, Alabama.

The first march was organized by James Bebel and Amelia Boynton on March 7, 1965. During this march, state troopers and county police attacked the protesters with billy clubs and tear gas after they passed over the county line, which was at the far side of the bridge. Law enforcement officials beat Amelia Boynton unconscious, and the media broadcast pictures that showed her wounded body on the Edmund Pettus Bridge. This event became known as "Bloody Sunday."

The second march occurred on March 9, 1965. Martin Luther King, Jr. was the leader of the march. The marchers confronted the state troopers and police at the county end of the bridge. When the troopers stepped back to permit the marchers to cross the county line, King had the marchers turn around and march back to the Brown Chapel AME Church where they started. He had spoken earlier on the phone with President Lyndon Johnson seeking protection for the protesters through the federal courts. He was obeying a federal injunction when he had the marchers return to the church. That night James Reeb, a Unitarian Universalist minister from Boston who had joined the second march, was beaten to death by a white group.

Martin Luther King, Jr. and James Reeb.

Reeb's murder and "Bloody Sunday" caused a national outcry and attacks on the government of Alabama and the federal government. The protesters demanded protection and a new federal voting rights law so that blacks could register and vote peacefully. President Johnson prepared a new voting rights law, even as Governor George Wallace refused to protect the marchers.

The third march started in Selma on March 21, 1965, and protesters were protected by the Alabama National Guard under federal command. Five days later, the marchers arrived safely in Montgomery at the Alabama State Capitol. Twenty-five thousand people had joined the march in support of voting rights. President Johnson signed the Voting Rights Act on August 6, 1965.

With all these fact in our minds, we left the Brown Chapel AME Church, marched over the Edmund Pettus Bridge, and crossed over the county line. I thought of Dorothy. I licked my right thumb, slapped it into the middle of my left hand, make a fist of my right hand, slapped the butt of it into my left hand and whispered, "Friends forever!"

The Edmund Pettus Bridge.

We marched back over the bridge to the church as the protesters had done on their second attempt, boarded our car and sped away to Montgomery where we planned to visit the Rosa Parks Museum on the campus of Troy University. This museum was built to honor icon, Rosa Parks, a black young woman, who refused to relinquish her seat in the "colored section" of a bus to a white passenger when the white section was filled. She was arrested for civil disobedience for violating the segregation laws in Alabama. The result was a boycott of the bus company for over a year. The lawsuit she filed, and the boycott made her an international icon of resistance to racial segregation. The United States Congress has called her the "First Lady of Civil Rights."

We entered the museum, which is located at the exact spot where Rosa was arrested, through a time capsule depicting the events of that day. When in the capsule, we studied the faces and heard the voices of the brave men and women who fought peacefully for freedom. The museum had interactive activities, exhibits and artifacts from the 1955 bus boycott. It also included original works of art and a restored 1955 station wagon that was used to transport protesters. One thing we all enjoyed immensely was being able to sit on a 1955 Montgomery public bus and actually take a virtual trip through time in the Rosa Parks Museum.

We all returned to Houston with a deeper understanding of the Civil Rights movement and a deep appreciation for all the brave men and women who devoted their lives to making the world a better place for all people, and they did it peacefully. We had learned so much.

I spent endless hours discussing the extraordinary experiences of Gee's Bend, Selma, and Montgomery with my grandchildren and the students at Furr. We all developed a richer appreciation of the struggles experienced by blacks before and during the civil rights movement. We also recommitted ourselves to the cause of social justice for all. Although it appears that it is still unclear who originated this quote, it has become epic and resonates with all who hear it: "Rosa Parks sat down, so that Martin could walk. Martin walked so that Obama could run. Obama ran so that our children can fly."

CHAPTER 42
In Search of a Dream

A common theme runs through many poems by Langston Hughes, one having to do with having and holding fast to dreams. It was clear that many of the students at Furr High School either did not have dreams or had dreams that they were forced to defer. Each day when I entered the campus, his poem "A Dream Deferred" ran through my mind like an electronic stock ticker.

This was the impression that everyone seemed to have of us. One of the local television stations came to Furr and filmed an award-winning documentary titled *Dropping Out of Options*. They chose Furr because of our reputation as a "dropout factory." I was disturbed when I heard many of our students say that their dream, if they had one, was to live at least to the end of the year because of the violence in the neighborhoods. Few of them had dreams of graduating from high school, and even fewer dreamed of attending college. Hearing the students' sobering dreams, I was reminded about another Langston Hughes poem and its description of individuals who had no dreams or hope. Furr was a campus filled with broken-winged birds that could not fly.

One student whose wings were broken was Tristan Terry. His mother, father, and two brothers were incarcerated, so he lived with his grandmother, who was dying of cancer. He came to talk with me often and wrote beautiful poetry, which I displayed in the hallways. I observed him smiling shyly when he saw other students reading his work. One morning around two thirty, the police called me to report that the alarm had gone off at Furr and that when they arrived, they had found Tristan asleep in a hallway. When I asked him the following day why he broke into the school, he replied, "Miss, this is the only place I feel safe. I have been in jail, Miss, and I have come back to the same 'hood filled with drug houses and the same old people. I am afraid in the 'hood, Miss."

Two months later, I saw in the *Houston Chronicle* that Tristan and three others had been present when the driver of an ice cream truck was murdered. Tristan had been arrested.

On Christmas Eve night in 2004, I was thinking about Tristan. I knew his grandmother was not able to visit him in jail, so I decided to go to see him to let him know I still cared about him. Despite my heavy coat, I was inexplicably chilled as I drove toward the jail. Snowflakes swirled in the air, transforming the city into a Thomas Kinkaid Christmas card. I had never been to the jail before, so I took Sharon Koonce with me. As I entered the building, shivers ran down my spine. I was required to go through several levels of security and was questioned repeatedly as to why I was there. When, finally, I was admitted into the visitation room and the door slammed behind me, I was overcome by a feeling of helplessness I had never known. Suddenly, an orange jumpsuit appeared, and Tristan rushed toward me. He placed his hands against the glass partition separating us, and I placed my hands against his on my side of the glass. He told me he was shocked that I had come to see him and especially at this time. I told him I could not let Christmas Eve pass without seeing him and described the snow scene outside. We talked about how it had never snowed on Christmas Eve in Houston. I suggested he write a poem about the occasion, and he told me he had neither paper nor pencil. I informed him I would leave money to purchase the writing material so he could continue to write. He assured me he thought the plan of his friends was to just rob the man, and he did not know the other kid was going to kill the driver. He said it made him sick at his stomach and that he had vomited in the ditch. He was beaming as he told me not to worry about him because he had a white attorney, and he was sure he would win his case because he was innocent. Tristan is black. I was later told he had been sentenced to forty years in prison for aggravated robbery. I still believe within my heart that, somehow, I could have helped Tristan to make the most of his talents and to see light at the end of what appeared to be his predetermined tunnel of darkness. I was determined to find a way to stop the violence at Furr High School and to replace that violence with hope, even if I had to do it one student at a time. I often asked myself if my caring was being soft on discipline as I had been accused. Perhaps time would answer the question. I wondered...

It was clear that I had to replace all teachers who did not believe in our students. Many teachers chose to leave on their own, and I assisted others in finding positions in schools more in keeping with their philosophy. In looking to replace the teachers who had left, we knew that not only did we need teachers who were well-versed in their subject matter and had effective teaching strategies, but we must also have teachers who could heal broken-winged birds. I was reminded of Harriet Peet's *The Creative Individual*, which I had read in the early 1960s. Her description of the two types of teachers to whom we should be grateful was so meaningful to me that I had committed it to memory. Upon my arrival at Furr, I had told the teachers that there were two things I wanted us to give our students. One was an academic attitude and the other was a view of life. They said it would never happen and made fun of me for suggesting that it could.

Bertie and Ebony Jackson.

We interviewed an endless stream of candidates and selected those who could take risks and mend broken wings. As it turned out, many of these teachers were from countries outside the United States. We had an international faculty with teachers from Russia, China, the United Kingdom, Cuba, Columbia, Africa, and India.

Working with these teachers, we realized that in order to curb the dropout rate at Furr, it was necessary to think about the classroom and instruction in a different way. We also realized that if we brought back students into the same environment from which they had dropped out, we would not accomplish our goal. We decided that we needed a charter school on our campus, one that would be designed specifically to meet the needs of overage students. Angela Borzon, a Teach for America corps member and one of the teachers who participated in the expedition to Estes Park, worked with me over two weeks to write the proposal for the new charter. Angela had been promoted to the position of literacy coach, when Sheila Whitford vacated it to serve as Furr's school improvement facilitator. In designing the new school, we used many of the ideas we had gained during the visit to Eagle Rock School in Estes Park.

One of the ideas we chose to use from Eagle Rock was a project-based instruction model that would be built around students' personality types, interests, and learning styles. It would also be a school that would operate on the quarter system, enabling students to gain credits more rapidly. It would have flexible scheduling to allow students with jobs to attend school on Saturdays or in the evenings. It would also be a school where the teachers and staff understood the affective and the academic needs of the students.

In 2006-2007, the district and the state approved the new charter school for implementation, which was named REACH (Realizing Educational Achievement in the City of Houston). The school accepted students from all over the district, and in the first year, enrollment exceeded 350 students.

Once the charter was approved, the district provided a small start-up fund of $225,000 to finance teachers, materials, and the salary of a dean of students. It took a very special person to work with these students, many of whom were adults and had families of their own. This group was sometimes challenging and required patience and understanding on the part of the teachers and the dean. We searched diligently for the right people for this program.

REACH met the needs of overage students who had already dropped out of school or were potential dropouts because of failures in elementary and middle schools. Many of the students zoned to Furr had been retained several times by the time they entered the ninth grade, and some were behind their class cohort by as many as three years. Research showed their chances of graduating from high school were less than 10 percent in a regular school program. The new charter gave these students hope by providing an environment that was different and engaging. They were, however, still required to pass the state accountability test to meet graduation standards. The students were also required to sign a contract stating that they would attend class on a regular basis, would not be disruptive, and would refrain from using drugs on campus. They must be serious about their work and be willing to go the extra mile in order to accumulate the required credits for graduation. Since its inception, hundreds of dropouts or potential dropouts have graduated from REACH and many have gone on to college.

Again wanting to show that I would not ask teachers to do work that I was not personally willing to do, I taught an art class in the REACH school and made it cross-curricular so that the work we completed would enable the students to receive credit in art, speech, and English. Bena Kallick assisted me in working with the students to develop a project around the needs of the school community. The students created a map of the Furr community and then decided which area they wanted to study. We provided each student with a disposable camera and instructed each to take pictures of areas of blight or areas that had created an unsafe environment that should be addressed by the city. They used those photographs to write a description of each area and to offer suggestions for what could be done to correct the problems. Those photographs and written descriptions were displayed in the classrooms and hallways. Students wrote speeches that were delivered to the city council to effect positive changes in the neighborhoods. All students eagerly participated in the project and could hardly wait to get to the class each day. They produced stirring photographs and stories and wrote and delivered exceptional speeches. We were all proud of them, and they were thrilled with themselves.

Bertie with the tile columns at the old Furr campus.

During this year, a local artist was commissioned to work with my art class to design visual art pieces that depicted the opportunities available to students and the careers they wished to pursue after graduation. Once the artwork was completed, the artist assisted the students in transferring their designs onto ceramic tiles, which were then broken. The broken tiles were used to create a mosaic of ceramic ideas on the four brick columns at the entrance of the school. These artistic symbols proudly welcomed visitors to Furr High School until the school was demolished in 2018.

One student, Juan Juarez, who was an amazing artist decided to try his hand at sculpture. He told me that the students in REACH had one arm chopped off, but I had reached out to them and designed a program that gave them hope. His sculpture depicting this story was so full of energy, movement and hope, we had a plaque made with the image and mounted it on the building entrance of REACH. I presently have a replica of his sculpture in my living room. The last time I heard from Juan, he was in college majoring in art and planned to become an art teacher.

Another teacher worked with the REACH students on a project related to nutrition. They produced a booklet with colorful pictures of nutritious foods, the number of calories in each serving, and attractive ways the food could be presented. The booklet included suggestions to the food services department and the results of a survey the students had designed and conducted at the school concerning the school cafeteria food, the nutritional value of the food served, and how the menu could be made more nutritious. They included the cost and cost-reduction measures, and suggestions for more attractive presentations. While the food services department made no changes, the students made a personal commitment to eat more nutritional foods and to cut down on their calorie intake. That is not to say, however, that I never saw them eating junk food after the study.

One memorable event in the REACH school was the year several REACH students were invited by Bena Kallick and Art Costa to present at the national Association for Supervision and Curriculum Development (ASCD) conference in Los Angeles that focused on best practice strategies to improve student achievement. The entire school was abuzz in the weeks leading up to the trip. The student representatives wrote their speeches and practiced delivering them for days. We had the Furr speech teacher work with them, and I listened to each one until I knew their speeches by heart. One student was unable to attend the presentation because he had to work in his father's pawnshop. I suggested I could work at the shop in his place, and he replied, "Miss, I don't think you have the skills to run a pawnshop." Well said!

After they had given their presentation, I received a call from the group on a Sunday afternoon. They excitedly told me that all the educators in the audience had cried when they presented. I asked if they were crying because the presentation was so bad.

"No, Miss," they exclaimed. "It was so good! They even invited us to come to Australia and New York and Las Vegas!"

246

When I asked where they would like to go, they yelled in unison, "Las Vegas!"

When they returned to Houston, they made a presentation to the board of education and told them of all their experiences. The students said they never thought they would speak to so many important people.

I must not mislead you. REACH did create problems on the Furr campus. Some principals in other schools saw the school as a place to dump their failing students and troublemakers. Members of rival gangs began to attend, and it was some time before we realized what was happening. We learned to spend more time interviewing applicants and refusing those who were not applying for the intended purpose of the program.

Some of the most effective teachers on the Furr campus taught in REACH, and they had remarkable success with the students. They worked well beyond a regular school day and got to know the students on a personal level. They rarely missed a day of school, and men came dressed in suits and ties to present a professional image for the students. I could not have been prouder of them as I observed them working with these struggling students.

REACH sculpture by Juan Juarez.

We all took great pride in the success of every student in the school. They were there despite their failures and their almost insurmountable problems. They were there because of their perseverance and their ability to find humor despite it all. Khalil Gibran expressed it best when he said:

Keep me away from the wisdom which does not cry, the philosophy which does not laugh and the greatness that does not bow before children.

CHAPTER 43
A Dream Interrupted

Furr High School had all the right people, and we were all headed in the same direction. The violence no longer existed on campus, and parents were becoming more involved. The climate was beginning to be one of caring and concern.

The entrance to the old Furr campus.

Teachers and administrators shared a common goal. The staff was committed to not just teaching academics but also addressing the socio-emotional needs of the students. We now had teachers who worked endless hours teaching the "whole child," which enabled the students to dream what seemed to be impossible dreams and gave them the support to make certain those dreams would come true. Angela Borzon met with core teachers in regularly held department meetings, and Sheila Whitford worked with all teachers to improve instruction. Bena Kallick and Marian Liebowitz were working with the regular school teachers and the REACH teachers on a monthly basis, and the school district professional development department was also involved. Finally, we could really work on improving the instructional program. The state had moved from the TAAS test to a more rigorous one called TAKS (Texas Assessment of Knowledge and Skills) in 2002. This meant that each grade level was held accountable as was each student group, including Caucasians, Hispanics, African Americans, and the economically disadvantaged. For three years, we had been able to meet the standards, as they steadily increased each year.

Bertie dancing at Furr's High School prom.

The entire Furr community was involved in repairing broken wings and being dream makers, and we had dreams of increasing our graduation rate. While the students in the magnet school did graduate from high school and go on to college, many of the students in the regular program, even after REACH was implemented, had no hope of graduating, and the graduation rate for the entire school remained at an unacceptable level. We also dreamed of raising the levels of student achievement and of producing students who were ready to attend college and ready to meet the future with hope and a positive attitude. To that end, we decided the school needed a new vision statement and a new mission statement. It was exciting to observe the teachers working to accomplish that task. They all agreed that the statements should not be the usual empty ones, which we had used in the past, but should really convey what we wanted our school to be. After much thoughtful work, they agreed upon the following:

Mission Statement:

We teach; we learn; we all succeed.

Vision Statement:

Furr High School, where academic success is achieved and hopes and dreams are realized.

The school district opened a stand-alone international studies magnet school in 2007, which was located near enough to Furr to eventually kill our magnet program. We were eager to replace the magnet with one that would better reflect the needs and interests of students on the East End of Houston.

After much thoughtful and arduous work, we submitted a proposal and received approval for a new magnet, which we called META (Mindful Exploration of Technology in the Arts). The arts were almost entirely absent in the schools in our area. I was told it was because our students need to spend their time preparing for the state-mandated test. Bena Kallick had been instrumental in suggesting a consultant from New York who worked with HBO to train some of our teachers in film production. This became a major focus of the magnet program, and we had difficulty getting our students to go home in the evening because they were so focused on their documentaries. We were soon able to hire a film teacher, Ms. Assol Kavtorina (Ms. K.), who had graduated from the Russian State University of Cinematography with a degree in screenwriting, and the program took flight. Students became highly adept at filmmaking and won national awards for their work. We formed partnerships with local colleges so that students could obtain dual credit, and local arts groups worked as partners with META as well.

META wall in theater lobby.

251

Everyone thought we were doing exactly what we needed to do to instruct the students—we were giving them more voice and not only preparing them for success after graduation but also ensuring they passed the state accountability test's continually increasing requirements. The teachers wrote common assessments in each of the core subjects and shared the results with the students. Even though many of the teachers were new to Furr, they worked cooperatively with each other and the administration. Elective teachers integrated the objectives being taught in the core classes into their classes. Student attendance was improving, and students were showing more effort.

I regularly monitored the attendance of students in REACH, Furr H.S., and the magnet program. I found one very bright student who was absent often. Tracey Clark, who was Furr's IT support representative for HISD, tells her story about my attempt to ensure that student would graduate:

> Once, we had a magnet student. Very good student! Just would never come to school. Come to find out, the girl was married. She had like two kids, and she was pregnant. So, Dr. Simmons called and talked to the girl, trying to get her to stay in school.
>
> The girl said, "I don't have a ride. We only have one car, and my husband takes it to work."
>
> Dr. Simmons volunteered to go and pick the girl up every day over on the southwest side. So, she leaves her home in West University and goes all the way to the southwest side. Every morning mind you. Picks this child up and her kids to come over to the school, goes past Furr, down off Federal Road, and drops these kids off at the day care, and then comes back to school. And she did this for the whole school year.
>
> What I'm getting ready to tell you is about the situation I saw that was troubling. One morning, everybody is always late behind Dr. Simmons because she gets there by the crack of dawn. But she's picking up this student so she's not getting there as early as usual. On this particular morning, I beat her. I was

walking across the parking lot when I saw her drive in. Now mind you, this parking lot had holes and pits and things like that. This morning, I turned to see Dr. Simmons drive in, and mind you, at the time Dr. Simmons had a BMW sport car. She turned in, and it was odd because the car was tilted to one side. I assumed that the struts or shocks had gone out on one side of the car.

I said to myself, "I cannot believe she drove that car all the way across town like that. I am going to fuss at her, and then I'm going to call her daughter, Paula. That is just ridiculous for her to drive that car like that."

So, I waited! While I was waiting, the car dipped into a hole and came back up. I'm just standing there, getting more upset.

I thought, "Oh my God! Look at this car. I cannot believe she let that car get to the point it was that bad."

There they go again! Hit another hole. The car pulls in the spot reserved for the principal. She jumps out, and before I could say something, the pregnant student got out and the car popped up! There was nothing wrong with it. I just turned and walked in the building. I didn't say a word. They made it there safe, and there wasn't anything wrong with the car. She did not hear one word from my mouth. Uh, uh. Not one word. The girl graduated.

We regularly used student data to track the progress of each student and provided interventions when needed. Our yearly review of the data revealed that only 20 percent of the students entering the ninth grade were reading at grade level, and few had passed the TAKS test in all four core subjects. Determined, we identified students who needed tutorials, and teachers volunteered to tutor. We notified the parents that we would be offering tutorials before school, after school, and on Saturday.

We paid close attention to each student group that was required to meet the state standards and those of No Child Left Behind. We were especially attentive to the students in grade ten because that was the grade that determined whether we made the annual yearly progress required in math and reading for the No Child Left Behind rating. In 2007, we failed to meet the requirements in that grade level in math for one student group. This meant that a letter would be sent from the district to our parents, informing them they could transfer their students to another school, with transportation provided. I was mildly amused when that letter was sent to our parents in English and Vietnamese, when most of our parents could read only Spanish. Many brought the letter to the school and asked if they were being deported. We were devastated by this cruel requirement of the No Child Left Behind law. Just when we were about to get it all together, this senseless law required that we be listed as unacceptable for two years. We also suffered the insult of our students being granted permission to transfer out of our school. We would make certain this did not happen again.

It was then that I received a phone call from a parent screaming into the phone, "No fat-assed whore is going to keep my daughter after school for no reason!" I told her the student was working three grade levels below her present grade in math and had never passed a TAKS test.

She replied, "I said no fat-assed whore is going to keep my daughter after school for no reason! What part of what I said did you not understand?"

When I asked if she had ever seen me, she replied, "No, and I don't want to see no fat-assed whore!"

I replied, "I am in my seventies, and if I am still whoring, that is the best compliment you could give me." She slammed down the phone and I never heard from her again, and I never again chased her daughter to get her to attend tutorials. I didn't mind her calling me a whore, but fat-assed? Now that is when I took exception.

Later, a parent called and threatened, "Get your ass ready, 'cause I'm coming up to whoop it 'cause you keep trying to get my son to go to tutorials."

I told her I would not get out of my chair, so she could not whip me. She came to whip me. She was at least twice my size, covered in tattoos and angry. I held onto the arms of my chair and began to laugh and tease her. She finally began to laugh, and we worked things out amicably. One of the Habits of Mind we had worked so hard on is finding humor. It worked in this case, thank goodness.

Simply offering tutorials clearly did not work, and almost no one attended. I met with the teachers to design a plan to get the students the help they needed. The plan that we finally chose was laughable in retrospect. The idea was that the leadership team members would go to each eighth-period class near the end of the class period, capture the students, and walk them to tutorials. It was like herding cats. They scattered, ran as fast as they could screaming and yelling, boarded the buses, and were beyond our reach in no time. This plan was a total failure. I often wished I could have captured this effort on video for posterity.

We then decided to change the schedule, double blocking the students in reading and math and adding one tutorial class in each subject during the school day. This meant the students had fewer electives, and this was a deep concern of mine. Still, as we religiously tracked the data, we saw progress being made, and it appeared that we would have the percentage of passing students to be deemed acceptable on the state rating.

Little did we know that all our hard work at mending broken wings, using effective instructional strategies, differentiating instruction, providing in-school and after-school tutorials, and attending professional development would result in the most disappointing happening during my tenure at Furr. In the spring of 2007, we anxiously awaited, as usual, the arrival of the preliminary results of the TAKS test. Our spirits sank as these results revealed that we were unacceptable according to the state accountability rating based solely on TAKS scores. It broke my heart to announce the results to the faculty and staff. Some members wept from the disappointment and pain.

I was immediately informed that I could appeal the rating if I could show data that indicated mistakes had been made. Several of us began to dig into the data feverishly. I personally investigated every angle and counted and recounted the numbers of students in each student group and in each core subject area. I pored over the data until late at night with a heart so heavy I could hardly breathe.

I was so desperate to find some explanation for our failure that it became an obsession. All the teachers and even individuals at top levels in the district were depending on me to find some evidence of miscalculation or oversight that would cause an appeal to be accepted by the state.

Finally, I decided that I would not appeal the rating even though it would probably cost me my job. It was the only decision I could make because we had simply made several mistakes, and the major one was that we had not prepared the students as well as we thought we had. Ultimately, we were unacceptable because three students in one student group did not pass math. Those three students had been sent to a disciplinary alternative school, and we had simply forgotten about them because we had no control over their instruction. I determined then that I would not send students to an alternative school again except when the law required it. When they were not on campus, we relinquished control over their instruction to others, even though we were still held accountable for their test results. I wrote the following letter to the staff and awaited the announcement of my job status:

May 12, 2007

To the faculty and staff of Furr High School:'

Last week was one of the most devastating and heartbreaking weeks of my life. I know it was the same for many of you as well. I saw it in your slumped shoulders, bowed heads, and weary eyes. It is truly amazing what a debilitating and deadly effect the arrival of the almighty TAKS test results can have on a school community. We all experienced this to the depths of our souls after our results were perused last Monday.

As you are no doubt aware, several of us have been crunching numbers all week to better understand what could possibly have happened that gave birth to the Grinch that stole our joy after all our hard work and high expectations. We have made several discoveries that I would like to share with you, which will help to partially explain how this uninvited and unexpected rogue caused such pain and despair.

 •   We had not prepared our students as well as we thought. There are ways we can and will address that deficiency.

 •   Five special education students were tested on TAKS who were scheduled to take a special education test. Even that small number has a significant impact on overall scores and student groups. We all own this problem and must take steps to make sure this does not happen again.

 •   In drilling deeper, I questioned the impact of junior students who were promoted at midterm since seniors' tests are not a part of those for which the school is held accountable on the TEA [Texas Education Agency] rating. I discovered that no students were promoted at midterm. While Chancery played a major role in this tragic drama, so did our lack of urgency in providing assistance in credit recovery and recording the grades in a timely manner, dealing with lost credit due to excessive absences, close attention to the use of our whole credit waiver, and providing credit for athletic classes.

All this should have been done before the end of January. In the past, this was not a major problem because the Schools Administrative Student Information (SASI) program permitted us to enter the information after January. We learned last week that the same could be done in Chancery, but we had been told it could not be done. The impact of this was highly significant because if the qualifying juniors had been promoted, we would have exceeded the state standards in all subject areas.

When I realized we could still enter the information effective in January, I began to discuss the possibility with others outside Furr. In every discussion I was told it should not be a problem, and I had a great deal of support from Thelma Garza, Pat Zumwalt, Dr. Lupita Garcia, Dr. Kelly Trlica, and Carla Stevens. (I tell you this to let you know you have much support from administrators outside of Furr). When I requested a statement in writing from the Office of State and Federal Compliance indicating it was appropriate to enter the student information effective in January, I was referred to Thelma Garza and Dr. Karen Soehnge for their approval. With proper documentation, Ms. Garza assured me she would sign my request. I immediately began to gather the documentation. Still, I always had a thought in the back of my mind that we were somehow manipulating the system and I did not feel good about it.

Last night after attending the prom and observing our delightful students, I was moved by their appearance and behavior. I was asked to dance several times and did so to the endless boom-booming music. That was a bit of a stretch for a 73-year-old grandmother, but I did it and loved it! I returned home exhausted, stumbled into bed and fell fast asleep. I awoke this morning with a feeling that could only be described as joyful serenity. Sometime during the night as I was sleeping, our frenetic behavior over TAKS scores was juxtaposed to the simple joy of the prom, and I awoke with a clear picture in my mind of where we need to go.

While I am aware that some of you may disagree with me, I have decided to drop our efforts to gather documentation to present to Thelma Garza so we might appeal the state's anticipated rating of Unacceptable. Even though we clearly have the documentation and technically are correct in what we are doing, is it morally right to ask another to sign off on something which was obviously, at least to a degree, our fault? Especially when all evidence I have leads me to believe we will still be Unacceptable in math, even after exhausting all avenues of appeal because of failing scores of three students in one student group. Our time could be better spent planning for next year so that we will be found to be a Recognized school. Then we can all hold our heads high and be proud of the work we have done with our students.

I have attached the results of the TAKS in a form I think will clearly and simply communicate them. Also attached is a sheet that compares the achievement of each grade level cohort of students this year with their achievement last year. I think this will clearly point out that we have much to celebrate. Remember, our comparison to ourselves is what is important; not our comparison with other schools.

I value you individually and collectively. Your value as a human being is not solely determined by test scores, but also by your integrity and your commitment to find ways to educate our students, some of whom show no interest in learning. I request that you put aside, for a time, what has happened and begin to look for the beauty in life, remembering that beauty is not out there, but is in your heart and your mind. While lines and bar graphs and numbers may inform us, they do not determine us. We are ultimately determined by what we think, feel, and how we behave. You have behaved admirably, and we will all work harder and smarter knowing Furr will be a Recognized school in the spring of 2008. Spring will come again!

Sincerely and with great admiration and respect,

Bertie

CHAPTER 44
Blood, Sweat, and Joy

The only word I can think of to describe the year after being rated unacceptable is humiliation. The school was invaded by "experts" from the outside, telling us exactly what should be done. I was reminded of the old saying "Experts have their expert fun telling others how nothing could be done." While they were likable and wanted to be helpful, their suggestions were all ideas and strategies we had been working on for years. Much of what they did was simply to document their work for the state, in the case of our state accountability rating, and for the federal government, in the case of No Child Left Behind. In addition, a series of meetings were scheduled for the principals of unacceptable schools. The meetings were less than informative and certainly not inspirational. I had difficulty finding the location of one of the meetings in a local hotel. I told an individual at the information counter I was the principal of an unacceptable school and she replied, "All the bad principals are meeting in room 102."

Now, I wanted to tell her I would like to "whoop her"—and well, you get the drift. But I smiled and moved on to the "bad" principals' meeting.

During these sessions, the consultants stressed one "revolutionary" practice. It required dividing all the principals of unacceptable schools into groups, each with an assigned leader. (I never knew if the leader was "acceptable" or "unacceptable.") We were to use the computer to communicate with each other on a regular basis so we could share best practices. Now, if we really knew "best practices," would our schools be "unacceptable?" This requirement was incomprehensible. I was on the verge of declaring that I had enjoyed about as much of this nonsense as I could endure when I received a call from the area superintendent.

Yes, it was the much-anticipated call. I was told that she and the superintendent of schools had decided my "contract with the HISD was being non-renewed," which meant I was being fired. I was to bring my school keys to the area office the following day. At that time, it was the district's practice to have principals bring their keys to the area office and to allow them to return to the school to retrieve personal items only when escorted by a police officer. I was a bit dismayed because, after all, she had requested that I come out of retirement to assume the position as principal of a school nobody else wanted.

Bertie and student at graduation.

Then, inexplicably, I received another phone call from her that night, telling me that she and the superintendent of schools had reconsidered their decision. She was leaving me at Furr. It goes without saying that I wanted the students to pass the almighty TAKS test, but I wanted them to learn so much more. I planned to continue to teach the whole child and struggle to stay under the radar.

Teachers began to participate in action research, a disciplined process of inquiry on how to improve our teaching strategies. They were to present their results at a district-wide exhibition in 2009. Doug Reeves, an educational researcher, was invited to Furr as a consultant to work with teachers on their research and grading practices. He stressed that feedback is a powerful influence on student achievement but that grades must be fair, accurate, specific, and timely. He even suggested that students should be given a menu of assignments and be permitted to choose the way they could make up incomplete work, rather than getting a zero. He also recommended that the weight of homework should be minimized. Following the session, although some thought this was cheating the students who completed homework on time, the teachers voted not to give zeros but to work with students to ensure the work was completed and to give a grade. Eventually the state ruled that a school could not enforce a no-zero policy related to grading.

At Furr, we believed we had a moral imperative to provide a rigorous program of instruction to the students. We got to know each student individually, learning the individual academic and personal needs of each. Each employee mentored and assumed responsibility for several students. When the student was absent, that student received a phone call not only from the school but also from the mentor. One of my mentees, Ray Ochoa, laughs about the time he was in the dentist's chair and received a call from me asking him why he was not at school. He was a freshman at the time, and as a senior, he still told the story about my thinking he was skipping and how I wanted to make sure he was always in school. In a given year, I personally met with over two hundred students and parents in order to ensure the students' success. Many other Furr staff did the same.

If we were unable to contact an absent student by phone, my Title I coordinator, Sharon Brown, and I went in search of them at their homes. Many of these areas were unsafe, with many abandoned houses and crack houses. We learned much about our students by making these home visits. We also built deeper rapport with the parents, which helped improve the image of the school and gave hope to the students. We participated in the annual Reach Out to Dropout program and were able to bring many of our students back to school.

Tracey Clark, an HISD IT customer service representative, described one such home visit that she made with me:

> So, Dr. Simmons called me one day in the hall and said she wanted me to take her somewhere.
>
> I said, "Oh, okay."
>
> I go to get my keys. When I came back, I'm thinking it is just she and I who were going, but no. Ms. Dixon and Ms. Aguirre were outside. All of us were going to be in my truck. I didn't even know where I was going, but Dr. Simmons was going to tell me the way.
>
> So, she told me, "No problem. I know where Clinton Park is."
>
> We got over there, and she said, "turn here and turn there."

So finally, we made it to where we were going. I pulled up outside the house, and I'm just sitting there. She had just said, "Drive her over." She opens the door and jumps out and was raring to go.

She stopped and turned around and said, "I'm not going by myself. Come on!"

I'm like, "Oh."

I got out of the car. Ms. Dixon and Ms. Aguirre were trying to get out. I walked with Dr. Simmons. She and I had already made it to the door. Before I completely got to the door, here she is, bam, bam, bam!

I said to myself, "Oh my God. This lady is going to get us killed. She's banging on the door like she is the poo-lice. I'm thinking, "You know, it's amazing."

Then the door opens, and it doesn't just fly open. Just a crack, about an inch wide, with an eye looking out. And Dr. Simmons is talking to it! She is just having a whole conversation. And I'm just standing there, and I'm like wishing I could be back in the car. When she finishes her conversation, the door closes. We stand there for some more, and I figure these people are not coming back to this door.

We are just standing here looking at a door. Nope! The door opens; it's the Mom. Dr. Simmons has a whole conversation. Mom closes the door again. We stand some more. This time the door opens, Mom comes out, and the boy comes out. We all go back to the car. We get in. I'm driving. I have a seat. Dr. Simmons is sitting in the front with me. She has a seat. Everybody else, they are all smushed in the back seat. I drive back to the school. Everybody gets out the car, everybody goes in. The mom and the boy head towards the office with Dr. Simmons, I go put my stuff back up. I thought I was going to have to take them home, but I didn't. She got somebody else to take them. The boy got in school, and he graduated! That was the situation with Dr. Simmons.

One interesting phenomenon happened as I reviewed the data of each student. I found that many of our students had never passed a TAKS test in their school career. I also found these students often had enough credits to be promoted to the next grade at midterm and some could even become early graduates, that is, they could graduate a half year early if they passed the TAKS tests. I called the parents and students in for individual conferences and told them this fact. The first year I tried this, I worked with a total of twenty-one tenth-grade students who were promoted at midterm. These students took all exit-level TAKS tests, and twenty of them passed all tests and, as a result, graduated a half year early. At that time, the state awarded money to early graduates for college: they received two thousand dollars for four-year college and one thousand dollars for two-year college. Nineteen of those early graduates went on to college. This was a possibility the students and parents had never thought about.

While our focus was on providing a rigorous academic environment for our students, we also realized that it was the relationships we established with them that would make the difference in their attitude about learning and about school. I was reminded of this many times over the years by former students. One example stands out in my mind.

It rarely snows in Houston, but during December 2008, it did. We were all excited as we watched the huge flakes drift slowly to the ground. Many students rushed to the window, mesmerized as they witnessed this rare occurrence. Years later, Carlos Rincon, a former student described his memory of the morning on Facebook:

> Most of the students had gone to class, but a select group of about twenty students skipped class and went outside to play in the snow. We're from Houston and we don't see it snow often. We were not about to be stuck in class while it was coming down outside. Straight up. So, these twenty kids, including me, started in the parking lot, full on scraping snow off the cars, having snowball fights, building snowmen, all that jazz. This was risky business for kids skipping class, yes, but it was snowing, and we didn't care if we got caught. Let those suckers stay in class. It was worth any getting whatever punishment was to be given to us.

Well, after about five minutes of building snowmen and fooling around outside the office, out comes Doc, followed by a few administrators and office staff. We all stopped for a minute and collectively go, "We are busted!" We knew we couldn't play outside forever, so we were ready to be punished and ushered back to class. Well, that's not what happened.

After giving us a hard time for a second and seeing why we weren't in class, Doc goes, "So are you all going to keep standing there looking frightened, or is someone going to get more snow?"

Doc didn't get angry at us. Doc understood. She knew sometimes kids will be kids and that it was snowing in Houston, Texas in December. Dr. Simmons AND a good portion of her administration spent the next two hours outside building snowmen and having snowball fights with all students who decided to skip class to play in the snow that day. It was AMAZING. That day, at least for a couple of hours, class didn't matter, periods didn't matter, and skipping class didn't matter.

Bertie and students with snowman.

Moments like these are why the students gave Doc so much respect. She was strict when she needed to be, but she knew how to let loose, and she knew when to be fair. Many principals would have just punished us, thrown us in school suspension, or sent us home. But Doc didn't. She and her administrators came outside to have a good time with us, and that is something Furr High School will never have again.

Doc and I had our differences on a couple of different occasions, but her commitment to students goes deeper than ANYONE I have ever met in the educational career field. Maybe some of the students did not understand that, but Doc gave everything she had to make that school a better place, and anyone who has ever spoken to her knows that. She brought that school back from the brink. She made it what it is today, and Furr High School will NEVER be the same without her.

Ugly snowman.

I clearly remember that event. We took pictures of the snowmen because they were so ugly.

All of us had a good laugh about the fact that none of the students knew how to really make a snowman. Students from the deep East End of Houston had no idea about rolling big balls of snow for the body, finding objects to create facial features, or how to add arms to the body. While I realized that they had missed class, this gave them the opportunity to be creative, to problem solve, and to experience joy. Others may not understand this philosophy, but it is what I think schools should be doing for our youth.

As we continued to implement strategies to meet the needs of students, we hired a reading teacher and began to implement online reading programs as well as teacher-directed lessons. We hired an English as a second language (ESL) teacher, and all the core teachers were trained in ESL strategies. We studied the data to determine students who had the ability to attend college successfully but also who needed extra training and encouragement. To meet their needs, we implemented the Achievement Via Individual Determination (AVID) program, which was highly successful. One AVID class was shocked when Goldie Hawn entered their classroom one day and participated in a Socratic seminar. Bena Kallick was aware Goldie would be in Houston and had invited her to Furr. The discussion that day was whether it was important to marry or if it was appropriate to simply live together. Goldie contributed greatly to the discussion, and it was a day the students will never forget. I later used the materials from her foundation to teach a group of girls who had great difficulty controlling their impulsivity. The girls completely changed their behavior, and I later chose them to be the jurors on the Principal's Court.

Bertie, Paula, and students with Goldie Hawn.

The Principal's Court, which I began in 2009, met each Friday to hear students who had received a ticket during that week for minor infractions of the rules. The purpose of the court was to enable the offenders of minor infractions to return to class immediately after the court, missing very little class time. This enabled us to close the in-school suspension program and end the practice of out-of-school suspensions. To add to the seriousness of the court, I served as judge, complete with robe and gavel. To meet the requirements of the Family Education Rights and Privacy Act (FERPA), we had parents sign an agreement and jurors to sign an oath of confidentiality.

I was amazed at how the student jurors made decisions about actions that they would require of the defendant. All decisions required academic work related to the infraction. Students were required to conduct research on the infraction, write a paper concerning the infraction, and even write an apology if the defendant had wronged someone. One of the many positive aspects of the Principal's Court was how it inspired students to become leaders. I was especially proud when the seniors adopted students who made frequent appearances before the court and mentored them for a year. The jurors learned to show empathy for the offenders, and at times, even pooled their resources to buy uniforms for those students who were repeatedly out of dress code because they could not afford to purchase a shirt.

One amusing situation was the day when, during deliberation, the jury decided the defendant had not told the truth and charged him with perjury. The defendant was to research the meaning of perjury and what would happen if the defendant perjured himself in court. He was to report back to the court the following Friday. The defendant yelled, "Perjury? What the hell is perjury?" The jury slapped another assignment on the defendant to write an essay on why one should not curse in court and present it to the court, also on the following Friday.

Furr had more than one hundred homeless students. A study, Mapping the Measure of America, that was conducted by the American Human Development Project and released in December 2010 listed our Congressional district as fifth from the bottom nationally in the areas of health, education, and income.

Victor Cardenas, a senior, was crying in the hallway one day, and I approached him, asking why he was crying. I was shocked at his reply. "Miss, I am living in the park now, and it is getting really cold. I don't have anything to cover with, and I stay awake because I am shivering. I'm afraid my grades will drop, and I really want to go to college."

I asked Victor to come into my office so I could find help for him. Fortunately, the film teacher, Ms. Kavtorina, saw us and joined us in my office. When she heard Victor's story, she called her family to see if they would agree to Victor living with them until he graduated in the spring. They agreed. Ms. Kavtorina is from Russia, and when I expressed surprise about their decision, she said, "This is no big deal. When a stranger came to my door in Russia, I would welcome that stranger. We would love to have Victor live with us. He is one of my favorite students, and he does great work. He will just be a welcome new member of our family."

In 2010, an article on Furr titled "Homeless High" was published in the *Houston Press*. It began by describing Victor Cardenas. Margaret Downing wrote, "When he was four his father walked out, overwhelmed by the debt and discord in their home. When Victor was 14, his mother threw him out, stabbed him in the neck with a knife and told him if he ever came back, she would kill him. He began sleeping on park benches."

Victor explained to Margaret Downing, "My mom had a real drinking problem, and my brothers all had problems with drugs. They belonged to Little Reds, a Denver Harbor gang. My mother was kind of unhappy because my dad left her. She had cancer. It was a really bad situation because she was gone much of the time. All of us got into trouble with the police. When we fought, we stabbed each other with knives."

In her article, Margaret Downing continued, "Victor Cardenas, a homeless wanderer for much of his high school career, graduated this past Memorial Day weekend as the valedictorian of his class at Furr High School, with a perfect 4.0 out of possible 4.0 average. He's the first person in his family to get past the tenth grade."

Victor had produced a documentary at school entitled *Just Being Victor*. Scenes from his documentary were flashing vividly through my mind, bringing tears to my eyes as I read Margaret's article.

It was that same year that the valedictorian from REACH was also homeless. The female student was a truly remarkable young lady who had experienced much trauma in her short life. She had been molested several times by a family member when she was seven and then by a different family member when she was fifteen. When her father found out about this, he called her "a female dog" and threw her out of the house. She had dropped out of her school even though she had good grades. She eventually enrolled in REACH, our charter school, and her speech at graduation was moving. I was glad she would be joining Victor at Texas A&M and the two of them could provide support for each other. The best was yet to come!

270

CHAPTER 45
A Deeper Dive

The teachers and administrators expressed a strong need to offer more rigorous opportunities to the students. We had spent years working on school safety, socio-emotional needs of the students, and creating readiness for academic rigor. The students were expressing a hunger for a chance to participate in more challenging classes that would prepare them for college.

In the spring of 2010, we decided to make an extra effort to ensure that our students were prepared to be successful on the Scholastic Aptitude Test (SAT). We organized an SAT boot camp which would be held during spring break. Each student was given a T-shirt with a picture of the principal in army fatigues saluting and pointing a finger on the front. The caption read:

"We want you for SAT boot camp!"

On the back it read:

"I SURVIVED SIMMONS' BOOT CAMP."

We had ninety-two students sign up to give up their spring break to prepare for the upcoming SAT. They all wore the shirts and the dog tags issued to us by the Army. Each day the students attended, they received a metal star to be put on the shirt, and if they attended all five days, they were recognized as five-star generals. The week was a huge success, and the scores did improve. The students attending all five days increased their SAT math scores by thirty points, their writing by thirty-one points, and their reading by twenty-one points.

We moved along, adding rigor when advisable and to the appropriate degree. We added a program called EMERGE which readied the students for acceptance to Ivy League colleges. Students attended special classes at Furr for six weeks in the summer and then one day after school every other week during the school year. The students who participated in this program learned for the first time about the possibilities of attending Tier I schools and participated in activities that enriched their lives in unbelievable ways.

EMERGE students.

In 2011, the new test, State of Texas Assessments of Academic Readiness (STAAR), was peeking its ugly head over the horizon. We were told it was far more rigorous and would require a minimum of forty-five days of testing. Here we go again!

Over a nine-year period, the graduation rate had increased from 50 percent to 78 percent, with a completion rate of 93 percent. The completion rate included those students who did not graduate in four years but did so in five. The percentage of students enrolled in a two- or four-year college was above 95 percent, depending upon when the count was taken. Many of our students were accepted into and attended Tier 1 universities.

Furr had begun to be recognized in district, regional, and state competitions. We had taken first place in one-act plays and had gone to state two years in a row in robotics and debate. This was due to the hard work of teacher Michael Ritch. To everyone's amazement, we took first place in the state's Russian Olympiada for fifteen consecutive years. The students who participated in this event were native Spanish speakers, had learned English, and were now fluent in Russian. This was quite a feat and was primarily due to an incredible Russian teacher, Anna Lavina.

One of the programs in which our students were involved was the grad lab. This lab was the idea of the superintendent of schools, Terry Grier. It enabled students who had lost credits to make up those credits online. Tracy Elam ran the grad lab twenty-four hours a day by using her phone to reset the computer when a student completed a task. This enabled the student to continue working online even in the middle of the night. Tracy was tireless in her efforts to assist students in gaining lost credits.

Ms. Lurlean Dixon, Sister Dixon, as I called her, worked with the school for much of the time I was principal. We had opened a family counseling center on campus where she provided family counseling, lessons in anger management, and financial planning classes. Through the center, she also worked to find students and their families employment by collaborating with Work Force Solutions. She worked on the Neighborhood Safety Council in Congressman Gene Green's office and sponsored job fairs for our families. I will never forget one afternoon when we had planned to take several of our students to interview for jobs. We told the boys they must wear a tie, but none of them owned one. Our teachers brought ties for the boys, and when I looked out my window, they were tying the ties on the boys.

We expanded Superintendent Grier's grad lab program into one of our neighborhood churches, North Shore Community of Faith, which was adjacent to several of the apartments where many of our students lived. The lab at the church enabled students who did not own a computer to work online in the evenings to make up lost credit and to gain original credit. Later, a computer repair class was opened there, where the students received dual credit working with the community college and were enabled to gain high school and college credit in those classes. Sister Dixon, whose son, Robert Irvin Dixon II, was the pastor of the church, supervised the program as students learned about building and repairing computers and about networking. Once the class was complete, the students were permitted to keep the computers.

Fall 2008
Reconnecting Youth Class
Furr High School

**Reconnecting Youth Class with
Sister Dixon, teacher Diana Littlejohn.**

We had decided earlier to take the plunge and place our students in Advanced Placement (AP) classes. We had dual-credit classes with the community college but believed that it was our moral responsibility to offer the AP classes. More than 75 percent of our students enrolled in an AP class that first year. It was a real struggle since this was the first time our students were expected to complete so much homework and extra reading outside of class. Several students wanted to drop out of the classes and had the full support of their parents. I spent endless hours talking to them about the importance of the classes and what it would mean to them when they attended college. This was not an easy task since many of our students worked until 2:00 a.m. and 93 percent of our students were on free or reduced lunch. In fact, we were likely close to 100 percent low income. The reason we appeared to be lower was because many of our students were undocumented and refused to fill out the free and reduced lunch form for fear of being deported. Still, we worked closely with the parents and removed students who were struggling, while encouraging others to remain in the classes. The students who remained stated they had learned more than they ever had, even though only a few of them scored a three or higher on any AP test. Angela Borzon, who had been promoted to dean of instruction in 2009, was primarily responsible for the success of the AP program.

I realized my dream of giving the students at Furr an academic attitude and a view of life, something that teachers had jeered at during my first year. It happened one day when we had purchased study books for all AP social studies classes. I made an announcement for all AP social studies students to come to the courtyard for a surprise. To be sure, I did not know how well received the books would be. I was delighted as the students grabbed the books, opened them, and stuck their noses into them to smell them because they were new. They thanked us profusely and then rushed to begin working with them. When the students returned to class, their teachers said they could not get them to do anything except work on the AP practice books. I knew then what an academic attitude looked like, sounded like, and smelled like.

Later in the week, I visited a Schools of Choice meeting where I saw a Furr student being approached by a principal of another school. I was shocked at his response to a question.

"Why don't you transfer to my school because it is a good school?" the principal asked.

"Do you have AP Chinese?" asked the student.

"We don't teach Chinese," replied the principal.

"Well, Furr does, and I am staying at Furr," the student stated.

Then he began to tell the principal the role that China plays in the world and why it is important to learn more about that country. There, I witnessed a student with a view of life. There is no way to express the joy I felt.

In the spring of 2011, we received a notice from the College Board that Furr High School was one of three schools in the nation to receive the Inspiration Award for providing rigorous AP classes to under-served students. A feeling of anticipation filled the school and the community. Could this really be happening to Furr High School? We laughed, we sang, and we danced with joy.

Civility Students with Congressman Gene Green in Washington, DC.

On the day of the celebration, which Furr had been expected to organize, the air was charged with excitement. We had worked hard to make certain the event went off without a hitch and that it exceeded the College Board's expectations. We arranged the refreshments in the Furr Coffee House and decorated the auditorium with strobe lights, bubble machines, and signs that read Working on a Dream. We could hardly wait for the arrival of our guests and the presentation of the award. Dr. Bena Kallick flew in for the event, and top officials from the city, district, and Congressman Gene Green's office were present.

Juliet Stipeche

This was by far the most exciting day we had ever experienced at Furr. Students all wore T-shirts with the inscription Working on a Dream. The superintendent of schools, Terry Grier, was there, as was our school board member Juliet Stipeche. The president of the College Board, Gaston Caperton, gave a moving speech and presented the Inspiration Award to the school. He is one of the most inspiring individuals I have ever met, and he deeply impressed our students and gave them

276

hope. The last to speak, I talked about the importance of having and holding on to dreams. As soon as I finished speaking, the auditorium went dark, strobe lights shot across the room while colorful bubbles poured from all sides, the band struck up the music, and the entire auditorium sang *"Working on a Dream"* by Bruce Springsteen. Wow!

Karen Banda, George Mendoza, and Bertie at the HISD Board.

The following fall, we took two students, Karen Banda and George Mendoza, to the College Board Forum in New York City. They each delivered poignant speeches, which grabbed the hearts of the more than one thousand people who were present. They talked about being poor and minority, but of having dreams of attending a Tier I college. They received many accolades and later presented their speech to the board of education in Houston. While in New York, they toured the city and saw *Memphis, the Musical* on Broadway, which they said they would never forget. On the flight back to Houston one of the students remarked, "I will be back here because I am going to college here one day."

As a result of this great honor and the hard work of many of the teachers and staff at our school, Furr High School was featured in an article in the September/October 2011 issue of *Texas Lone Star* magazine. The title of the article was "A Throw Away School No More," and the title page was covered with hearts. This is a publication that is sent to all superintendents of schools and school board members in the state of Texas. Furr was also named by the *Washington Post* in 2012 as among the top 5 percent of the best schools in the United States because of our efforts to provide rigorous programs to under-served students.

The Texas Lone Star article included comments from two Furr students. Keweyn Chandler, a struggling senior, said, "This school has been a lifesaver to me. I say lifesaver because beyond an education (and I needed a lot of education), this school and its staff led by Dr.

Bertie Simmons, have clothed me, fed me, encouraged me, supported me, and housed me. They helped me to find refuge when my own family didn't care where I slept. When I was crying because it was all a bit too much, this school stepped in and let me know I was not alone. That's what I mean by the word lifesaver. I didn't think I had a chance of graduating, but now that is within reach. I owe that to Furr High School. I have been to many different schools, and I didn't know a school existed that would do the things Furr has done for me. They changed me and helped me become a better human being."

Sebastian Obando, a brilliant student said, "Furr changed my view of the world. It showed me the art of reality through the documentaries that the film department allowed me to work on. It made me into someone who was able to defy the odds of being a foreign student from a low-income economic background and reach a top-tier university. Furr was home, and Furr was a teacher. It taught me life as well as academics, and it was a cradle where I was allowed to become who I need to be."

As I read the student comments in the article. I thought how far we had come and how proud I was of all the students and the hard-working staff. I was also proud of our community involvement and how we had been working to educate the parents as a result of our covenant with them. I was reminded of Ray Ochoa whom I had mentored for the four years he had been a student at Furr High School and had watched him grow into an accomplished young man.

When Ray was a 2012 senior, he addressed the HISD Board of Education, and among other things, he said, "At times I find myself not wanting to leave Furr because of its warmth and the numerous educational opportunities. I was in an AP psychology class where I was learning about Maslow's hierarchy of basic needs. I left that class and walked into the school coffee house where I found my parents learning about the forty developmental assets." He added, "It is like Furr feeds the community hope and inspiration while it teaches them things that will build a better relationship between student and parent. No matter where I go, I will always return to Furr because Furr is more than a school. Furr is a last name because it is a family. Thank you for giving me this family." Sitting in the audience that night were Sister Dixon and Tiphaine Shaw, both of whom were big supporters of all our students and were there to support Ray. Tiphaine was one of our most creative staff members at Furr, and she always knew the individual student's academic and emotional needs.

At that same board meeting, the Furr Glee Club performed a moving rendition of "Seasons of Love" from the Broadway musical *Rent*. The students informed the audience that this song described how they measured a year (525,600 minutes) in their lives at Furr. Remember when schools could provide this type of environment for students and not be required to do it "under the radar"? What more evidence do we need to show that we must teach the whole child if public education is to survive?

**Students in Washington, DC with the
Institute for Civility in Government.**

We had a long-standing working relationship with the Institute for Civility in Government, a grassroots, nonpartisan, nonprofit organization that is building civility in society. Each year through this relationship, selected students spent four days in Washington, DC, where they had an opportunity to meet with members of the House of Representatives and Senate to present and discuss issues that the students felt important. One year, they discussed the economy, immigration, and the need for a change in education to reduce the time spent on mandated tests. They implored the leaders on the Hill to put education back into the hands of educators and remove control of the school system from politicians and business people.

As a culminating activity, we held a Civility in the Park event to celebrate the civility we now experienced within the school and the entire school community. It was a brilliant, sunlit day, and the whole community came out to join the celebration. Students performed, and the band played loudly and on key. Parents provided games and food as we all shared the joy of oneness. Each participant was given a Civility in the Park pin and a Furr Passport, in which they were to record any acts of civility they witnessed. As I watched the joyful celebration, I was reminded of the time when the local parks were unsafe, and we dared not take students there. Sister Dixon reminded us of the song "Let There Be Peace on Earth, and Let It Begin with Me." It was, indeed, a grand closing of a grand Civility in the Park event.

CHAPTER 46
Intentionality

Furr was an invitational school built on intentionality, trust, mutual respect, and optimism. We were intentional in how we created an environment that invited members to do their best. With all the obstacles our students faced, we did not leave the school environment and student success to chance. As a result, our students were given opportunities to participate in numerous projects and competitions that made learning purposeful and personal. We believed that students would be more engaged and have bigger dreams if the school activities were somehow relevant to their lives, passions, and talents.

Five students were finalists in the Youth About Business National Championship Camp at Columbia University in New York City. This was the result of participating in the HISD EMERGE Program which had helped many of our students attend Tier I schools. In addition, eighteen students participated in an internship program with the HISD media services department. The students' expertise in media technologies grew exponentially as a result.

Furr was one of only six schools in the district to be chosen to participate in the Houston Innovative Learning Zone (HILZ), a program of study offered in conjunction with Houston Community College. HILZ offered students courses in developing technology skills that would prepare them for the workplace. It was a dual-credit program that would give students both high school and college credit. Through this program, students would qualify for an associate's degree while still in high school.

The Furr after-school robotics team competed in the regional competition in Dallas. The goal was to inspire students to pursue careers in engineering, science, technology, and math through participation in a sports-like robotics competition. Michael Ritch, an excellent teacher and role model, led these students as they learned the intricacies of robots and their importance to our future.

We were involved in Project Lead the Way's programs and received national accreditation in 2011. The mission of this program was to prepare students for the global economy through a world-class curriculum, high-quality professional development for teachers, and an engaged network of schools from throughout the nation.

During the 2012–2013 school year, twenty-two students participated in the Coca-Cola Valued Youth Program. They worked as tutors in two local elementary schools and received thirty-five dollars a week in compensation. Furr students placed second and third in the district-wide Valued Youth Essay Contest. The students were selected based on their academic strength and interest.

One of the most effective programs we added was No More Victims. This program was designed to give support and encouragement to students whose parents were incarcerated. The program was designed and taught by Marilyn Gambrell. The class usually had in excess of 30 students who fell in love with Ms. Gambrell. She saved many lives and was responsible for most of her students graduating from high school. Many of these students completed college successfully.

In 2013, Furr implemented Linked Learning to provide a viable structure for problem-based learning, which had been our focus for several years. Linked Learning is based on the belief that students work harder and dream bigger if their education is relevant to them. It integrates rigorous academics that meet college-ready standards and high-quality career technical education and work-based learning. Many of our students came from turbulent worlds. Many were immigrants who had fled the violence of Honduras and El Salvador, and most experienced gang violence or economic instability every day. Through these programs, we gave students a sense of hope and an abiding belief that they could be agents of positive change.

We offered a choice of three interconnected pathways that provided our students with opportunities to experience voice and choice; to be creative, collaborative, and innovative; and to solve problems in their community. Students chose the pathway they wished to join based on their passions and interests. There was the Environmental Communications Pathway, which focused on conducting research and producing documentaries to highlight environmental challenges in the East End. The Place-Based Pathway focused on classrooms outside the brick-and-mortar rooms and connected people to people and people to nature. The third pathway, Alternative Forms of Energy, focused on ways that Houston could diminish greenhouse gases and reduce the city's carbon footprint. These three pathways worked in union to bring the East End of Houston and the whole world a breath of fresh air, both literally and figuratively. They helped ensure that the pollution of the San Jacinto River, which threatened the lives of many of the families of the East End, was brought to the forefront of the Environmental Protection Agency's agenda. This was authentic learning in action.

The Environmental Communication Pathway students took samples of the water in the river and worked with the University of Houston to test the samples for toxins. They reported the findings to the EPA and sent the agency persuasive essays concerning the urgent need to remove the toxic waste pits left by two paper mills. They produced a film, Jacque's River, that movingly depicted the adverse health effects, including cancer, experienced by those living near the San Jacinto River. The film was selected by the Texas Environmental Justice Film Festival to be shown at the River Oaks Theatre during the festival. The students even filmed a story on the high cancer rates in the Manchester area of the East End. At Furr High School, they tested the water and discovered exceedingly high copper levels. The students presented the results to the HISD Board of Education, emphasizing the health hazards to which students were exposed every day.

The Environmental Communication Pathway, led by Assol Kavtorina (Ms. K.), wrote the film scripts, filmed and edited the footage, and produced the films about their work on the environment and social justice. They competed at the state level and always placed at the top, even winning first place. Because of the accomplishments of students in this pathway, Ms. K., Victoria Martinez (one of the students), and I were invited to present at the national Linked Learning Convention in San Diego, California. Ms. K. and Victoria made me so proud. Victoria had always seemed rather shy, but she came into her own there. She spoke with such self-assurance, and the audience was enthralled as she recounted what she had learned. I thought we would not be able to get her to return to Houston. "This is the most beautiful place I have ever seen," she whispered over and over.

The East End of Houston is where some of the largest chemical plants and refineries are located. Toxic materials are spewed into the air from these plants and into the homes, parks, and schools in the area, where Furr students live, play, and learn. On a few occasions, the Environmental Communication Pathway students experienced how their efforts to investigate these issues troubled the companies that create these problems. When the pathway was focused on the Manchester area of Houston, Ms. K., and two students went to film the area. They were approached by security guards from the Valero petroleum plant and told that they could not film the area. When the Valero guards learned that one of them was from Russia and one was from Ecuador, they grabbed the camera and asked them to reformat the memory card in their presence and erase everything on it. They complied with the demand. Then Ms. K. put her jacket over the camera and lowered the window so the students could continue to film the area after the guards had gone. Later, they filmed around the railroads in Fifth Ward. Around dusk that afternoon, two policemen arrived at Ms. K.'s house and questioned her about the filming. They did the same thing when students went on toxic tours to learn about the Superfund sites in the East End with Texas Environmental Justice Advocacy Services (t.e.j.a.s.), an organization founded by the Parras family. This East End family was committed to developing awareness and promoting corrective actions to address the environmental issues of the area. We learned that individuals who lived in our side of town were 22 percent more likely to develop cancer than those who lived in other parts of the city.

Media Students:
Milburgo Mora, Victoria Martinez, Elmer Milla.

The Placed-Based Pathway worked with Texas A&M to also study water and air samples in the Manchester area of Houston, which has the highest cancer rates in the city. Students from all three pathways reported their findings to the Houston City Council and the HISD school board. They also organized a group of students called Green Ambassadors, who visited elementary and middle schools and trained students on the "greening" of the East End. They worked with the Parks and Recreation Department to plant and maintain a community garden in Herman Brown Park, which was a block from our school, and delivered fresh vegetables to elderly residents in the Songwood neighborhood.

The Place-Based Pathway set up what they called a "STEAM" Room, where they kept unusual animals, reptiles, and spiders, including a huge tarantula, a Texas white rat snake, and a beautiful mink. The students were thrilled to tell visitors all about the animals. Elementary students visited the school to see the STEAM room. The Place-Based students also grew hydroponic plants in a room that would also sometimes be used as a home for bunnies that they were raising. It was not unusual to look through the hallway windows of the room to see high school students sitting on the floor mesmerized by the antics of the baby rabbits. Another of their projects involved raising chickens in a fenced-in area on campus. The flock included exotic hens that laid multicolored eggs.

Our Place-Based Pathway students often visited other parts of the country to study the habitats of birds. Ours was the only school in the country to receive the Abraham Lincoln Award for diversity and inclusion because of the work of this pathway. When one of the students heard we had received the award because of their hard work, he rushed into my office and breathlessly shouted, "Miss, did you know we just won a national award for adversity?" That gave me the opportunity to discuss the meanings of adversity and diversity and why we had received the award for diversity. At the end of our conversation he remarked, "Well, I don't think we have a lot of adversity, but I surely am glad we won for being diverse." He hugged me and ran to tell others the good news.

The Alternative Forms of Energy Pathway was interested in learning whether there was enough wind in Houston for a wind farm to produce electricity. We purchased and the students erected an anemometer at the back of the school. Each day they checked and recorded the readings. They learned that the only time there was enough wind was during a hurricane when the wind was recorded as blowing ninety-three miles per hour.

Students in Dr. Zakar Hovhannes Mnjoyons's class made a potato clock for my office. The students who presented it to me were studying how to reduce pollution by creating clean energy. They had used a battery from an LED clock, two potatoes, a zinc nail, a copper nail, copper wire, and two alligator clips. They explained how they had connected it all and then set the clock. They often checked to make sure the potatoes had not rotted, and when the potatoes were deteriorating, the students replaced them for me. I used the clock until I left the school, and it was always a good topic of discussion. This group also studied solar and kinetic energy. I was always surprised at their creativity and innovative ideas.

At the end of each semester, students in the pathways delivered capstone presentations to an audience of business and industry partners, HISD personnel, parents, and university professors. The depth, comprehensiveness, and professional quality of the presentations was remarkable. The audience invariably expressed their amazement at the students' and teachers' commitment to their projects.

One year, Cynthia Cantu presented a study she had conducted on the adverse effect of sugar on health. She happily exclaimed, "As a result of my study and the actions I have taken, I have lost fifty pounds. It also has helped my family because they have sugar diabetes. I have learned so much by conducting this study."

For a capstone project one semester, the Alternative Forms of Energy Pathway planned to serve omelets cooked in solar ovens. The weather was cloudy for four days before and on the day of the presentation. As a result, the solar ovens did not function, and the students took the opportunity to tell the audience the disadvantages of solar energy. Fortunately, they had also planned to use lamps to demonstrate how solar power (represented by the lamps) would have enabled them to prepare the omelets.

Another student explained how he harnessed the kinetic energy of the traffic on his street to create electricity. He constructed a speed bump and attached an electric bulb at the end. When he rolled an object over the bump, it generated enough electricity to cause the light to burn. I could not believe my eyes! During this same presentation, another student created kinetic energy by turning the back wheel of an upside-down bicycle, which caused a light to shine.

Things were moving quickly, attendance was up, and more and more students were attending and completing college. Karen Banda, who was a speaker at the College Board Forum in New York City, graduated from Furr in 2014. When she had entered ninth grade, she told me her family had told her doors would be closed to her because she was Hispanic. I had promised her then I would take the hinges off the doors for her.

"Dr. Simmons, I would like to apply for the Gates Scholarship," Karen told me. "Would you write a recommendation for me? I doubt that I could win, but I would like to give it a try."

"I would love to recommend you," I replied. "And I think you have a good chance." I could just see, in my mind's eye, those hinges flying off Karen's door.

Karen graduated from Furr as the class valedictorian and was the recipient of the Gates Millennium Scholarship among many others. She was granted a full ride to Smith College, where she studied until 2016 when she transferred to a university in Cordoba, Spain. Karen graduated cum laude from Smith in 2018 with a double major in government and Latin American studies. She accepted a job as a paralegal in a law office in New York City. Karen's wonderful parents are so proud of her as we all are. Her father still works as a custodian in an HISD school, and her mother still does everything she can to help others.

The Texas Promise, a documentary produced in 2014 by Vanessa Roth, was filmed after the eighty-third Texas Legislature cut $5.4 billion from educational funding during the previous session. Nearly two-thirds of the public schools sued the state, and Texas lawmakers fought furiously over school funding. The film depicted the lawmakers' actions and the impact of these cuts on students and on the future of public education in Texas.

Vanessa called me and said she had been told Furr High School should be one of the schools featured in the film. She and her film crew spent days at Furr asking us about state funding for education in addition to issues related to charter schools, schools of choice, and high-stakes testing. Clearly, high-stakes testing had been a painful thorn in Furr's side.

On October 25, 2014, *The Texas Promise* was shown at the Austin Film Festival. I took a busload of students, parents, and staff to the event where we were treated as royalty.

CHAPTER 47
Restoration

For many years, I had been deeply concerned about police officers' general eagerness to quickly enforce zero tolerance policies and impose severe consequences for minor infractions. The consequences sometimes included jail time. "Such criminal charges may have been most prevalent in Texas," stated Deborah Fowler, the deputy director of Texas Appleseed, a nonprofit organization whose mission is to promote social and economic justice for all Texans. In 2013, the federal Departments of Justice and Education had proclaimed new guidelines against the harsh policies of zero tolerance. Secretary of Education, Arne Duncan stated, "The need to rethink and redesign school discipline practices is frankly overdue." This was music to my ears and to the ears of Officers Craig Davis and Danny Avalos, who had worked with me since 2008. We shared the same philosophy about discipline. They developed relationships with the students, and students with minor infractions were sent to the Principal's Court, where other students decided the consequences. This was especially true of Officer Davis, who worked with me for as long as I was principal and who is truly an exceptional human being. He showed great compassion toward our students, understood their backgrounds, and knew how to build rapport with them and get them to change their behavior. Unlike many police officers, he made every effort possible to settle problems at the school level and avoid the direct pipeline from high school to prison. He did not believe in zero tolerance.

In 2013, a reporter from the *New York Times* had visited the school to interview Officers Davis and Avalos and me about how we had built relationships with the students. Later the same year, reporters from Spain and France visited Furr to report on a similar story. They explained that their countries were experiencing harsh punishment by school police officers, just as in American schools. In 2014, the documentary Zero Tolerance was produced and directed by Sara Gibbings, and Furr was one of the schools featured throughout the film. The documentary is available to stream on Amazon Prime.

I began studying the use of restorative discipline as a way of handling student discipline in schools. Although I found little literature on the subject, I decided we could start our own restorative discipline program. I worked with several teachers and gained input from the staff about what might be included in our program.

We decided to begin with the classroom. Teachers would establish respect agreements for their own classroom based on student input in four categories of respect: teachers respecting students, students respecting teachers, students respecting each other, and all respecting property. When a problem could not be solved in the classroom, the student would be sent to a "Thinkery," where a mediator could work with the individual or individuals to restore the relationship. At the end of the mediation, each person involved chose a Habit of Mind to remember when faced with the same situation in the future. The teachers and staff received extensive training in the restorative discipline and all strove to be consistent in its use.

One day I saw a female student in the hallway near the Thinkery. "Baby, why are you here?" I asked. Her response surprised me.

"Miss, I was in the Thinkery with my boyfriend because we had a fight. When we restored our relationship, I chose the Habit of Mind 'Thinking about Thinking.' The more I thought about my thinking, I became so angry with him that I wanted to beat the hell out of him. So, I am going back to the Thinkery and learn more about the habit 'Learning to Manage Impulsivity.'"

On one occasion, a student was sent to me from the Thinkery. She was crying when she entered my office. I hugged her and asked what had happened.

"I cannot do my work, Miss, because all I can think about is my little cousin. My uncle lives in Mexico and owed a bunch of money to the drug cartel. When he couldn't pay the money, they kidnapped my eight-year-old cousin. My uncle finally paid them all he could, but that was only half of what he owed. The next morning when they opened the front door, the top half of my cousin's body was laying on the front porch. I just can't stand it." I held the girl as she whispered, "I just can't get that picture out of my mind. I don't even sleep at night."

I was overcome with empathy. I called the district, and a grief counselor was sent to the school to work with the student. I clearly understood why she could not concentrate in class.

The implementation of restorative discipline required extensive training and the restructuring of our discipline policy. Below are the questions teachers and the Thinkery mediator used as a part of the plan. We never gave up on students, and as a part of our continuity of care philosophy, we always found ways to leave the student with a deep and abiding sense of hope.

1. What happened?

2. What were you thinking or feeling at the time?

3. What have you thought about since?

4. Who has been affected by what happened?

5. How were they affected?

6. What do you think needs to happen to make things right?

When parents in the community had disagreements, they would call and schedule a time to meet in the Thinkery with Ms. Brown, the mediator. One day a local Presbyterian minister, Cassandra Dahnke, visited the Thinkery and was moved by the warm encouraging ambiance. She just stood there for a minute and then remarked, "This place has a spiritual feeling. There is no wonder relationships are restored here."

CHAPTER 48
Breaking Boundaries

I n March 2015, two students, Esmeralda Valdobinos and Romelius Pendleton; Instructional Technologist Brad Pearl; and I presented at the National ASCD Conference held in Houston. The title of our presentation was "Breaking Boundaries, Empowering Student Voice through Personalized Learning." The students who represented all the Link Learning pathways used film and technology to demonstrate how staff members at Furr identify students' passions and talents and how these strengths can be nurtured through cross-curricular teams of teachers using project-based instruction. The strategies gave students a voice and encouraged them to assume responsibility for seeking solutions to social issues. We discussed projects such as environmental justice, immigration and the Dream Act, banned books, and civility in the public square.

Bertie chatting with students.

Following our presentation, Namji Steinemann, director of the East-West Center's Asia Pacific education program, approached us. The center, which is based in Honolulu, was established in 1960 by the US Congress as a public diplomacy institution with the mandate to promote understanding and human relations between the peoples of America, Asia, and the Pacific through cooperative study, training, and research. Namji wanted to discuss the possibility of her visiting Furr. We were eager to have her visit.

Students showed her around the school the next day. She then asked me if I would be interested in partnering with the East-West Center. We quickly agreed to become partners and to make plans for a teacher and several of our students to join her and educators and students from a school in New York on a trip to Cambodia. They would work to bring fresh water to an elementary school in that country. Through our partnership with the East-West Center, we sent two groups of students to Cambodia and a group to Japan. These experiences provided rare learning opportunities for the students and teachers. The students told me they thought they were poor until they went to Cambodia.

Furr students in Cambodia.

On September 16, 2015, a tragedy occurred that knocked the wind out of our sails. I picked up the phone and heard the voice say, "I am calling from the HISD Transportation Department to tell you that there has been a terrible school bus accident involving several of your students. One student died at the scene, and several others have been taken to Memorial Hermann Hospital."

"Who was the student who died? And who was injured?" I frantically asked. "Oh, my goodness. Tell me!"

"I cannot release the names because the parents have not been notified. You can call the hospital, and they may be able to help you," was the reply. "I will get back to you as soon as possible."

I immediately called the hospital, identified myself, and requested the names and conditions of Furr students. I was told they could not release that information until next-of-kin were notified. I then obtained from the HISD bus barn the number of the bus involved and a list of the students riding that bus.

When the news finally arrived, I learned that Mariya Johnson and Janicia Chatman had not survived. One had died at the scene and the other at the hospital. Two other students, Brandon and Lekesia Williams, had been injured and admitted to the hospital. I knew all our students and was overcome with sorrow. Janicia was an outstanding Furr student, and the other three were in the REACH school. Mariya was new to REACH, and I knew the Williams siblings very well. They were all well-behaved and transferred to our school from the south area of the city.

I took some comfort from the fact that I was able to speak of each personally when I was asked to make the announcement on local television. I also visited each family to offer condolences, and we prepared a celebration of their lives, which was held in the school courtyard. Many of our students presented during the program, and artwork received from other schools in memory of those who lost their lives was presented to their parents. I visited the two students in the hospital and worked with them to catch them up on their lessons when they returned to school. I was saddened when I thought about the fact that all four of these students had chosen to come to Furr from the other side of Houston because they wanted to be involved in the activities at our school.

This tragedy overshadowed my feelings of appreciation when I received several awards later that year. I was especially proud of the Apple Legacy Trailblazer Award, which I received from the Iota Phi Lambda Sorority's Beta Pi Chapter. This award was given for "fifty-four years of dedicated service to the students, parents, teachers, school, staff and the entire city of Houston." I also received the Excellence in Leadership award from HISD. In retrospect, it is ironic that I received these awards just prior to a devastating blow that attempted to discredit my service.

The Possible Impossible

So we thought public education was really on the brink
And we thought we could make it better by giving high schools a rethink.
We would focus on the students by giving them more voice.
We would tap into their passions by giving them more choice.
We would personalize instruction so that each student would know
Exactly how he/she learns best and which strategies are needed to grow.
We would develop partnerships with business, colleges, and the city.
We would revamp our educational system to reduce all the nitty-gritty.
We would emphasize the skills needed for century twenty-one.
And work on real-world problems that are engaging and fun.
We would apply for the XQ grant, which appears out of our reach.
But we will improve our skills along the way as we all learn how to teach.
So here's to you, XQ, we will give it our best shot.
We will all be better for our attempt whether we actually receive it or not.

-Bertie Simmons
2016

CHAPTER 49
The Possible Impossible

"**D**oc, I think you might be interested in this." It was a text from an assistant principal, Marjorie Martinez, concerning a grant Lauren Powell Jobs was offering to ten schools to "rethink" high school. Each recipient would receive ten million dollars. Margie and I chatted about the possibility of applying and decided to present the idea to the entire faculty. They embraced the idea enthusiastically, and we submitted the name of Furr High School as a school that desired to participate in the process. I held a weekly, after-school staff meeting for anyone interested in this journey to learn and to give input.

This began in October 2015, with only ten staff members in the trailblazing group. XQ, the organization founded by Jobs and administering the grant, provided the planning team with learning modules to guide our thinking about the possibilities of rethinking high school. Gradually, others joined the planning team. Several students joined too and provided invaluable input.

The first step of planning was the discovery phase, which consisted of three modules focused on what today's high school students need to learn in order to be successful in the twenty-first century. We studied a module titled "The Science of Adolescent Learning," and we learned about the most recent research on learning in psychology and neuroscience. We asked numerous students to tell us about what and how they wanted to learn. What were students' dreams and aspirations? The planning team would study the modules during our weekly meeting and leave with assignments for deeper study. The goal was to learn what and how students wanted to learn, which was a question we had pursued for several years. The XQ activities reinforced what we had been doing and gave us hope that we were on the right track.

We spent the fall working through the modules and inviting others to join us. I paid each member of our team extra-duty pay for the time spent after their normal workday. We were always aware of those staff members who looked at us with skepticism about the value of this new endeavor.

After we completed each set of modules, we were required to respond to questions posed by XQ to define the ideas we were developing for a rethought high school. In January, we submitted the first phase of the application process and anxiously awaited to hear whether we would move to the next phase. We were shocked and thrilled that we were approved to continue to the second phase.

The second set of modules was called the design phase. It was during this time that we developed our vision of what the school would be. We defined the school mission and culture, teaching and learning, student agency and engagement, and school partnerships. Our Linked Learning pathways, project-based instruction, and numerous partnerships assisted in our design. During this phase, we also held Jeffersonian luncheons to gather input from community members, politicians, college and university instructors, and business and industry employees. We asked what they thought the school should be to meet the needs of students for the twenty-first century. As with the first phase, we ended the design phase by submitting our responses to XQ's questions relating to our design.

Again, we were approved to move on, this time to the development stage. In this stage, we focused on six areas related to the implementation of our design, giving specific information about each. These areas were talent and training, performance management and evaluation, use of time, space and technology, our financial model and sustainability, and governance. The goal was to paint a clear picture of what these aspects would look like when our vision was implemented.

We began to talk about the profile of an excellent teacher and created a new teacher selection process called "Escape the Interview." I had taken our entire staff to an Escape the Room event as a part of our team-building professional development. Without exception, everyone stated it was the most effective training we had ever had, and they had learned so much about each other. We decided to use this model for employee selection. Rather than being interviewed individually, applicants would participate in group activities designed to demonstrate their problem-solving, collaboration, leadership, and creative thinking. Tiphaine Shaw, one of the brightest staff members, designed these activities. Sebastian Obando, our technology genius, set up an observation station in another room where the selection team could observe the applicants using wireless internet cameras.

During the "interview," the selection team scored each participant on a rubric that included creativity, teamwork, leadership, persistence, attention to detail, and collaboration. The interviewees enjoyed the experiences, and the interviewers learned so much about the applicants. It was an informative, innovative way to interview prospective teachers and staff members.

Ms. Khan later told me about the experience: "I had just escaped my house and had driven farther than I had ever driven before and to an unknown part of Houston. I was afraid I would never find Furr High School. My former husband never wanted me to drive because he was from Pakistan where some men do not look favorably on women driving. Then I get to Furr, and you said we were to 'escape a room.' I thought, Just bring it on! But I loved the exercise and thought it was a good method for selecting teachers.'"

School went on as usual while we continued to work on our XQ proposal. I kept a close eye on student attendance and noticed that Harold, a sophomore, had missed several days and was not responding to phone calls. I decided to make a home visit, fully aware of the fact it was a rather dangerous area. When I arrived at the house, I was greeted by an angry pit bull. When I attempted to open the gate, he charged, barking loudly with streams of saliva dripping from his mouth. I loudly called to Harold, but there was no response. I continued to call until I heard a car coming to a screeching halt on the street behind me. I froze in terror. Do I stand here and take the shot in the back, or do I turn and let them shoot me in the front?

Suddenly, I heard a voice from the street yell, "Baby, you still out here trying to get kids to come back to school? Ain't you eighty-two years old?"

"Did I ask you how old I am?" I asked without turning around.

"Well," replied the voice. "I'm one you brought back. Now I gots me a job, I gots me a car, and I gots me a diploma. I just wanted to say thank you."

I turned to see one of my former students. I went to the car to talk with her and told her how proud I was of her. It was then I knew it was worth my many trips to students' homes to get them to return to school. Harold never responded to my attempted visit, but he did return to school the next day, and I discussed his absenteeism with him. He graduated.

One of our greatest honors occurred on April 16, 2016, when Furr was granted the International Habits of Mind Learning Community of Excellence Award. Our honored guests at the award presentation were Art Costa and Bena Kallick. It was a community event where we had invited special guests and district and community representatives. The award recognized the fact that Habits of Mind had become a way of life at Furr High School and all students could speak of them and practice them. The Habits of Mind had been painted on the walls of the campus and were an integral part of our restorative discipline. We were thrilled to be a recipient of the award, and the celebration marked another step toward our goal of bringing civility to the Furr campus and school community.

Three forces of nature: Dr. Bena Kallick, Margie Martinez, and Dr. Art Costa.

Our work on the XQ grant application continued throughout the spring semester. By May 2016, we had completed all the questions from the last module of the development phase and were certain we would submit the result of our hard work by the deadline. Much to our surprise, we were notified that there was one additional step that we would need to complete. We were to assemble a group of the planning team members to respond to a scenario. Once we received the scenario, we would be given four hours to develop, as a team, a plan of action that we would submit electronically. When we received the scenario on May 13, 2016, I walked into the library to meet the planning team. I was startled at the large number of individuals assembled after school to complete this challenge. This group included about fifteen students; my boss, Mario Marquez; and thirty-four staff members. While we worked in small groups to address the demands of the scenario, the Environmental Communications student film crew produced a short documentary about our process. They filmed, edited, and produced the finished product within the four hours we had been given. I was nervous that we would not be able to submit the film and our written response to the scenario by the deadline. When Sebastian hit the submit button, we had two minutes left. We all let out a huge sigh of relief. Then a week later, we submitted our plans based on our response to the scenario, and we waited!

We were asked by XQ to describe our feelings after submitting our final work. I responded that I felt as if I had given birth to a baby. Several days later, the film crew students produced a film of a baby shower that showed the planning team members celebrating and me holding an infant, the baby of one of our students, in my arms.

Lee Hirsch, an American documentary filmmaker from New York, and Leslie Norville, one of his assistants, had been contracted by XQ to make frequent visits to Furr to film activities, so it was not surprising when XQ alerted us that the film crew would be there on August 3, 2016, to film one of our planning sessions. The planning team assembled in the school cafeteria where the film crew was interviewing various teachers and students. Lee set up a laptop and said he wanted to show us some of the videos they had shot during the year. When the picture appeared on the screen, it was Laurene Powell Jobs and Russlynn Ali, chief executive officer of XQ, chatting with each other. They suddenly started talking to our planning team, telling us what they liked about our proposal.

At the end of their comments, they congratulated us on being one of the ten national winners of a ten-million-dollar grant to rethink high schools. We were shocked and thrilled. We grabbed each other, questioning whether this was really happening. We were blown away! Since we never thought we had a chance of winning, this was beyond belief. We finally calmed our emotions enough to thank them profusely. There were only twenty members (staff, teachers, and students) of the planning team there, and we were told we could not tell anyone about this until the "big reveal" in Washington, DC on September 12, 2016. We all promised to keep it a secret until that date, but I had real concerns that someone might spill the beans.

I cannot tell you how difficult it was to keep the secret during the preservice with staff in late August. Bena Kallick provided professional development on Habits of Mind, personalized instruction, and project-based instruction. We administered the Kirton Adaption-Innovation personality inventory as well as the Myers-Briggs Type Indicator inventory. We gave the staff voice and choice in carrying out the activities planned for two weeks of training. We were modeling the way we wanted them to continue to work with the students, the way they had been for several years. I am not aware that any member of the planning team divulged the secret that was clawing to escape from our promise of confidentiality.

Bertie, Adrian Sendejas, Dr. Bena Kallick, Sharon Koonce, David Salazar, and host Roland Martin at the XQ Reveal in Washington, DC.

On September 12, 2016, several planning team members flew to DC for the big reveal. During our visit, we received training from XQ staff for two days. This added more detail to our implementation plan for the XQ grant, which would take place in our new building, one that we had been planning for two years with input from the entire community. The new school would be named Furr Institute for Innovative Thinking. In Washington, DC, we were treated as royalty, and on the last day, the big reveal occurred on a nationally televised program. Each school was introduced by a celebrity. Roland Martin, a journalist and television commentator, introduced us. Roland was a graduate of Yates High School in Houston. He told about having been zoned to Furr when he entered high school but chose to attend Yates because of their School of Communication. Following the introductions, we were treated to a first-class celebration. Furr staff and faculty members learned on national television that we would become a part of the XQ family, one that we had never thought in our wildest dreams we would become a valued member.

Wisely, XQ would not place the funds in the HISD budget, and we were informed that we must identify a non-profit foundation to receive the grant and oversee its use according to the proposal we had submitted. We searched diligently and eventually selected the Greater Houston Community Foundation to receive the funds.

**Bertie,
the Rap Queen.**

On October 29, 2016, the XQ bus came to Furr to celebrate our receiving the XQ grant. Students and teachers showcased products and activities which had been created as part of our regular Genius Hour, a weekly period that allowed students to pursue their own passions and interests and encouraged creativity. XQ financed the cost of food trucks, which offered free food to the approximately two thousand guests, which included staff, parents, students, and community members. A special guest was Dr. Billy Reagan, the former

HISD superintendent, who thoroughly enjoyed and contributed to the event. Our film students interviewed Russlynn Ali, XQ chief executive officer, in our new film studio, which had been created by the Environmental Communication pathway students. Paula and my grandchildren, Brook and Austin, performed with the Joy band. We also had a mariachi band. It was a glorious day for all.

Shortly after the bus event, Furr received a site visit organized by Monica Martinez, our XQ school support representative. We had been informed we would have a special guest and we assumed it would be an XQ board member. We were all ecstatic when Laurene Powell Jobs and her two sons appeared. We simply fell in love with them. They visited classrooms, the STEAM lab, and the community garden which was maintained by our Place-Based Pathway students. They all were down-to-earth and seemed caring and interested in helping our students. I was especially impressed with Laurene, who seemed to be shy but deeply interested in our students.

Furr's staff celebrating success!

A Reckoning

I listened as they tore a dream castle down;
Some pseudo educators on the east side of town.
With a smirk and a sneer and the stroke of a pen,
They ripped out the heart and the hope within.

And I thought to myself, do these acts require skill
As that which was required as we struggled to build?
And a small voice inside me awoke and said,
"You know the answer in your heart and your head."

Jealousy, ignorance, shallow souls, and greed
Are absolutely all the traits they need.
They thrive on destruction, defamation, and shame
In their quest of fortune, attention, and fame.

They care nothing for students; they care nothing for change.
They care nothing for those caught in their firing range.
Their vision is limited to self and the dollar.
They float in the sewage of souls that are hollow.

I turned my head from the heartbreak and pain,
And vowed to build bridges in the days that remain.
I resolved to rise above their hate and their lies
And work to lift spirits from stygian depths to the skies.

I will live my life so the whole world will know
Helping less fortunate are seeds we should sow.
I will build with love, and I will build with care
So, the world is a better place because I was there.

-Bertie Simmons
2018

CHAPTER 50
Unexpectedly, the New Normal

I had been making presentations in various parts of the country and was experiencing more and more difficulty breathing. Thinking it was the result of medication I had been taking, my daughter spoke with a physician, who suggested I stop taking the medication. Still, I had great difficulty walking from my car into my office without stopping to rest.

Bertie with MC Hammer at an XQ conference.

We had thought we would be moving into the new building that had been designed with input from parents, students, and staff gathered in planning meetings over the previous two years. The expected move-in had been changed from May until July. We moved in August 7, 2017. The furniture had not been delivered, and the elevator did not work in the new three-story building. The workers from the moving company had to carry every stick of furniture up two or three flights of stairs to place it all in the correct locations.

Teachers were to report on August 14. We had two weeks of training planned but modified our plans to enable teachers to work in their classrooms for the first two days they were allowed on campus. Once the security system was operational, all doors could be locked, and staff members could re-enter the building if they left during the day, but we had not received the key cards that were to be passed out to the teachers. The security system was also not functioning so Officer Davis was required to spend the night in the building for security reasons.

Bertie in her office in the new school.

I had been assigned a new area superintendent, Jorge Arredondo, with whom I had never worked. When he visited the school, he always appeared to be playing a game of Gotcha. He rarely checked in with me. But I would hear reports that he was nosing around the building. Instead of assisting with the construction problems, which included security, he appeared to be seeking problems which he could blame on me. He often complained about the security system, which was out of my hands, but he never tried to help. Any time he was in the building, I had that strange feeling again, the one I had when my baby brother was born, the one I had when I met Dorothy when I was ten years old.

Several committees had worked since January to enable us to implement the XQ proposal in the areas of teacher selection, student government, mentoring and student support, professional development, and teacher evaluation in collaboration with the Houston Federation of Teachers. The new ninth-grade academy had been planning and attending XQ workshops with individuals from the Massachusetts Institute of Technology. Numerous other teachers had spent the summer working on units of study that would include elements from the XQ proposal. They were each paid extra-duty pay to complete the units to be implemented throughout the fall of the upcoming school year. Bena Kallick and Heidi Hayes Jacobs had assisted them during the year with their planning. They were both present again at the beginning of August and worked with the teachers in thinking about alternative use of space, unit planning, Habits of Mind, and personalization of instruction. During the first week of professional development, other optional sessions were offered on the socio-emotional needs of students and restorative discipline. These were conducted by Sharon Brown, Paula Fendley, and me.

Educators extraordinaire:
Dr. Heidi Hayes Jacobs and
Dr. Bena Kallick.

The following Tuesday, August 22, I was unable to get out of my car. Officer Davis came out to help me and insisted, "Doc, you need to go to the emergency room. You don't look like yourself, and you certainly don't act like yourself." Turning to my friend, Sharon Koonce, he continued, "Ms. Koonce, will you drive her to the emergency room? Doc, you need to take care of yourself. I love you."

I was sent from the emergency room to be checked immediately into the hospital, where I was told I had experienced heart failure and I had lost three pints of blood. I stayed in the hospital for five days while physicians ran test after test in search of cancer. On the fourth day, they had me swallow a camera, which discovered the culprit. I was told that as one ages, it is not unusual that blood vessels in the small intestine pull away from the intestinal wall and bleed. Mine had done just that, but they had healed. I was given three pints of blood over the five days I was there and went from the hospital to my daughter's home, where I stayed three days while Hurricane Harvey devastated the Gulf Coast. The entire school district closed, and I returned to school on September 5 when administrators were permitted to enter the building. Teachers reported to duty on September 8. Students returned on Monday, September 11.

While I was in the hospital, I heard nothing from my new boss, Jorge Arredondo or Debbie Crowe, my school support officer. Angela Borzon, who had worked with me for several years at Furr, visited me, as did one of my teachers who was ill and in the same hospital. When the teachers returned to school, several of them remarked that Arredondo and Crowe had spent the week snooping around and asking questions. Some said they were trying to get staff members to say something unkind about me. I was told that Arredondo held a faculty meeting where he implied that I would not be back and that I was suffering from cancer.

When the students returned, we learned that many of the transfer students did not have schedules because they had not been released from their former schools due to a problem in central administration. In addition, we had finalized the master schedule and the bell schedule in August after responding to teachers who requested that the Genius Hour class would be once a week and at the last period on Friday. After school began and we implemented the Friday Genius Hour, the coaches asked that it be moved to last period on Thursday because of conflicts with the athletic schedule. The change was made to accommodate their needs. As a result, the clerk would need to make changes to the schedules, and this must be done manually. We were told if it was not done correctly, the entire schedule would be "wiped out." The clerk clearly understood how to complete this change.

Hurricane Harvey had caused the students and many staff members great trauma. Many of their homes were flooded, and the neighborhood streets had become swirling oceans of water. Several students had called me to see if I could come to rescue them. Once I was permitted to enter the area, I was heartbroken to see all their belongings stacked out in front of their houses. Block after block revealed the struggle and loss. I contacted several agencies to obtain food, clothing, bedding, and cleaning supplies. Staff members assisted in organizing and distributing the donations. Several thousand people came to get the supplies, which had been generously donated.

On the evening of September 8, there was a nationally televised XQ Goes Live program, which was broadcast on ABC, NBC, CBS, and Fox News. Laurene Powell Jobs had purchased the airtime, and several of the XQ schools were featured. Tiphaine Shaw; Ms. Ochoa, a parent; her daughter Alice and her son Ray; and others attended the event in Los Angeles. We also held a viewing of the program in the auditorium of the new building, and I invited the superintendent, Dr. Carranza; Diana Davila, our school board member; my bosses, Jorge Arredondo, area superintendent, and Deborah Crowe, my school support officer; Juliet Stipeche, who represented Mayor Sylvester Turner's office; and Mario Marquez, my former boss. Parents, teachers, community members, and notable individuals were also invited. We registered well over two thousand attendees, and we had standing room only in the auditorium for the program.

We were amazed by the enthusiasm of so many people. Furr was no longer the dropout factory, the school that no one wanted to lead, teach in, or have their children attend. No, Furr had a large family of parents, community members, and partners who supported each other. For the parents and students who attended even though they were still struggling after Harvey, we made sure they were well fed and gave out clothing, food, and supplies. We also had a program, before the television broadcast, where Dr. Carranza, Juliet Stipeche, a student, and I spoke. Dr. Carranza sang a love song to me in his soaring tenor. When the XQ Goes Live program began, Furr was the first school featured, and they returned repeatedly to our school. We rather felt that we were stars!

Not everyone was celebrating with us. Diana Davila, our school board member, arrived late and rarely looked at the screen. She appeared to be texting on her phone. I noticed that Arredondo appeared to be doing the same thing. It was common knowledge that the two were great friends. I got that strange feeling again. I sensed that my days as Furr principal were limited and expressed my concern to my family after the program. I was also aware that Diana was fond of neither Juliet Stipeche nor me. She had defeated Juliet, whom we all loved, in the school board race. Juliet had also been very supportive of the school when she was on the board. I felt Diana Davila was the "music woman" who had come to town, and there was going to be trouble, trouble, trouble right here in Houston, Texas, RIGHT HERE! And it starts with C, and it rhymes with TRASH and it stands for CASH.

I had always made it a practice to arrive at school before daylight and sometimes stayed until after dark. One morning, I pulled into my parking space, and I could see from the streetlights that I was the only one in the lot. Before I could get out of my car, a big black pickup truck pulled in behind me, blocking me in the space. The driver opened the door of his truck, and the light came on inside it. I could clearly see in my mirror two men, both Hispanic with tattoos on their faces and necks. As they moved toward my car, one on each side, I froze, managed to lock my car and wanted to call my daughter to tell her what was happening. At that very moment, two cars drove into the parking lot, and I recognized them as teachers. The two men immediately turned and ran back to the truck and sped away. I was terrified and totally confused. I walked with the teachers into the school. Later in the day, two employees told me they had received calls from two different members of a newly formed adult gang. My loyal assistant principal Margie Martinez told me she knew some of them. One had called her and asked her to tell me not to come to school before daylight and not to leave after dark because the gang planned to kidnap me and hold me hostage until I turned over the ten million dollars we had received from XQ. I had appeared on television and radio shows and in numerous newspaper articles, and it was common knowledge that Furr had received the ten-million-dollar grant. As soon as I was told about the calls, I called my daughter and told her I had almost been kidnapped. She replied, "Mother, that would not be kidnapping. That would be 'granny napping.'" Her humor escaped me at the time.

Even as the school year began, we continued to struggle with the schedule and the lack of adequate furniture. Some teachers panicked and began to bring furniture from the old building over to the new building. Jorge Arredondo complained about the numerous boxes that had been delivered from the old building and were now stacked, unopened, in the makers' space room. Many of those boxes contained trash brought over by a teacher, Fredalina Pieri, who never threw anything away. We were unpacking boxes as quickly as possible

312

during the ongoing construction and regular school activities.

I had a growing distaste for Jorge Arredondo, and he was apparently not aware enough to know I knew of his intention to get rid of me and to get control of the ten million dollars. To add insult to attempted injury, I learned that one of my English teachers was boasting that she did not have to do anything I said because she was friends with Arredondo. She had taken one of the new tables, which had finally arrived, and was having the students paint the top black. She denied having done that until I showed her pictures that the students had posted on Facebook showing them painting the furniture.

I decided I was dealing with an element in society unknown to me. Jorge Arredondo's behavior was curious because I knew he had been told that I intended to retire at mid-term. I later learned that he also knew that many community members wanted my daughter to replace me when I left. Perhaps that bothered him and Diana Davila.

Toadstools

Toadstools
have always fascinated me.
The way they spring up overnight
and stand as a phalanx of soldiers
holding dew-sprinkled flags of surrender.
As a child I longed to touch them somehow
feeling that in so
doing I could
capture the secret
of their essence.
I was warned that
their looks were
deceiving and that it
was difficult to tell
the harmless from
the deadly.
I think I have just touched a deadly toadstool!

-Bertie Simmons
1988

CHAPTER 51
The Beginning of the End

Officer Davis and my hard-working assistant principal Margie Martinez came to me concerned that our new ninth-grade students were flashing gang signs and tagging. They were also wearing gang colors. We had not enforced our dress code because Dr. Carranza had informed principals that schools would not adhere to dress codes because of hardships caused by Harvey. I checked with other principals, and several of them informed me they had imposed the dress code despite the district's pronouncement. So, I purchased uniforms for all students and made an announcement that by September 29, every student must be in dress code.

I called Arredondo and informed him about my decision. He said I was in violation of the superintendent's directive and was prohibited from doing it. I named the other schools that were enforcing the dress code and the fact that we were beginning to see gang activity at Furr. When he insisted that I must follow what Dr. Carranza had ordered, I asked to speak directly with Dr. Carranza. Why would Furr be the only school prevented from enforcing a dress code? I told him that I had evidence of other schools' decision to require the dress code. I had copies of the communications that these other schools had sent out to parents and posted on their website. He refused to let me talk to the superintendent. I explained that if I did not enforce the dress code, he and Carranza would have to deal with the gangsters. I had been at Furr when assemblies and after-school activities were impossible because of gang warfare. Perhaps Carranza and Arredondo did not know how effective we had been in controlling violence on campus. Perhaps they did not know that during the previous year, five Furr students had been killed during off-campus gang conflicts, but we still had maintained a safe campus with very few disruptions. Jorge Arredondo had not supervised Furr at that time, and he was clueless about previous gang activity on our campus.

When a group of students came to school out of dress code, I made an announcement over the intercom: anyone out of dress code should come meet me in the gym, and I would bring my bat to work them over. This had been a running joke in the school for about fourteen years and had been a way I built rapport with the students. Everyone knew the joke. The joke turned out to be on me. One of my employees taped the announcement and gave it to some students, along with Arredondo's and Dr. Carranza's phone numbers. She told the students to send a message to Arredondo and Dr. Carranza saying they were afraid because they were undocumented.

I met the students in the gym. I did not have the bat but told them they were to be in dress code in the future or be sent to the Thinkery or be issued a ticket to Principal's Court.

The bat had been given to me by Margie Martinez and was inscribed with some of my saying, such as "Don't make me take my earrings off" and "Are you cray cray?" She had also included on the bat several inspirational quotes that I often used with students and staff: "Hold fast to your dreams!" and "I am determined that ALL kids are going to have a chance." I was eighty-three years old and five feet two inches tall. I could hardly lift the bat.

Late that afternoon, I was about to leave for home when a stranger tapped on my car window. When I rolled the window down, she said to me, "I want you to know I am doing this with a lot of respect for you. Dr. Arredondo asked me to deliver this to you."

I took the letter that placed me on administrative leave pending the outcome of an investigation into my threatening students with a bat. I asked why Debbie Crowe, my school support officer, had not informed me. I then asked to return to my office so that I could speak with Mrs. Crowe. The stranger accompanied me to my office where I learned from Mrs. Crowe that she knew nothing about this. She had stayed home that day with an ill child.

I left and decided I needed an attorney since I felt that my rights had been violated. I contacted Scott Newar, attorney for employment law and civil rights, explained my situation and asked if he would take my cases. He readily agreed. Other principals had required dress codes, and no punitive action had been taken against them. The old bat joke was just that, a joke that I had used for years. All my other effective bosses had known of it and understood the importance of establishing rapport with the students by joking and using language that made sense to them.

It had also been rumored in the East End for some time that Diana Davila had been saying that the predominately Hispanic areas had too many white administrators. She had already removed one principal, and I knew she intended me to be the second. Later during the ensuing investigation, I received a copy of an email, dated October 16, 2017, in which Diana Davila stated to one of our parents, "Let's pray all is cleared and that we can move forward with a stronger academic focus so that Furr can be a nationally recognized school—not for its leader, but the student academic gains." My lawsuit also uncovered credible evidence that confirmed the fact that she had publicly stated that we had too many white administrators in HISD. This statement was documented in affidavits by participants at a fund-raiser that Diana Davila ostensibly held for her "mariachi band" in one of her schools. A select group of individuals, including Jorge Arredondo, were charged five hundred dollars to attend the event.

My mind drifted back in time more than twenty-five years before. I had been removed from the superintendent position of District VIII by a Hispanic school board member because I refused to place one of her friends into a principalship. I had always fought for equity for all people, and I had finally realized I was being discriminated against because of race and age.

In early October, I received a call from HISD's Human Resource Department to come in to be interviewed concerning my threatening the students with a bat. I was eager to attend the meeting. My attorney was not able to accompany me, so I went alone. Investigator Kaneetra Bass questioned me concerning the threat. I explained that the bat had been an ongoing joke. The students all knew it was a joke. I had often used it to build rapport with them. And while I did threaten them with a bat if they did not adhere to the dress code, I also threatened that they would be sent to the Thinkery or be issued a ticket to the Principal's Court. I told her that I believed in honesty and integrity, and if I had done anything wrong, I would admit it.

A week later, my exceptional attorney, Scott Newar, accompanied me to a meeting at central administration. There, Arredondo stumbled through reading a memo that stated I would be written up for threatening students with a bat. He said that the district had been made aware of other problems at Furr, so I was being relieved of duty indefinitely, pending the outcome of the investigation. I was fully aware of what those "other problems" were: Ms. Vivian Smith, Furr's union representative, had submitted twenty-four problems to the Houston Federation of Teachers in 2017. The complaints had been investigated by Zeph Capo, president of the Houston Federation of Teachers, and no evidence was found to support them. I wrote a letter at that time to the entire faculty responding to each of the allegations. I ended the letter by stating, "In the spirit of restorative justice, if I have not responded to your problems in this open letter, please come to see me personally so we could talk." No one ever came to see me. I later learned that Ms. Smith was still angry because I had removed her as attendance clerk and assigned her to another position.

Scott Newar stated during the meeting with Arredondo and his attorney that if I were not reinstated by the following week, we would be filing a lawsuit. HISD did not reinstate me. I was assigned to my home and paid my full salary while the district attempted to complete the investigation of my "wrongdoings." I would remain there for over eleven months.

The following week, Sharon Koonce, was notified her services were no longer needed. She had volunteered to lead the XQ applications process and after we received the grant, she was hired on a part-time basis to manage its implementation. Officer Davis was stripped of his officer badge and all official credentials. He was assigned to drive cars for other HISD officers. Sebastian Obando, a non-certified staff member was removed from his postion for sponsoring a extra-curricular media program that fell under the supervision of the pathway lead and superior teacher, Assol Kavtorina. He was assigned to a cubicle in the HISD warehouse. These remarkable individuals who had changed the lives of many students at Furr were all ousted with me.

When I was not returned to my position, my attorney called a press conference, and we announced the filing of a federal lawsuit against HISD claiming age and race discrimination. I was swamped with media requests. I could not respond to their overwhelming volume.

The Monday after the Friday I was removed, Arredondo called the Greater Houston Community Foundation asking questions he apparently hoped would prove misappropriation of funds. As the investigation proceeded, all allegations regarding the use of the XQ funds were quickly dropped from HISD's correspondence with me. All expenditures charged to the grant were documented according to the grant guidelines. An individual from HISD's central administration office called XQ concerning the funds. I was told they wanted to move the funds into a budget in the HISD. I later read communication describing how Anitra Piper in the grant office was concerned we had not worked with her to obtain the grant. In times past, we had worked with her and she had taken a sizeable percentage of the money after doing very little of the work required to enable one to receive the grant. This had been done when the district had moved to a "fee for service" policy. Several of the central office departments charged schools for their services since they were required to sustain their own departments at that time. This policy was even true of donations made to the school, even those that I made. Also, this was a different type grant that was solely intended to be given to a school.

Dr. Grenita Lathan appointed Rosa Hernandez as the interim principal at Furr High School. I was told by some of the teachers that Mrs. Hernandez informed the staff she had been sent to Furr to clean up the mess. It appeared that she had been directed to do so by Lathan. Neither she nor Lathan knew me, I did not know them, and neither had ever been to Furr.

Approximately two weeks after my removal, students and parents staged a walkout at Furr. They were hoisting signs that read Bring Bertie Back! Lisa Falkenberg wrote in the *Houston Chronicle*, "They included students from the predominately low-income campus—freshmen and seniors, marching band members from Spanish-speaking homes and athletes with dreadlocks." The protesters also included an activist with the Nation of Islam, elderly ladies from the community—and, interestingly, the students who had made the initial complaints to my bosses about the bat threat. They told Falkenberg that they had not intended anything bad to happen to me. One of the students, Yulisa Cabrera, said I was stubborn but that was what made me special.

Falkenberg's article stated that many of the students praised me for coming out of retirement seventeen years ago to turn around Furr, once known for gangs and dropouts. Yulisa said I had completely changed her life, that she went from not wanting to go to school to planning to go to college.

Johnathan Camacho, a seventeen-year-old senior, said that he was upset about no longer having Genius Hour, where he would be teaching philosophy. He said students had been able to learn nearly anything, from cooking to 3-D printing. Others were upset over the loss of the Principal's Court, with hearings and sentences by their peers, and the Thinkery, where relationships were restored.

Jordan Davis had staged the walkout. Falkenberg reported that he said he was staying out here to stand up for a principal who inspired him to do better in school and at one point even reached into her own pocket to pay for a motel room when his family didn't have a place to stay.

Ann Estes, a community member, told Falkenberg how it was once too dangerous to walk in the neighborhood because of gangs and that property values had plummeted as a result. She described how much things had changed, with students stopping to hug her when they saw her walking.

"For me personally, this is heartbreaking because I love Bertie Simmons," Dr. Carranza told Falkenberg. "Our intent is to clear her name and get her back." Falkenberg stated that Dr. Carranza seemed genuine when he insisted on a fair, prompt investigation. I believe that is what he wanted, but the same individuals who were after me were after him.

We had all been instructed that we could not speak with staff, students, or parents at Furr. Any attempt we made to do so would be reported to the interim principal, Rosa Hernandez. Scott, my attorney, went back to court and that decision was overturned.

In late October, I received a call from an extremely upset parent. The parent told me that a clerk who was a friend of Arredondo's had called the parent's daughter into the school office and asked her to provide written documentation of something condemnable about me. When her daughter said she did not know of anything, she was told to just make something up and write it. Her daughter had refused and was treated badly.

More and more of the talented staff members who were supportive of me and participated in the writing of the XQ grant were being eliminated. Margie Martinez was removed with unclear cause and assigned to Ryan, then the HISD's professional development center. Her clerk, Eva Olivares, was accused of changing grades on Ms. Martinez's computer when she was out of her office. The investigators were unaware that neither of them had access to grades on the computer. Olivares was also accused of selling drugs to students. She, too, was assigned to the warehouse, a suspiciously absurd punishment. Had Olivares in fact been selling drugs, she would have been breaking the law and should have been arrested.

Margie Martinez had been a loyal employee at Furr for many years. As the school's basketball coach, she built a strong rapport with students. That rapport continued when she was promoted to assistant principal. In this position, she worked closely with district personnel from the central office to establish attendance and grading guidelines. Ms. Martinez was one of the hardest working individuals on the campus. She was the go-to person when a job needed to be done, and the job would be done efficiently and in keeping with HISD guidelines. She worked with students in making up no-grades, a term used on report cards to indicate when students passed a course but had excessive absences. She developed contracts, signed by teachers and students, that detailed how the students would make up the time missed. Texas Education Agency guidelines state specifically that the time was not required to be made up in a classroom setting, and the hours were not required to equal the exact number of absences. I do not believe that the individuals who conducted the investigation were aware of this fact. Ms. Martinez was involved from the beginning of the development of the XQ proposal and was one of the most faithful participants of the planning committee. She retired at the end of the school year, but I believe that she has an abundance of energy and drive and would make an excellent assistant principal for a school in another district.

Eva Olivares, her clerk, was one of the most dedicated, capable individuals I have ever known. It is mind-boggling that she would be accused of selling drugs and of changing attendance when she did not have access to attendance records. This was yet another indication of the ignorance of those investigators who also found that I had signed off on changes to grades after I had been removed from the school. The HISD's acceptance of the charge only demonstrated their own ignorance and corrupt intentions. Olivares sat in the warehouse all year, with no purpose, and became more and more distraught. She was never found guilty of any wrongdoing, but she was so disgusted with the district that she resigned in June. She now is employed by the City of Houston, doing manual labor to support her family. Another loss to the district.

Next came Mrs. Samuel, the registrar. She had been employed by the district over forty years, had always had excellent district audits, and had trained many new registrars in HISD. It was unclear what her wrongdoings were, but she was treated with disrespect when she was walked off campus and assigned to the warehouse for the remainder of the school year. At the end of the year, she retired due to illness in the family.

We had submitted the 2017–2018 School Improvement Plan, in which Furr had received a waiver from HISD to allow us to embed health into the physical education curriculum and to teach the TEKS for both courses simultaneously during the physical education classes. This meant adding an additional class period as a placeholder for the health grade. HISD actually sent individuals out to walk the building looking for students in the eighth period. Since they found none, all counselors were removed and assigned to the warehouse. This included Tiphaine Shaw, Katherine Augustine, and Andrew Horne. None of the three were guilty of any violations of board policy. This also showed how little central administration knew about the waiver we had received and the use of embedded classes.

Mrs. Hernandez was critical of the way Ms. Dianna Littlejohn, chair of the special education department, and Mrs. Deborah Ross, teacher assistant, performed their duties and she made disparaging remarks about them in the presence of other employees. Ms. Littlejohn and Mrs. Ross both retired at midterm. They told me they had been treated with great disrespect by Rosa Hernandez.

Then there was Seema Dwivedi who was in the newly formed ninth-grade academy and held a doctorate in biochemistry. She had completed the work in the Alternative Certification Program (ACP) to receive her Texas teachers' certificate. When Rosa Hernandez received the notification, which required her approval, she refused to sign it, stating to Dr. Dwivedi that she was not an effective teacher.

When I heard of this and that she had paid a sizeable amount of money to the ACP and earned excellent grades in her classes, I told her that I would sign the document. After considerable back-and-forth with the university, they agreed, and she received the certificate. Mrs. Hernandez called her in for a conference for the record, which meant she was making a recommendation for termination. Dr. Dwivedi resigned. One more brilliant, caring teacher from another country gone.

Then came Mrs. Nishtha Pant, Mrs. Mirela Khan, and Mrs. Niloufer Jivan. All three staff members were from countries outside of the United States. It was interesting that all three were eventually removed since they were among the best teachers in the HISD.

Mrs. Pant had worked with me for years and had been named outstanding science teacher in the county. I had promoted her to dean of instruction at Furr, and she was doing amazing work in that role with the teachers, who adored her. She was called in and given a short period of time to find another job, which she did. She is presently teaching science in a middle school in HISD.

Mrs. Khan was a new teacher. When I visited her room a few weeks after she had begun teaching in September, I was excited about the way she was able to engage the students and the rapport she had developed with them in a short period of time. She told me she went to see Rosa Hernandez about taking her students on several very interesting field trips. Mrs. Hernandez prohibited her from taking her students on field trips and told her that she was unhappy with her teaching. An assistant principal was sent to visit her class. During the observation, a young man became upset when he made a mistake while working a problem on the board and blurted out the f-word. In the meeting that followed, Mrs. Khan explained that she had dealt with the problem after class. Mrs. Hernandez handed her a resignation form and told her she had two options, which Mrs. Khan interpreted to mean that she could either resign or be harassed. She signed the resignation form, returned to her classroom, and asked the students to assist her in packing her belongings and taking them to her car. Some of the students were crying. Mrs. Khan held a degree in geophysics and was working on her Texas teachers' certification, for which she had paid a significant amount of money. With her resignation, she lost the opportunity to be certified in Texas and the money she had paid.

Mrs. Khan called me to tell me she had taken two jobs, each paying minimum wage. She was divorced with four children and was at risk of having her electricity disconnected and possibly being evicted from her home. I offered to pay her electric bill. She replied, "I am from Romania, and we are taught to find ways to earn our own way. Thank you." She is now working three jobs and seeking a position at a university. The district lost a brilliant, caring individual.

Mrs. Jivan came to my house and expressed her frustration about the way Rosa Hernandez had treated her. She had returned to Furr after having taught science for several years at The High School for Health Professions magnet school. She was seeking a transfer from Furr, but each time Mrs. Hernandez was called by a prospective school, she would give Mrs. Jivan a negative reference. She asked if there was any way I could help her. I did call a principal in a school outside the HISD. Mrs. Jivan was offered a job, and the HISD lost an incredible teacher.

The dynamic duo: Tiphaine Shaw and Bertie.

Tiphaine Shaw was a highly intelligent, creative individual who had been pivotal to the XQ proposal and innovative changes at Furr. She and I did not always agree, but I had nothing but great respect and admiration for her work. She was suffering from jail fever every time I spoke with her during her confinement in the warehouse. This broke my heart. After spending an entire year in the warehouse, she was exonerated and reassigned to an elementary school as a counselor. Mr. Horne, a fellow counselor confined to the warehouse, was assigned to a middle school.

This unfair and unprofessional treatment of some of HISD's most effective staff members tore at my heartstrings until they became frayed. I had difficulty sleeping and could not wrap my mind around the purpose of destroying a school and the major players who had brought about positive change.

I was concerned about all those who had been banished. The warehouse was known as a "teacher jail," and yet none of the employees at Furr had been proven guilty of any wrongdoing. This went on for a full school year. They were all receiving their salary while others had been hired to replace them. What a waste of funds and an indication of poor management and greed when the district was in dire financial need.

These are the kinds of actions that could lead individuals to commit desperate acts. I am ashamed of the HISD's actions and am embarrassed that I worked for a district that proved to be heartless, uninformed, corrupt and backward. It is no wonder Dr. Carranza left when he did.

Jorge L. Arredondo @Drjlarredondo · 30 Oct 2017
@HoustonISD @FurrHS **Great parent meeting today to empower parents** as "owners" of their school of innovative thinking! @HISD_Supe – at Furr Highschool

Is this what they wanted?

CHAPTER 52
The Final Blow

After only 564 days as superintendent, Dr. Richard Carranza left HISD. He assumed the position of chancellor of schools in New York City, to everyone's surprise. Even school board members were taken aback at his sudden departure. In an interview after his departure, Dr. Carranza stated that the HISD was simply not ready for innovation. I had a great deal of respect for him and liked him as a person and as a leader.

I recalled the day when he had visited Furr and we went into our Thinkery. When I explained how the Thinkery worked, he remarked that he needed to bring his school board members there. Then he said jokingly, "But what do I know? I am just a wetback." We were laughing as we entered the front office, and I introduced him to my secretary, Diana Marroquin, and said he had called himself a "wetback." Diana told students and teachers I had called the superintendent a "wetback" and wrote it in the statement she gave to the auditors during the eight-month investigation. Confusingly, her statement also mentioned that I was "hell to work with," even though she had previously also told many people I was like her mother and that she did not know what she would do if anything ever happened to me. At least she had a chance to speak with the investigators, an opportunity that was never afforded to me during or after the investigation of the other concerns as reported by Vivian Smith. I was shocked that I was never interviewed. I was never afforded a semblance of due process after fifty-eight years of service.

The departure of Dr. Carranza necessitated the selection of a new superintendent. At the HISD school board meeting on March 22, 2018, the board voted to name Dr. Grenita Lathan as the interim superintendent. She assumed the role on April 1, 2018, April Fool's Day. All hell broke out as tensions mounted in the community and among board members. Was this an April Fool joke?

Fredalina Pieri, a disgruntled employee and an individual who had given me cause to distrust her, became a teacher assessor and Mrs. Hernandez's chief ally. She went to Ms. Kavtorina and told her Mrs. Hernandez wanted her to replace my image from the XQ Goes Live film with footage of Mrs. Hernandez. Ms. K. told her that was illegal because the film was copyrighted. Later, when Ms. K. returned to her room, her furniture had been removed. She was pressured all year, and at the end of the year, Mrs. Hernandez sent an email to the Furr staff stating that Ms. K. would no longer be teaching the Houston Community College dual-credit film classes at Furr. She was being replaced by Juan Elizondo, a novice film teacher. Ms. K. resigned and took a job at MD Anderson Cancer Clinic.

This was a huge loss to the district. Her talent and ability had given Furr High School an award-winning film program. In the following statement, she tells the story of her experiences at Furr after I was removed. I am disturbed by her present feelings about our country and democracy and feel compelled to do something to change her perceptions since she came to America from Russia in search of hope.

> After Dr. Simmons was removed from the Furr campus, HISD investigators started interrogating faculty and staff. I was called in to be interrogated by investigators, and I was shocked by the way they spoke to me. There were two investigators in the room with me, and they were cross-interrogating me for two and a half hours. They kept asking the same three questions over and over again. The questions were the following:
>
> •Did Dr. Simmons make you change grades?
>
> •Did she make jokes that were offensive to you?
>
> •What did people say about her behind her back?
>
> They were very persistent to get the answers they wanted. They were rude and pushy. They were implying that if I wouldn't cooperate with them, I would get into trouble. They mentioned that Mr. Elizondo took them into the studio storage and told

them that some cameras were missing. They tried to accuse me of this. I felt like I was being interrogated by the Gestapo or KGB. My blood pressure went so high that I was throwing up in my car on my way home.

The atmosphere of terror and witch hunt was established at Furr by HISD after Dr. Simmons was removed. HISD officials came to our pathway meetings and told us that we could not discuss with students what had happened, and that we couldn't post anything on our social media accounts either. For the whole school year, we lived under the threat of being fired.

People were disappearing from campus every day, and nobody explained to us what was happening to these people. They were not allowed to talk to us.

I felt as if I were back in the thirties of the 20th century somewhere in Hitler's Germany or in Stalin's Russia. They ruled the school with threats and fear. They knew very well that all of us, being enslaved by our mortgages and car payments, couldn't raise our voices to defend anybody and to stand for the right cause.

The atmosphere of brown racism was established at Furr campus. Principal Hernandez, as well as her gang, were accusing black students of all the discipline problems. They were harassing teachers who were not Hispanic, too. People who were not qualified to appraise teachers were put as appraisers and were making threats during the conferences.

I left Furr. I have mixed feelings about this time in my career. I miss teaching. I miss my students and my coworkers. But now I work in a safe place. Furr High School was ruined completely. A lot of people's lives and careers were ruined completely.

I don't believe in democracy or justice in the United States anymore. There is a dictatorship of stupidity and incompetency at HISD going on now, or maybe not just at HISD, but in the whole country because

NOBODY was able to stop HISD officials from their actions. They destroyed a wonderful school and many people. What a shame!

Later I learned that Ms. K. was diagnosed with post-traumatic stress disorder as a result of the oppression she had experienced at Furr under the leadership of Rosa Hernandez. She was told by a psychologist that she was not the only one from Furr with the same problem.

Karen Taylor, my friend and neighbor, had previously sent the *Houston Chronicle* information concerning the oppression of students and teachers at Furr and requested that they investigate. She had even included the names of people who were willing to speak to them. The *Chronicle* took no action. When Karen read Ms. K.'s statement, she was furious. She immediately sent the *Chronicle* a new message, which ended, "This tragedy is on your shoulders. The *Washington Post* is right. Democracy does die in darkness, and the *Chronicle* made it even darker by staying silent while evil triumphed."

One by one, Mrs. Hernandez closed every program we had written into the XQ grant. The Newcomers' Center, where we had planned to teach our limited English-speaking students using the Accelerated Integrated Method, was closed. We had sent teachers to Canada to be trained in that method, but this was now a wasted investment. The neighborhood clinic that we had planned was also closed. The restorative discipline system was abolished, and students began to be suspended and expelled. I was told she said in a faculty meeting, "I am taking this school back from the students." Student voice and choice were gone.

Competency-based and personalized instruction were also dropped, and the integrity of the ninth-grade academy was destroyed. I wondered how she expected to continue to receive the funds without implementing the plan that had won Furr the grant. She and her select group did participate in XQ meetings out of state. I was told she and Pieri had planned a vacation to New Zealand in late spring using XQ funds, but that was not approved by the district. Stories concerning Hernandez's unprofessional behavior flooded the school and spilled over into the school community.

While this chaos was transpiring, my attorney, Scott Newar was in court requesting the district provide us with the evidence found in their investigation. He was also attempting to establish a date for the depositions he was requesting. Davila and Arredondo were never available. It appeared we were going to be denied access to any comprehensive evidence concerning my wrongdoings because of "attorney-client privilege." I had become aware they were accusing me of changing grades and attendance, neither of which I had done, but I never knew what evidence they had other than a grade-change form where someone had signed my name and dated it after I had been removed.

On May 14, 2018, a conference for the record was held for me. Present were Arredondo; his attorney; my attorney, Scott Newar; and I. I was told that I was being recommended for termination from the HISD for a series of allegations that I knew were false. Arredondo stated during the meeting that the district no longer had confidence in my ability to act as principal. I thought that statement sounded a bit like age discrimination, even though I had been restored to excellent health.

Scott requested a copy of the memo that Arredondo read to us. His attorney denied us that right, again citing "attorney-client privilege." I had always given to the employee a copy of the memorandum of record when I held a conference for the record. I simply smiled confidently and left, knowing the charges were unfounded, and realizing the ineptness of the HISD.

I found one of the charges amusing. I had been accused of requiring that teachers not give a grade below fifty, regardless of student performance or completion of assigned tasks. I have always believed in and fought for equity. I believe that in grading students we should make every effort to ensure the completion of assigned tasks, even in the case of homework when students work all night, as many of ours did. I had invited Douglas Reeves, founder of Creative Leadership Solutions, a nonprofit organization created to improve education opportunities for students, to Furr to work with the staff on grading. When I arrived at Furr, teachers were giving zeros to students who had not completed homework. When Dr. Reeves met with us, we learned of the negative impact a zero had on a student and that student's chance of passing the course. When there was no hope, there was no effort. Zeros further damaged our broken-winged birds.

They resulted in deferred dreams and ultimately explosions all over the campus. Over time, we participated in studies on the purpose and value of homework. My purpose here is not to debate the issues but rather to point out the depths of our training and how it influenced our thinking and beliefs. Teachers were never directed not to give a grade below fifty. They were, however, directed to inspire students to want to complete assignments and to succeed academically. That was one of the reasons we built the concepts of competency-based education and personalized learning into our XQ grant and intended to make them pillars of our school philosophy. It is interesting to note that, in the end, the HISD reworded this charge, claiming instead that I "created a climate" rather than "directed teachers" not to give a grade below fifty. Of course, this assumes that such a climate is undesirable, which I do not believe, and it shows the ignorance of the HISD.

Immediately after I was removed, one of the new employees hired by Hernandez went into the online master and bell schedules and attempted to change them. That was when, just as I had feared and we had warned, the entire schedule disappeared. One of the things the district accused me of was not being able to build a schedule. When I was removed, a total schedule was in place and students had been scheduled into the classes. We had spent months building the schedule that would be aligned to our XQ vision.

I had always had bright, knowledgeable, involved, and supportive superiors who spent a great deal of time at the school. There was Thelma Garza, Sam Sarabia, Natalie Blasingame, Dino Coronado, and Mario Marquez. Both Dino Coronado and Mario Marquez were deeply involved with the development of the proposal for the XQ grant. Sadly, Arredondo's actions never reflected the characteristics of these capable and supportive leaders.

Dr. Grenita Lathan was chief academic officer of HISD at the time I was removed. She was fully aware of actions taken at Furr during that time and after she was named interim superintendent. Rosa Hernandez thanked Dr. Lathan during a school board meeting for sending her to Furr as the interim principal. Could I take this act as evidence of Dr. Lathan's complicity in all the actions taken by Hernandez at Furr? I had met Dr. Lathan only once, and she had never visited Furr High School. She had also never spoken to me concerning the happenings at the school. Again, she appeared to not be interested in knowing me, and therefore, I never knew her. What I did know was that Dr. Lathan was being recommended for termination in Peoria, where she had served as superintendent. I also knew that she resigned from Peoria just before she was scheduled to be terminated and that the parents and communities of the Peoria Public School #150 and the citizens of Peoria had declared a declaration of no confidence in her leadership for several reasons. They indicated that her tenure had been marked by unprecedented turmoil and confusion within the district. It is interesting to note that the same occurred after she became the interim superintendent in Houston.

I watched the board meeting on June 14, 2018, when the board approved Dr. Lathan's recommendation for my termination with the HISD. The following day, the local news reported that I had been terminated for changing grades and attendance. I had done neither and knew I could prove it in court.

I assumed I was terminated so I began gathering my data, which I planned to use in court to prove my innocence. Among this was a stack of report cards from the end of the previous year, which I had received from an employee to review. Since the district prohibited me from taking any records when I was removed, I was fortunate that I had these available to me. Numerous report cards reflected grades below fifty, and I thought how easy it would have been for the investigators to check the report cards before issuing a false report. I had other records that could easily have disproven charges of grade and attendance changes. It appeared that the investigators apparently took the words of disgruntled employees who were eager to find fault and report it.

A little more than a month later, I received a letter from Dr. Lathan informing me that the district would be sending a recommendation for my termination to the board. We had a limited number of days for me to appeal this recommendation to the Texas Education Agency, which I did immediately. Scott handled all the legal actions involved in the appeal and the pending lawsuit. I had full confidence in him and his ability. He reported actions taken to me, and I always felt I would be ready for the September trial. Many employees from Furr and other schools had called, requesting to testify on my behalf. Students and parents did the same. Many also posted statements on Facebook, hoping to help clear my name.

Joel Romo, a former student:

Ladies and gentlemen,

I want everyone to know my story of Dr. Simmons and me. I grew up in the East side of Houston, Texas, in a barrio called El Dorado. I was young at the time. I was 16 wanting to know all in life. It was rough measures when life took its toll on me. Drugs were my escape. Drugs were my source of income, but it was a hard job receiving all kinds of calls at night. That was the only way I could make money and make ends meet. So, I decide to drop out of school and go full time selling drugs, even though I realized education was what I needed in this world. Boy, I was crazy and dumb. All my homies that hung around me were getting locked up or else going to the military, so I was being alone in this game. The thing that hurt me most was what it did to my grandma. She was my protector; she was my best friend. She kicked me out because I wanted to deal drugs, so I had to be on my own and think no education and only think of dealing drugs. Then a couple of years later my grandma suffered 14 strokes, not all at once, but she was in the hospital. It tore me up so bad that my heart collapsed. That day I prayed, "Father, take me instead. I will change, but don't take her."

So, when I came back to school, Dr. Simmons said, "Joel, I have faith in you. Dreams are for you to believe, Joel, and your grandma was a good friend of mine."

My grandma had been an active lead mother for the PTA at J. W. Oates. I was like, "I can't do this." But I'm proud to say my journey through life was positive. I left drugs; I left the gang life. On the day I graduated, I kneeled to my grandma. "I love you and miss you. This is for you."

I was 21 when I graduated but thanks to the courage and dedication of you, Dr. Bertie Simmons, you made this possible. I love you with all my heart and I'm writing my poetry book as we speak. Also, thanks for making me the writer I am today. Dr. Simmons it's you that had faith long ago in me.

Karen Banda's mother (translated from Spanish):

> In more than one occasion you dried the tears of my daughter and changed them into smiles. You, Dr. Simmons proved to be an excellent tutor. It was like a substitute mother. You gave that unconditional love to each of your pupils. For my daughter you are the maternal granny she can't get to know. You deserve our most sincere admiration, love and will always be reflected in our memory. All your sacrifice is written in our history. Thank you for your unconditional help to my daughter.

Mattie Adeleja, a teacher:

> Dr. Bertie Simmons, you make the world a better place for the good of all people. God still has greater things for you and others to do. I love you and I am ready to help you, too.

Treachell Moniee Buylley, a former student:

> I love this lady she changed my whole mentality she made me such a better person.

Jordan Davis, a former student:

> And the coolest principal award goes to.... Bertie Simmons Dr. Simmons you have done so much crazy things for your students! All out of love and respect HISD lost a well-respected principal but Dr. Simmons continues to do what she loves best which is making the world a better place one student at a time in honor of her Granddaughter. Her legacy is instilled in the community of Houston through the lives she has touched over a 50+ year dedication to education.

I was prepared and ready for the trial when Scott called and said the school district was ready for a settlement. I received the news with mixed emotions. I wanted to prove my case in court and to clear my name. I believe in honesty, integrity, and transparency. On the other hand, I was eighty-four years old and had family members to consider. This unexpected and unbelievable disaster could continue for years before we ever went to trial, even though a date had been set for September. I agreed to go to mediation on September 6, 2018.

There are times in one's life when something happens that is so morally wrong it simply should not happen. Those are the times that test one's character and reminds one that character matters. As I made the decision not to pursue a court trial, I had no hatred or animosity in my heart—only heartbreak, sorrow, disappointment, and loss.

Bertie and former Mitchell student, Adam Perez.

CHAPTER 53
Absolution

We met starting at nine thirty on the morning of September 6, 2018. The skilled mediator, Alan Levin, had the two sides meet. The district had four attorneys, and we had the brilliant, capable Scott Newar representing Sharon Koonce, Officer Davis, and me. After individual introductions, one of their attorneys read the charges. I wanted so badly to respond, but of course that would not have been appropriate. I did, however, have a chance to tell Elnita Hutcheson, the attorney who worked with me when I lost two students in the school bus accident, how helpful she had been at that time.

Scott Newar made a PowerPoint presentation showing the awards I had received over the years, including one naming me best principal in the State of Texas from Howard E. Butt, a businessman supportive of public education. He then demonstrated a clear indication of racial discrimination by the HISD, by showing the number of white administrators who had been replaced recently by Hispanics. His presentation was impressive and eye-opening.

The mediation began. The mediator placed the two parties in different rooms, and he moved gracefully and flawlessly from group to group. Money was not the purpose of my lawsuit. All I wanted was to make a statement about the way the district was treating its employees. I was not an opossum and would not roll over and play dead, as most of the others who had been terminated did. Still, I was told that money was all that mattered to the district.

Late in the afternoon, Alan Levin came to our group and said he thought it would expedite the settlement if Elnita Hutcheson and I sat together and talked. We did that, and then the mediation continued. The district included a statement in the settlement that required us to make no disparaging remarks about the district, and the district would thank me in a public statement for my fifty-eight years of service. Scott asked me if I cared whether they thanked me for my service to which I quickly replied, "No." How phony would such a gratuitous remark be after they had destroyed a dream and the reputations of so many talented and intelligent employees? That entire section was removed, thanks to Scott and his negotiating skills. Any little derogatory remark about the district made by any of us could have resulted in litigation, which none of us wanted.

We were well into September 7, and no settlement had been reached. I marveled at the seamless and thoughtful way both Scott and Alan worked. Finally, at approximately 3:30 a.m. on Friday, Alan came in with the final settlement. Exhausted and eager to close the mediation, we all agreed to the offer. I was sincerely happy that both Sharon and Officer Davis had received money, though I felt Officer Davis should have been paid for all his lost compensation since he had been cleared of all charges. I vowed to use a portion of my one hundred thousand dollars to assist some of the employees who had lost so much.

After all the papers had been signed, I asked if I could go to the other room and speak to the HISD attorneys. When I entered the room, one of the attorneys jumped back as if she thought I was going to attack her. I hugged her and told the group how much I appreciated their hard work in settling the case. We all laughed and Elnita said, "We came here to settle, and we settled." As I left the room, someone said, "That was unprecedented." I was not aware until then it was unusual. I went home and went to bed as the sun was peeking over the horizon. I had just spent the night with three of the most remarkable men I had ever met.

The following day, my attorney issued the following press release:

> Today, Dr. Bertie Simmons, Sharon Koonce, and Officer Craig Davis, have held HISD accountable for its discrimination and retaliation against them during the 2017–2018 school year.
>
> Regrettably, many of the members of Dr. Simmons' team—a team responsible for Furr High School being named one of ten Super Schools and winning

a $10 million grant from the XQ foundation in 2016—remain uncompensated, unemployed and/or in prison in HISD's warehouse solely because they helped Dr. Simmons re-invent public school education.

Additionally, HISD has yet to hold to account HISD District 8 Trustee, Diana Davila, and Furr administrators—specifically, East Area Superintendent, Jorge Arredondo and Interim Principal, Rosa Hernandez—who were responsible for the mistreatment and abuse of Furr's teachers and students during the 2017–2018 school year. Dr. Simmons will not rest—and HISD's taxpayers should not rest—until Trustee Davila and the HISD administrators have been held accountable and all members of her award-winning team have been made whole.

Scott Newar

CHAPTER 54
We Are Better than This!

In the spring of 2018, eleven months into HISD's investigation into the claims against me, war was raging within the HISD family. There was talk of a Texas Education Agency takeover of the HISD board and the possibility of charter schools assuming responsibility for some chronically low-performing schools. It boiled over on April 23, 2018, when the board was discussing the future of ten struggling schools. Chaos broke out after the president, Rhonda Skillern-Jones, closed the meeting to the public. Several parents refused to leave. Some of these individuals were dragged out by police, and two women were arrested. The district claimed a police officer was injured while he attempted to escort parents from the room. Charges were dropped the following day against the parents arrested. This was just the beginning.

Growing frustration and behind-the-scenes anger at the district became volcanic six months later at the October 11, 2018, board meeting when trustees considered whether to give a short-term contract to Dr. Grenita Lathan as interim superintendent while conducting a national search for a permanent leader. Tensions on the board grew as some members expressed a desire to "call a spade a spade" and divulged comments made in private or closed sessions. The tension centered on the support that the three black members were lending to the candidacy of Dr. Lathan, herself a black female.

Trustee Elizabeth Santos responded, "The most important thing we have to do is select a superintendent. It has been put off for 203 days. No one is asking Dr. Lathan not to apply."

Another trustee stated there was a race war among the members of the board. She implied that board meetings were like a soap opera, calling the meeting "As the Board Turns."

Loud insults were being shouted by individuals in the audience, and trustees yelled at each other. Trustee Sergio Lira, who is usually mild mannered and unemotional, held up an article written by a black activist who had stated that opponents of Lathan were members of a new education "clan." Lira denounced the claim as "despicable."

The three black trustees made various allegations of unethical behavior and racism against trustees who did not support Lathan. They claimed that their colleagues' refusal to support her was because of her race. They called the Hispanic board members hypocrites and accused them of saying one thing in closed sessions and quite another in open meetings. They accused them of warning Lathan not to fire certain individuals.

As a surprise move, Trustee Diana Davila moved to remove Dr. Lathan as interim superintendent and replace her with Dr. Abe Saavedra, a former superintendent of HISD, and to assign Dr. Lathan to her former position of chief academic officer. The audience went wild as did the black board members, who loudly confirmed what I had been told about Davila: she had wanted to oust Dr. Carranza because he refused to bend to her demands. After much haranguing and slinging insults back and forth, a trustee called Davila corrupt and a disgrace. One said, "How dare you disrespect a black female." Individuals in the audience moved to the podium to make remarks. Police officers removed them.

There was total chaos when Trustee Jolanda Jones called the question so they would vote, and she could see who was involved in this action with Davila. When the vote was taken, the results reflected five for and four against. Sue Deigaard, who is white, voted with the three black members. She represents my part of town, but she did not represent me when I needed her. The audience erupted. The results of the vote drew an outburst from members of the black community who felt those who voted for the motion were being unethical and deceptive. I agreed. Jolanda Jones assured the audience she would refuse to attend an upcoming weekend board retreat where they were to engage in team-building activities led by Cathy Mincberg, a former HISD board member. As far as she was concerned, Jones said, there would be no "Kumbaya" there.

Mayor Sylvester Turner expressed his displeasure at the decision, and a group of powerful leaders from the community, including

Congresswoman Sheila Jackson Lee, met in Emancipation Park to plan actions to be taken. Emancipation Park is the oldest park in Houston and in Texas, and it is in the city's Third Ward area. It was the only public park available to black residents during portions of the Jim Crow era. This was truly a symbolic meeting.

Shortly after they had engaged in personal battle and disharmony, the HISD board met for team-building activities. It was reported that they got to know each other better during the workshop. This was the first step toward a new beginning for the board and a repairing of their image as individuals responsible for the education of over two hundred thousand students in the HISD. Dr. Saavedra would not be a part of this new beginning He had withdrawn his agreement to assume the interim role stating, "The dysfunction is not at the superintendent or leadership level. It is at the board level."

The day following the team-building session, the board held a press conference and apologized for the unprofessional behavior at the recent board meeting. They expressed their intention to project a more professional image. With the problems they were facing concerning funding and chronically low-performing schools, I believed they were sincere in hoping they could put away their differences and be more focused on meeting the needs of students in the HISD. Sadly, it did not happen.

As I watched the results of the great political upheavals in our country and on the HISD board, I felt disturbed. It appears we all feel entitled to say anything we want to say, lie if it fits our needs, and place blame for our shortcomings on others. I keep thinking, We are better than this. I thought of my granddaughter Ashley, who looks down on us from her Wyeth window, reminding us of our unwavering commitment to hope.

I think of my friend Dorothy. I think of watching her house burn while white men in white robes howled. From deep in my memory, that feeling of sorrow and disbelief tugs at my soul and wrings tears from my eyes. I find it difficult to believe that the dark cloud of racism still hangs menacingly over our country. I think of the years I have spent attempting to erase from the face of the earth, not the images, but the reality, of injustice. I was always certain that by now, we would be better than this. Today, I wish to erase the reality of the identity politics I witnessed at the HISD board meeting on October 11, 2018. I, with Elijah Cummings, say, "We are better than this."

When I think of my life, my goals, and my desire to make the world a better place for all people, I do not view myself as a victim. I must "hold fast to my dreams" and continue to strive to help create a better world for those who come after me. I must help to create a world where honesty matters, words matter, character matters, all lives matter, and global warming is real! I must not catch the self-indulgent narcissistic plague that is sweeping across the country at a swift pace.

I was encouraged by the behavior of the school board members when they listened to each other and, hopefully, realized that we are all more alike than different. I hope they realize that nestled deep inside each of us is a need for respect and acknowledgment, and that our differences are to be cherished and do not make us less than anyone else. That we are all better when we embrace our differences and celebrate them as a part of the patchwork quilt that protects our right to be our unique selves, and step to the music of our own drummer. It is my hope that my life has, in some small way, made the world a better place for all people. I feel as President Abraham Lincoln must have felt when he wrote, "I have an irrepressible desire to live till I can be assured that the world is a little better for my having lived in it." I am uncertain of the amount of time I have left on this earth, but it is my sincere hope that my willingness to freely disclose my life struggles, dreams, and hopes will touch someone in a profound way such that a new movement sweeps the nation that broadcasts honesty, kindness, caring, forgiveness, and justice. Hope will no longer be a whisper. Let the broadcast begin!

EPILOGUE

I had completed my memoir and was lying in bed, replaying the events of my life and wondering if I had made the world a better place for anyone. It was then that I received a message notification on my phone. It was almost as if the universe had answered my question, and I had the closure I was seeking. The message I received was a letter from a former student of mine.

Dr. Simmons,

I am writing you this letter in hopes of somehow sharing with you the deep, profound effect that your 4th grade class at Mitchell Elementary had on my life. I am 58 years old, and although it has been almost 50 years, I have never forgotten those days and particularly the lessons learned in your classroom. I didn't know it at the time, but you designed the teaching in that classroom with a great purpose. It was a beautiful combination of students that were both advantaged and disadvantaged. I always kind of joked that I was not sure which group I was in, but it really did not matter. I was very blessed to have a lot of support from my parents, and my Mom was the room-mother.

I was involved in a lot of outside activities including Camp Fire Girls, church, twirling and piano lessons. We lived on a great cul-de-sac street in a middle class neighborhood that had old-fashioned block parties, and I truly experienced the wonder years. About half of the students in the class were experiencing the same type of advantaged life. However, the other half were the ones that were struggling for a variety of reasons. I remember that many of them lived in the nearby trailer park. Some could not read or write very well, and some were very poor. Many of them had major behavioral issues and had spent a lot of their time in previous grades at the principal's office. It was two sides of the track in that classroom and it was just the way you wanted it.

You took the whole class and united us together with common goals. You encouraged us to follow our dreams, and to work together to achieve a huge variety of amazing results. In the process, we all learned so much from each other. Unity is such a beautiful thing.

Instead of focusing on our weaknesses, or what we were doing wrong, you brought us together by inspiring us to do good things that built character and made a difference. You taught us how to be considerate of each other and how to work together as a team. It bonded us together with great hope and a purpose.

Here are a few of the activities that we accomplished in your class:

We created a puppet show for the Texas Teachers Association. This included everyone working together to construct a giant puppet box and the puppets. I don't really remember what the show was about, but I remember that I pulled the puppet strings for the dog!

We all participated in a televised jump-roping performance at the half-time show for the basketball game at the University of Houston.

We produced a phenomenal cakewalk for the classroom's booth at the school's fundraising carnival, and we raised a lot of money.

We performed a musical show at the Royal Coach Inn, where I actually got to play my ukulele for a large audience.

We hosted a lady from Japan who visited our classroom and did a presentation about the Japanese culture. Each of us contributed to the Japanese day with our own original origami art on display.

We were able to listen to a missionary from India who came and did a slide presentation about her travels and experiences in third world countries.

We held a massive school-wide newspaper drive. We collected so many newspapers that we were able to fund the plane fare for the famous author, Doris Gates who flew to our school to talk about her books and about being a writer. This talk was also televised, and I remember that we were actually featured on several different television shows for other events as well.

I have never forgotten about the experience in your 4th grade classroom. I do not even remember anyone going to the principal's office that school year... Probably because we were so busy learning life skills in an interesting way! I remember that you led us by example, and we discovered that when we worked together, we could really make things happen. I have been a student in many classrooms over the years, but can mostly only recall the names from my 4th grade group; Homer, Glenn, Mary Beth, Laurie, Sheila and Donna to name a few. I have not seen any of them since those days, yet I will never forget their faces, nor the times we shared. Thank you so much for those memories.

I have followed your career, and was I so excited when they were able to convince you to come out of retirement to be the principal of Furr High School. They were so fortunate and blessed to have you at the helm with your compassion and fearless determination. Your ability to think outside of the box and relate to the students is what really sets you apart. I thank God for the thousands of students that you were able to encourage and redirect. You do not give up on anyone, and you are a beacon of light for the ones that have lost their way. You see potential in young students and you champion their cause. No doubt this is how you were able to turn the school around, and receive the grant. There will always be opposition, especially when we are trying to do something for good. But God sees, and He has a heart for the lost as well. He will multiply your efforts and your legacy will endure forever.

I thank the LORD for placing me in your 4th grade class. The experiences that I learned during that time were able to shape my life in so many ways. I have been very involved with jail ministry and juvenile detention mentoring. I've volunteered with homeless outreaches and I am very involved with animal rescue. I live to make a difference, something you taught me at an early age.

I have such great admiration for you, and I want to thank you again for your servant's heart, your passionate leadership, and your great love for all of us. You are definitely a hero in my book and in countless others.

God bless you, Dr. Simmons. I can't wait to see what you do with the next chapter of your life.

Sincerely,

Terri McKinney Neely

Disclaimer

I have tried to recreate events, locales and conversations from my memories of them. In order to maintain their anonymity, in some cases, I have changed the names of individuals and places of business.

For more information, address:
bsimmon82@gmail.com

First published - November 2019

Hardback
ISBN 978-1-7340604-0-9

Paperback
ISBN 978-1-7340604-1-6

bertiesimmons.com